Praise for *Po...*

'Real-life black ops – a must have' Frederick For...

'Our elite forces in blistering action against all odds'
Bear Grylls

'Reveal[s] the entire operation as well as the ugly story of how they were left to possible capture or death by their senior commanders' *Independent*

'This account is so gripping that I read the review copy from cover to cover within 48 hours of receiving it just before this issue went to press' *Combat and Survival*

'A truly extraordinary book; fast-paced, gripping, authentic. A taut telling of an elite mission that helped change the course of a war. I joined the Regiment with David Blakeley and served alongside him in Kosovo and Iraq. He was a dynamic and inspirational leader' Dan Jarvis, MBE MP

'Blistering action behind enemy lines – a true soldier's story'
Big Phil Champion, author of *Born Fearless*

'An incredible story of heroism and honour beyond measure. Men may want to be David Blakeley, and women will surely want to date him!' Olivia Lee

'A fascinating and gripping tale of daring do'
Military Machines International

Captain David Blakeley was second in command of the elite Pathfinder Platoon and fought in the Iraq War in 2003 and in Afghanistan after 9/11. Before that, with 1 PARA he saw action in Kosovo, Sierra Leone and Northern Ireland and was, at one point, the youngest captain in the British Army. After being seriously injured in Iraq, he fought his way back to physical fitness and went on to undertake SAS selection. He now works as a military consultant to TV and film production companies. He lives in London.

By David Blakely

Pathfinder
Maverick One

PATHFINDER

A SPECIAL FORCES MISSION
BEHIND ENEMY LINES

CAPTAIN DAVID BLAKELEY

An Orion paperback

First published in Great Britain in 2012
by Orion
This paperback edition published in 2013
by Orion Books Ltd,
Orion House, 5 Upper St Martin's Lane,
London WC2H 9EA

An Hachette UK company

1 3 5 7 9 10 8 6 4 2

A CIP catalogue record for this book is available
from the British Library.

ISBN 978-1-4091-2902-8

Printed and bound in Great Britain by
Clays Ltd, St Ives plc

The Orion Publishing Group's policy is to use papers that
are natural, renewable and recyclable products and
made from wood grown in sustainable forests. The logging
and manufacturing processes are expected to conform to
the environmental regulations of the country of origin.

www.orionbooks.co.uk

For my mother and father,
for always being there for me.

'It is not the critic who counts, nor the man who points out how the strong man stumbles, or where the doer of deeds could have done them better. The credit belongs to the man who is actually in the arena; whose face is marred by dust and sweat and blood; who strives valiantly; who errs and comes short again and again, because there is no effort without error or shortcoming; who knows the great enthusiasms, the great devotions, who spends himself in a worthy cause; who, at the best, knows in the end the triumph of high achievement, and who, at the worst, if he fails, at least fails while daring greatly, so that his place shall never be with those cold and timid souls who know neither victory nor defeat.'

PRESIDENT THEODORE ROOSEVELT
Speech at the Sorbonne, 23 April 1910

'Happiness shall always be found by those who dare and persevere; wanderer – do not turn around, march on and have no fear.'

ANONYMOUS
Unofficial collect of the Pathfinders

ACKNOWLEDGEMENTS

A very special thanks to my sisters Anna and Lisa, for all your support over the years and especially when I was away on operations with the military: I love you and you continue to inspire me.

I would like to thank Damien Lewis, the master of jack brews, for the time spent searching for inspiration while staring into the blanket fog of a southern Irish rain; publishers Rowland White and Alan Samson, for their inspiration, vision and guidance from the very earliest stages; Jillian Young and all at Orion who did so much to make this book a success. Thanks also to Annabel Merullo, literary agent, and her assistant, Laura Williams, for their support.

Thank you to: my steadfast friends Ewan Ross, Gareth Arnold, David Green, Azim Majid and Stefan D'Bart. To the most loyal friend Jimmy Chew – thank you for being there. Also thank you to Lara Fraser, Alice Clough, Rob Mussetti, Francesca Mussetti, Matt Taylor, Andy Jackson, Sabina Skala, Janice Dickinson, Sophie Ball, Laura Pradelska, Olivia Lee, Bonnie Gilmore, Josh Varney, Emma Rigby, Richard Allen, Charles Towning, Luke Hardy, Andrew Chittock, Patrick Hambleton, Katie Rice, Charlie Birch and Katerina Konecna. And thanks of course to Eva, Chubbs, Logs and Podge, for putting up with my repeated impositions upon your hospitality.

Very special and heartfelt thanks to the men of my patrol, *Mayhem Three Zero*, with whom I shared so much and as is depicted in this book, and especially Tricky, who saved my life on more than one occasion.

To the Pathfinders (PF): many great men have put huge amounts of effort into developing this elite unit. The PF are the best in the world at what they do because of your efforts. To the fallen; we will remember you. To the current and future Findermen – move fast, stay low and enjoy it while it lasts.

'FIRST IN'
Pathfinder Platoon Motto

David Blakeley
March 2012.

Find out more about David Blakeley at:
www.davidblakeley.co.uk

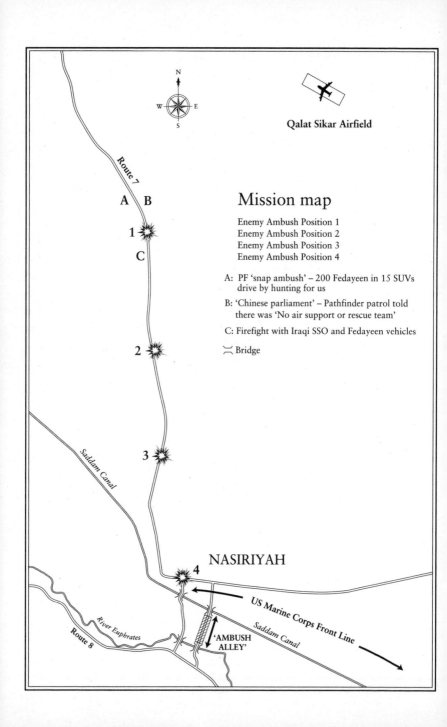

Qalat Sikar Airfield

Mission map

Enemy Ambush Position 1
Enemy Ambush Position 2
Enemy Ambush Position 3
Enemy Ambush Position 4

A: PF 'snap ambush' – 200 Fedayeen in 15 SUVs
   drive by hunting for us

B: 'Chinese parliament' – Pathfinder patrol told
   there was 'No air support or rescue team'

C: Firefight with Iraqi SSO and Fedayeen vehicles

⊃⊂ Bridge

Route 7

A B

1

C

2

3

NASIRIYAH

4

US Marine Corps Front Line

Saddam Canal

Saddam Canal

River Euphrates

Route 8

'AMBUSH
ALLEY'

N
W   E
S

AUTHOR'S NOTE

I have changed some of the names of the soldiers depicted in this book, and a handful of geographical locations, for operational and personal security reasons, and to protect the identities of members of the British and Allied elite forces.

My story as told in this book concerns my tour of Iraq as I fought it. It is written from my own personal memory and recollections of the events portrayed, and from the memories of others I have spoken to from the mission who were able to assist, and from my notes of that tour. I have done my best to portray accurately and realistically the events as they happened. However, my memory is no doubt fallible, and any mistakes herein are entirely of my own making. I will be happy to address them in future editions.

PROLOGUE

I t was last light, almost time to load up the C130 Hercules and take to the darkening skies. I strolled down the deserted runway to get a little space to myself. The sun was sinking below the rumpled, grey mass of the mountains several kilometres to the west of us, with the vast expanse of the great semi-arid desert lying beyond.

The airstrip was deep in the shadows of a sunken valley and well out of sight, which was just as we wanted it. From high above me an eagle emitted a lonely, high-pitched screech. A dust devil came swirling across the bush, whipping up dry grass and debris as it skittered across the runway. The scene was so utterly deserted, it was hardly possible to imagine all the hidden men-at-arms making their last-minute, fevered preparations.

You can mount an airborne mission from just about any service-able length of tarmac – from London's Heathrow to a battle-scarred Baghdad International Airport, or a disused airfield in the middle of the bush. Mostly, conventional military operations go out from one of the big airbases, with little need to keep them hidden. With missions such as ours we needed to be well away from the public gaze, and the prying lenses of the media.

With this airstrip we'd got exactly what we were looking for. It was so ancient it didn't even possess a working control tower. There was just a ragged, sun-bleached, dull-orange windsock hanging limp in the air, plus a couple of semi-derelict hangars. Since its arrival the previous night under cover of darkness, there was also the fat, powerful form of a C130 Hercules transport aircraft squatting on the apron, looking well out of place next to the pitted runway, half-overgrown with weeds.

One of the two hangars housed our vehicles, a pair of cut-down Land Rovers bristling with machine guns, which we affectionately referred to as the 'Pinkies'. The building dated from the 1950s, with brick walls topped by a sagging corrugated-iron roof. The rust-red metal had been patched with scores of repairs, like dull silver sticking plasters. Still, it served our purposes fine. From there we could load the Pinkies aboard the C130 for deep insertion missions, or on to a Chinook heavy-lift helicopter for shorter-range operations.

In the wild, empty quiet I took a moment to reflect upon what lay ahead of me. It was only recently that I'd taken over as second-in-command (2IC) of our unit, the Pathfinders, and here we were poised to jump into the darkness and the unknown. A number of the guys had many more years' experience than me: no doubt about it, I was going to be tested as never before.

They say that war is long periods of boredom interrupted by intense periods of action. We'd waited a good few days for this one to get the green light. But even now, two hours away from brakes off – the aircraft take-off hour – we could still get stood down. In fact, we could get called back at any moment before we dived off the Hercules aircraft's open ramp, high above hostile terrain.

Once we were out of the aircraft's hold we had reached the point of no return. No one could call us back. You can't use a radio on a HALO (High Altitude Low Opening) jump, which was how we'd be inserting. There was no way to hear a radio message, or to speak into a mouthpiece, when freefalling from extreme high altitude and plummeting to earth at speeds in excess of 100 mph. In any case, the slipstream would rip any earpiece or mouthpiece away.

We'd be incommunicado as we fell. Once we were on the ground we'd be in the midst of hostile territory, so radio silence would be paramount. The earliest we'd have communications would be at our first 'Sched', one of the two daily radio reports we had to make to mission HQ. Our first would be at 0800 the following morning, by which time we'd have reached our objective and completed our CTR (Close Target Recce), so what were the chances of getting called off then?

If we could just get our arses out of that Hercules and into the air, then we'd be free-running to target. It was an awesome proposition, and I could feel my pulse thumping just at the thought of it.

I made my way across to the Herc. Tom, the C130 pilot, served with the RAF's 47 Squadron, their Special Forces wing. I knew him well from previous jobs, and we'd been out on the piss several times together. He was a big drinker and a larger-than-life character, plus he was a superlative Special Forces pilot – a king at what he did, which was flying guys like us deep behind enemy lines.

At my approach he slid back a side window in the giant aircraft's cockpit, and poked his head out. 'Latest MET report is all good, mate. No change to weather conditions at the IP, and no change to the flight path we'll take in.'

The IP was the impact point, the exact landing spot that we'd pre-identified from the maps and sat photos.

I couldn't suppress a grin. 'Looks like we're on then?'

He glanced at his watch. 'Wheels-up minus ninety. I reckon this one's a go.'

Wheels-up meant aircraft take-off time. I felt around in the left-hand breast pocket of my smock, and pulled out a CD. It was AC/DC's album *The Razors Edge*. I tossed it up to him.

'Track three mate …'

He rolled his eyes. 'Not bloody "Thunderstruck" *again*? How many times am I going to have to listen to that racket as you guys pile out of my backside. Can't we have something a bit more classy – like Wagner's "Ride of the Valkyries" maybe?'

'RAF wanker,' I cut in. 'Anyway, you know the form. We always jump to "Thunderstruck". It's PF tradition.'

He shrugged and turned to the co-pilot beside him. 'Pete, can you get this crap racked up on the CD and test the Tannoy system's working?'

I hurried over to the hangar. There was still one hell of a lot to get done before we got airborne. As I approached the building I could hear music blaring out. Tricky most likely had revved up the Foo Fighters' heavy rock on his portable CD player. Out here in the midst of the deserted bush it didn't matter how much noise we made: about the only things that we were likely to disturb were the local ostriches.

This bone-dry mountainous region was renowned for its herds of ostrich. We'd seen them running in wild confusion across the valleys, their fat legs pumping and their plumed tails flapping, as they tried to get away from one of our Chinooks flying at 180 knots and at treetop level. Over the past few weeks our quartermaster had got very adept at flipping ostrich steaks on the makeshift barbecue we'd rigged up at the rear of the airbase. Tasty they were, too.

I stepped into the relative darkness of the hangar. The lads were busy doing their last-minute preparations. I made one final check of my weapons, my mags of ammo, the pouches on my smock and my webbing. The last thing you wanted was one of those falling open during the jump, and a vital bit of war-fighting kit spinning down to earth. I stuffed my belt and chest webbing kit into my bulging rucksack and shut the flap, tightening the straps to the max.

To one side of me Jason Dickins, the second-in-command of my six-man patrol, jammed his massive rucksack into a large canvas coverall. He turned to speak to a tall, awkward-looking figure standing next to him. We'd been tasked to parachute an extra body in on this mission. He wasn't a Pathfinder. He was some sneaky-beaky mystery type, whom we'd nicknamed 'The Ghost.'

'You got your bergen ready, mate?' he demanded.

None of us had particularly warmed to The Ghost. Ever since he'd joined us a few days back, he'd treated Jason and the other rankers as if they were one step removed from the mice and other vermin that infested the hangar. He'd managed to exchange the odd civil word with me, but only once he had realised that I was a Sandhurst graduate and an officer. Pathfinders wear no marks of unit or rank, so it had taken him a while to do so.

His attitude had gone down like the proverbial turd in a punch-bowl. In the PF, as our unit is known, each man is treated as an equal regardless of education, class, background or rank. No one can enter the Pathfinders without passing the brutal selection course, which rivals that of the SAS. Selection is the first great leveller. And once in the PF, patrol command goes to the most experienced and capable soldier for the mission in hand.

Jason was one of a tiny number of operators in the British Army who'd qualified as a military tandem master. As such, he was able to freefall another human being from extreme high altitude into target. I'm not permitted to reveal from what height exactly we jump, but suffice to say it is from far above what any civilian parachutist would ever do so.

On this mission Jason would be parachuting with The Ghost strapped to his torso. Jason was the last person the guy should ever have treated with disdain or disrespect. Pretty shortly his life would be 100 per cent in Jason's hands, when they jumped out together into the dark and howling void.

'Erm, I imagine I've got everything I need,' The Ghost remarked, gesturing at his bulging pack. It wasn't our need to know what was in there, or what he'd be using it for exactly. Our mission was just to get us, and him, to target.

'Hand it over then, mate,' Jase prompted, impatiently.

Jason stuffed the guy's rucksack into the canvas coverall along-side his own, and laced the whole tightly closed. He'd freefall with The Ghost strapped to his front, and the canvas sack hanging on a strap suspended below him. Not counting his own body weight, he'd be steering some 130 kg into the IP. It was one hell of a tasking.

Being the most experienced parachutist amongst the six of us, Jase would lead our stick out of the C130. As 2IC Pathfinders and a well-experienced high-altitude parachutist myself, I'd follow.

Jase turned to me. 'Wheels-up minus sixty,' he grunted. 'Best we load up the bergens.'

It took the three of us – myself, Jase, plus The Ghost – to man-handle the canvas sack containing their two packs the 200 metres or so to the waiting aircraft. We staggered up the open tail ramp and dumped it in Jason's place, nearest to the rear. We ferried the rest of the bergens across the apron, mine going next to Jase's, then Dez's, Steve's and Joe's, with Tricky's last of all. You'd always put one of your most experienced operators last in the stick, for he'd have no one to watch his back.

You placed those with the least experience between your better guys. So, Dez Vincent would come after me, for he was a bit of a meathead and not long with the PF. Steve Knight, the Pathfinders' armourer, came next, so Dez was sandwiched between the two of us. Between Steve and Will 'Tricky' Arnold – an unbeatable PF opera-tor – we had Joe Hamilton, who at twenty-three was the young pup on the patrol. No one could quite figure out if Joe had done enough soldiering to qualify for the PF, but he'd passed selection and that made him one of us.

With the bergens loaded we headed over to the second hangar. We paused for a nervous piss outside, before strapping ourselves into our HALO gear.

Inside, the lead PD (Parachute Dispatcher) greeted us with a crink-ling around the eyes. 'Ready, lads?' he queried. 'Parachutes on?'

Alfie was a warrant officer with the RAF. His one and only role in life was to serve as a parachute dispatcher, ably assisted by the two other PDs who made up his team. Our state-of-the-art BT80 chutes were lined up against one wall in the order that we were going to jump.

There were a couple of the RAF's parachute packers to the rear of the hangar. It was their job to ensure that our chutes were stored, repaired, checked and documented properly. They'd unpack and re-pack them at regular intervals, to check they were in good order and free of tangles. They were hanging around the hangar just in case one of us had a problem with our chute, not that it had ever happened.

Those guys were consummate professionals and we had absolute faith in what they did, which was fortunate, because our lives depended upon it. We couldn't keep our chutes with us at all times, for often we'd deploy far behind enemy lines on foot-mounted or vehicle-borne operations, and we couldn't lug our BT80s on those. They remained under the care of the parachute packers until the very moment that one of us strapped himself into his parachute harness.

The BT80 is effectively a massive oblong of silk, one that is finely engineered to carry 90 kg of bloke slung beneath it, together with another 60-plus kg of kit. It's a hugely durable yet delicate piece of equipment, and it needs to be treated as such. We each flipped open the top of the para-rucksacks in which our chutes were packed. Inside were two wires, each of which was encased in red cotton thread. We checked that they were present and correct, which meant that the seals hadn't been broken since the chute last was packed.

That done, Jason turned his back to his BT80 and Alfie stepped up beside him. His para-pack was noticeably different from ours, for it had been specially configured by the parachute packers to enable him to strap The Ghost to his front.

'Here you go then, lad,' Alfie remarked with a grunt, as he lifted the heavy pack.

With Alfie's help Jason slipped his squat, powerful form into it. He straightened up and took the weight, the shoulder straps pulling tight as he did so. He bent down and began to fasten the loops that go around the top of the thighs. By the time he was done Jason was standing there with the equivalent of a sack of coal strapped to his back, but showing no visible sign of the weight he was carrying. Jase was always one of the last on PF training runs, but on a tab over the hills carrying serious weight he was unbeatable.

Alfie helped him tighten his para-pack until it was immovable. To one side of us The Ghost was standing around looking lost. It was quite possible that he'd never done a jump before. He'd certainly never have done a HALO. He wouldn't be getting strapped on to Jason until the last possible moment, for trying to shuffle around a C130 at altitude whilst bound tightly together wasn't any fun. It looked as if the reality of what he was about to do was starting to dawn on him, and that he was shitting his load.

I was next to load up. We'd only had the BT80s for a couple of months now, and the harness felt stiff and hard, like it still needed to be properly worn in. At six foot four I'm not small, but the shoulder straps were large enough to half-cover my chest. As I fastened the heavy titanium chest buckle – *Kerthunk!* – I felt my torso being tugged into a stoop by the pressure of the harness. By the time I'd clipped the chunky leg-buckles together and pulled the straps tight, it was like I was in a straitjacket.

I could well remember the agony of getting my tackle caught on a previous jump, and even now the leg straps were cutting into my groin area. But it was vital to strap on the BT80 until it was tight as a vice. The last thing you wanted was a loose harness. You'd start the freefall and it would immediately shift and saw its way into you. By the time you reached the ground you'd have rubbed your shoulders and groin raw, which would bugger you for the next stage of the mission – the long tab under a crushing bergen through hostile terrain.

The BT80 was exactly what we'd needed to replace our previous kit, the GQ360. The GQ360 was strapped to your back with your bergen below it, which meant that you were backside-heavy when you jumped. If you caught a fierce air current it could send you into a violent spin, which could render you unconscious. The GQ360 would be triggered by the altimeter to release automatically, but if you were lying on your back it would open under you. You'd fall through it, the chute wrapping itself around you, and you'd be toast.

By contrast, with the BT80 you had the weight of the bergen hanging from your chest, which meant it was all but impossible not to fall front-first. Even if you were unconscious, the chute would open on your back and should still function properly. We'd joined forces with the SAS in order to get the BT80. Together, we'd managed to sidestep the MOD's laborious procurement system, and had gone straight to the parachute's French manufacturer. And thank God we'd done so: it was a fantastic bit of kit to have in service right now.

The BT80 Multi-Mission System is made by Parachutes de France. At £50,000 a throw it's no snip, but it's arguably the best military parachute in the world. It has the best glide ratio, which means it can cover great distances in relation to its rate of descent. When dropped from extreme high altitude we could glide an enormous distance, crossing borders and infiltrating deep into hostile terrain. It was also designed in such a way that when you pulled the chute it released more or less silently, so we could descend unnoticed and unobserved.

Having got myself into my chute, Alfie helped me fix my personal oxygen canister pack to my front. It went on with a series of straps, which Alfie looped below and behind the BT80's harness, before pulling them tight so my stomach felt it was being crushed. He passed me the oxygen mask, and screwed the black, ribbed rubber tube into the nozzle on the oxygen pack. I placed the mask over my mouth and nose, and fastened the metal clips to either side of my helmet. Pathfinders use light, open-faced fibreglass helmets, a little like you'd see a Hells Angels biker wearing.

I pressed the oxygen mask into my face, and breathed hard. If the latex rubber of the mask wasn't making a proper seal with my skin, I'd feel air leaking around the sides. I gave Alfie a thumbs-up, and he switched the oxygen cylinder valve to the 'on' position. I breathed in and felt the cold, clear burst of oxygen entering my lungs, and an instant later I got the rush to my head. We weren't breathing pure oxygen, but pretty close, and it was fantastic. There was no better way to clear a hangover if you'd been on the piss the night before.

Prior to doing the HALO course every PF operator has to undergo a hypoxia test, to check his ability to function under conditions of lack of oxygen to the brain. You're placed in a compression chamber, which to start with replicates the atmosphere at sea level. Gradually, the chamber takes you up to 10,000 feet, where the oxygen level is noticeably lower. You then have to take your mask off, and yell out your name, rank and serial number, plus do some clapping games to demonstrate your co-ordination is still okay.

It kept taking you higher, until everyone in the chamber was pretty much scrambled. Human beings react differently to hypoxic conditions, just like individual mountaineers on a high-altitude climb. The aim of the hypoxia tests is to prove that you can operate for a few minutes at such extremes of altitude on little or no oxygen, in case your mask fails.

Alfie switched off the valve and moved on to the next bloke in line. I grabbed my main weapon – my battered M16 assault rifle – and slung it over my left side, barrel pointed at the floor. My 13-round Browning pistol was in my rucksack, for if I strapped it to my thigh I'd risk it getting in the way during the jump. My grenades and most of my spare mags of ammo were in there too. But you'd always jump with your main weapon strapped to your body, just in case you lost your bergen during the fall.

We all carried a knife, usually strapped in a sheath on our left shoulder. You needed it within easy reach, in case one of the many lines from your chute got tangled and you had to cut it free.

Lastly, I pulled on a pair of thin leather gloves. When freefalling from high altitude it can get bitterly cold, but the gloves were more to protect your hands. The handles with which you steered the canopy were made of a tough canvas material, and you'd often have to do a good deal of work with the chute as you fell. Even a blacksmith's hands could still get cut to shreds, which would be the last thing you'd ever want at the start of a mission.

I had my altimeter strapped to my left wrist, to tell me the distance I was from the ground during the fall. I'd set it to zero before take-off, with an adjustment for the height of the terrain we were jumping over. If you didn't account for that change in terrain, your altimeter might indicate you had bags of height still to go, when actually you were about to smash into the earth. We'd each be checking our altimeters as the C130 climbed to altitude, to ensure they were working properly.

With all six of us strapped into our HALO gear we made our cumbersome exit from the hangar, looking like a bunch of astronauts about to board the Shuttle. As we did so I heard the whine of the starter motors on the C130's four turbines, followed by the cough and splutter of the first firing. Tom was getting the big bird ready for brakes-off. We stepped towards the Hercules as it began to spool up to speed, and I felt the first flush of goose pimples.

I reached up and pulled down my HALO goggles, which were strapped around my helmet and secured at the rear. They were much like a scuba diver's mask, with a glass eyepiece and squidgy rubber sides. I checked to make sure they made a good airtight seal. If not, the goggles would get torn off my face during the freefall. Our terminal velocity would be approaching 150 mph, and it would be impossible to see without goggles. It'd be like riding a motorbike at that speed with no visor.

Ahead of us, Alfie and the two other parachute dispatchers were waiting. We were so heavy and cumbersome that it would be easy enough to take a fall, and they helped each of us up the C130's open ramp and into our places. Alfie lowered me into a red, fold-down canvas seat, the third from the rear, and buckled the safety strap across my knees. The last thing he did before moving on to Dez was to plug my mask into the C130's main oxygen tank.

As the aircraft climbed we'd be breathing 100 per cent oxygen, to flush any nitrogen from our blood stream. We'd breathe from the C130's on-board tank, to save our own supply. At higher than 22,000 feet a rapid ascent or descent can lead to decompression sickness, more commonly known as 'the bends'. By breathing pure oxygen on the way up we hoped to minimise that threat.

The C130 was completely dark, and we'd be flying into target on black light. Outside the aircraft the runway was also devoid of illumination. There was a faint glow emanating from the cockpit, and the parachute dispatchers had broken out Cyalume light sticks to help show us to our seats. But otherwise all was in shadow, my fellow jumpers presenting a dark silhouette to either side of me.

– 11 –

The dispatchers plugged into the C130's intercom, so they could talk to the aircrew. Tom would be doing his last checks by now, as the four-bladed propellers spun at speed in the darkness. There was no soundproofing in the Hercules, so unlike in a commercial airliner the noise from outside was deafening. There was the roar of the turbines pulsating in my ears, plus the odd whine of hydraulics as the aircrew tested the flaps, and the scream of the fuel injectors.

I was acutely aware that if we were going to get stood down, this was the most likely moment. It had happened to us before. We'd been pumped up with adrenaline and waiting for the take-off when the engines had powered down, and the mission had been postponed for twenty-four hours. The deal was never done until the money was in the bank, as they say.

All of a sudden the aircraft jerked forwards, and we began the taxi to the far end of the runway. I turned to Dez and shouted a couple of words of encouragement into his helmeted ear, but I doubted if he could hear me. There was a flurry of gripped leather fists between the six of us, as we realised we were that much closer to making the jump.

We reached the end of the darkened runway and I felt the Hercules doing an about turn, as Tom spun it on the spot through 360 degrees. There was a momentary pause as we waited for the final go. I could feel my heart pounding in my chest as the engines revved up to take-off speed, and the familiar smell of the exhaust seeped into the C130's interior.

A fleeting thought flashed through my mind. I remembered being jammed with ninety men in a C130 during my days with 1 PARA, as we headed into Sierra Leone. We'd done this low-level insertion through horrendous turbulence, and there were guys puking up to the left and right of me. Now, we were six soldiers – plus The Ghost – about to climb for an hour or more to the still and silent heavens, whereupon we were scheduled to do an epic freefall into the unknown.

Needless to say, there was nowhere else that I'd rather be right now than here in this aircraft with these blokes. There was a massive boost to the roar of the engines outside, the sound of which tore into my thoughts, and suddenly the C130 was surging forwards. It had hardly gone more than 500 metres before the aircraft lifted off and began to climb steeply.

I reached under my chin and unhooked my helmet strap. I yanked it off, and pulled on a set of intercom headphones, so I could listen in on the chat. I heard Tom's voice giving a running commentary to his co-pilot and the navigator to his rear, plus the parachute dispatchers in the aircraft's hold.

'Airspeed 700 knots. Altitude 1500 feet. Rate of climb …'

Tom was speaking so calmly he sounded as if he was some kind of British Airways pilot addressing his civvie passengers. I was waiting for him to say: *We're about to start our in-flight entertainment, but first the hostesses will be serving you some complimentary drinks and snacks. Our expected flight time to New York's LaGuardia airport is eight hours and fifteen minutes …*

The only threat to the mission now would be a drastic change in the weather conditions at the IP. If severe winds blew up we could still have the jump canned. It wouldn't matter much what the wind speed was at altitude, for we'd plummet to earth like stones. But at the IP anything over 20 knots could prove fatal. You'd come in to land under your chute, the wind would knock you sideways like a battering ram, and you could break a leg or an arm, or even get yourself killed. We just had to pray the weather stayed good at the target.

'Altitude now at 10,000 feet,' Tom's voice announced over the intercom. I felt a surge of adrenaline as we kept climbing toward our jump height. 'P-Hour minus sixty.'

P-Hour (Parachute Hour) was the moment we'd jump from the C130's hold. We had sixty minutes to wait and we'd be gone. I turned to Jason and mouthed 'P minus sixty'. Jason was a taciturn individual at the best of times, so all I got in return was a barely noticeable nod of the head. Sandwiched between Jason and me was The Ghost. He was staring at the Herc's cold metal floor seemingly in a daze. Reality was sinking in big time, I figured.

'P minus forty,' Tom intoned. 'MET conditions and flight path unchanged.'

Even with the C130's ramp closed there was still an icy draught seeping in from the rear. I stamped my feet to force some life back into them, then I leaned forwards and glanced left, towards the back of the plane. Tricky caught my gaze, and there was the barest hint of a smile in his ice-blue eyes.

A hard-as-nails Jason Statham look-alike, Tricky was the operator that no one ever tried to mess with. To de-stress from operations he'd go sparring with Lance Green, another PF stalwart. During his weekends off Lance used to bare knuckle box in a cage in front of mega-wealthy London bankers, and to see him and Tricky going at it you'd think they were trying to kill each other. Tricky and I were dead close, and I took huge comfort from having him back-stopping my patrol.

'P minus twenty,' Tom announced. 'P minus twenty.'

It was the moment we'd been waiting for. I removed the headphones and pulled on my helmet, as the three parachute dispatchers started to help us on with our bergens. You couldn't lean back in your chair, due to the BT80 strapped to your back, so you had to stand and heft your bergen on to your seat. Then you had to squat down and clip the bergen on to the two titanium D-rings set into the front of your para-harness. There was no way we could manage this on our own, so the PD boys were really earning their pay now.

That done, the six of us were left standing by the C130's starboard side, with one hand grasping the top of the bench seats in an effort to steady ourselves. We each were carrying 30 kg of parachute gear and a 30 kg bergen, plus weapons and oxygen weighing another 15 kg or more. Fortunately, there was very little turbulence at this altitude, and Tom was keeping the C130 steady as a rock. Even so my back felt like it was bent double, and it was starting to ache like hell.

My mind blanked the pain as Alfie reached out to grab the tube of my mask, whilst signalling with his other hand that he was going to swop over the oxygen supply. This was the single most dangerous moment prior to making the jump. One gulp of the rarified atmosphere at this altitude and I'd get a burst of nitrogen into my bloodstream, which could balloon to dangerous levels. If that happened I'd get the dreaded bends as soon as I jumped.

I took a massive in-breath and held it, and as quick as a flash Alfie plugged me out of the C130's tank and into my personal oxygen bottle.

'P minus ten.'

I couldn't hear Tom's announcement any more, but Alfie's hand signal compensated: ten fingers held up in front of each of our faces, to make sure none of us had missed it.

'P minus five.' Five fingers were waved in front of our begoggled eyes.

Alfie held up a closed fist and blew into it, spreading his fingers as he did so, like his breath had blown them apart. This was the signal for wind speed at the IP. Having blown into his fist like that, Alfie next held up five fingers. Wind speed was 5 knots at the IP. Perfect for making the landing.

Above the roar of the C130's engines I suddenly heard the first guitar riffs screaming out of the aircraft's speakers. AC/DC's 'Thunderstruck': the signal for three minutes to P-Hour. High-pitched, fast, crazed; each whine of the guitar was punctuated by a mad, breathy, spooky chant, which built and built to a climax.

Thunder! Wahahahahahahaha.
Thunder! Wahahahahahahaha.
Thunder! Wahahahahahahaha.
Thunder! Wahahahahahahaha.
Thunder! Wahahahahahahaha.
THUNDER! WAHAHAHAHAHAHAHA.
THUNDER! WAHAHAHAHAHAHAHA.

Drums started crashing and more guitars kicked in, howling and echoing down the C130's hold, as the chant kept building in volume and intensity.

> *THUNDER!*
> *THUNDER!*
> *THUNDER!*
> *THUNDER!*

Then the lyrics proper kicked in, deafeningly loud over the Tannoy system. In spite of his earlier comments, Tom, God love him, was cranking up the volume.

> *I was caught in the middle of the railroad tracks.*
> *THUNDER!*
> *And I knew, I knew there was no turning back.*
> *THUNDER!*

To the rear of the aircraft there was the hollow *thunk* of a seal breaking, and the whine of the tail ramp starting to lower. To our left and right the PD boys were helping us as we shuffled towards the rushing void. The nearer we got the louder grew the noise of the aircraft's slipstream, the wind howling above the music and threatening to drown out the lyrics.

> *Sounds of the drums, beatin' in my heart.*
> *The thunder of the guns tore me apart.*
> *You've been thunderstruck …*

The icy blasts of air were mixed with the powerful, heady scent from the engines, a combination of burning oil and aviation fuel. It was the kind of smell you'd only ever get when you were about to jump, and it set my pulse racing like a machine gun. I saw Alfie and the other PDs strap themselves to one side of the ramp, to prevent themselves from getting torn out of the opening by a sudden blast of wind.

I glanced towards the void. Nothing. Swirling darkness. I took a step closer, and gazed up into the massive expanse of the starlit heavens. We were on the very roof of the world here. During the long ascent our eyes had adjusted to the gloom. Our natural night vision had kicked in, which meant we'd have as good a chance as any of keeping sight of each other as we began the freefall.

There was no way you could use NVG (Night Vision Goggles) when doing a HALO: the slipstream would rip them from your face in an instant. In any case, NVG tended to channel your vision into a narrow corridor of artificially boosted fluorescent light, which meant you lost your spatial awareness, and that was the last thing you ever needed during a HALO jump. The NVG were stashed in the bergens, along with all our other gear.

We were seconds to the 'go' now, eyes glued to the red bulbs glowing faintly to either side of the open ramp. We each did a final check on the bloke in front of us, making sure his BT80 hadn't managed to snag on anything.

To one side Alfie was strapping The Ghost to Jason's front. Jase's squat form held the bloke upright and jammed up against him, as he shuffled him closer to the ramp. I could see from the guy's expression that he was screaming, his eyes wide with panic, but not a sound was escaping from his oxygen mask. In spite of the massive adrenaline high we were feeling, we couldn't help exchanging exultant looks. *Payback time.*

Then Alfie, yelling: 'Tail off for equipment check!'

At the rear, Tricky whacked Joe on his right shoulder. 'SIX OKAY!'

Tricky's oxygen and chute were all good. Joe repeated the move and the shout, and it rippled down the line. It reached Jason, who was face-to-face with Alfie, and the old hand just gave him a thumbs-up: *Good to go.*

We shuffled tighter together. Too much space between blokes would result in too much separation in the sky, and we mightn't find each other. As we steeled ourselves for the go, I felt this incredible high coursing through my veins. We might have done this a hundred times before during training, but still nothing came close to the buzz of doing the jump for real. *Nothing.*

There was no way down for us now but the freefall, and we all knew the dangers involved. Too many good men had died doing exactly what we were about to do now. We might have total trust in our kit, our ability and each other, but still any one of us could perish out there. And who knew what might await us on the ground? The intel said the IP was clear of hostile forces, but how often had the intel been wrong?

We stood on the edge of the ramp, cold air buffeting and rocking us. The green light flashed on. Alfie stepped back, and yelled: 'GO! GO! GO!'

I saw Jason forcing The Ghost towards the void, and suddenly he was diving forwards, the two figures plummeting as one into the darkness. I dived directly after him, hit the C130's slipstream, and felt the powerful blast flipping my legs over my head, and twisting me around. I ripped out of the slipstream, stabilised my dive, and began searching below me for Jason and his jump-buddy.

I pushed my weight forwards on to my bergen, and felt myself accelerating into a headfirst dive. I felt like a giant shuttlecock plummeting directly towards earth. There, right below me was the form of my stick leader, a black spot against the darkened terrain far below. All I could make out of the landscape we were dropping into were the different shades marking out the mountain ridges and valleys.

To increase my velocity I got my body into a delta shape, arms by my side, legs streamlined behind me. Jason had turned to the right as he began his freefall, and I brought myself down beside him so I was facing the opposite direction. I steered myself by moving my arms and my head gently in the direction I wanted to go. I'd done over a hundred HALO jumps, and I'd learned that if I stuck an arm or leg out sharply I'd flip myself over and be well messed up.

I got to within 50 feet of Jason and brought my arms and legs into more of a star shape, to slow myself down. I stabilised at that distance, so I could maintain this position for the duration of the freefall. Then I turned my head gently into the roaring slipstream, so I could check on Dez. When I caught sight of him he was maybe 80 feet behind me, but catching up fast. I counted four other dark human-shaped blobs strung out behind him. So far, so good.

We were falling in a staggered line formation. Keeping eye contact man to man was vital. If I lost Jason we'd all lose him, and we'd get scattered across the ground, which would be a nightmare. Having made sure the line was complete I did a quick check of my altimeter. Even when jumping from such height we'd be just ninety seconds in the freefall. If you didn't keep one eye on your altimeter you could easily lose track of time, and crash through your release height.

Release height was set at 5000 feet above ground level, and we were going to manually open our chutes. You could opt for automatic release, but the auto systems can and did fail. Manual was the failsafe. As we hammered towards earth I kept checking on the position of the blokes to either side of me. At the same time the mission plan was running through my mind at lightning speed.

We'd set the release point almost directly above the Impact Point (IP), and the IP was set some 30 kilometres back from the target. That way we should hit the IP undetected, but should still be able to make the target on foot before sunrise.

As the stick leader, Jason would choose the exact spot to put down. There was no way you could read a map when doing a HALO, so the only way to select a landing spot was by visual means. He'd be scanning the ground as it rushed towards him, trying to choose a spot devoid of trees or other obstructions and away from any obvious danger.

The key responsibility for the rest of us was to stick on his tail, and not to lose him. If you lost one guy during the jump, it was all but impossible to find him again. You couldn't radio each other to try to work out where you were and you couldn't afford to show any lights, for obvious reasons. Keeping the stick together was the absolute number one priority.

Below me Jase hit the 5000-foot mark. I saw the flash of his canopy blossoming grey in the darkness, before I reached my right hand down and grabbed for my own release. The 'throwaway' release is a mini-parachute-shaped piece of material that deploys your main chute. You have to grab it out of its pouch on your right thigh, and throw it into the air. The mini-chute opens and drags your main chute into the void behind you.

Trouble was, as my gloved hand flailed around my right thigh, I couldn't seem to get my fingers on the throwaway. I plummeted past Jason, and made a second grab for it. *Still nothing.*

My right leg strap must have shifted slightly and trapped the throwaway. I'd tried to grab it twice now, and lost 1000 feet in doing so. Every second brought me 300 feet closer to a pulverising impact with the earth. There were just seconds before I hit, and the adrenaline was bursting through my system like a massive punch to the head.

Instinctively, I reached my right hand up and ripped away the emergency release strap from my left shoulder strap, so jettisoning my main chute. I slid my left hand into the wire handle on my right shoulder strap, and ripped it forwards, so triggering my emergency chute. An instant later I felt as if some giant was reaching over me and yanking me violently upwards by the shoulders. A second after that it was like I'd driven a car into a wall at 150 mph, and the air bag had just gone off.

I'd gone from deafening wind-noise and the sense of death rushing towards me, to total silence and quiet. I counted in my head: *one thousand, two thousand, three thousand.* I looked up to check my reserve canopy was good. Then I reached up with my hands, grabbed the steering toggles, and gave them a sharp series of pumps, which forced more air into the chute. Thank God it felt and looked perfectly okay.

I'd gained a good 1000 feet on the others, so my priority now was to slow myself down. Fortunately, the BT80 reserve is more or less a carbon copy of the main chute, with the same glide properties. I knew the rest of the stick would be trying to catch me, steering sharp left in a series of turns that would make them descend more quickly. I kept trimming my chute with the toggles, making small adjustments to steer it and slow myself, as I waited for the guys to appear.

I sensed a faint swish of air beside me in the darkness, and there was Jason, two-up with The Ghost. He didn't even bother looking over to check I was okay. If there was a problem he knew I'd let the blokes know about it. We had barely a couple of thousand feet to go, and Jase's priority was getting us down safely. We formed up in line, and began serpenting after Jason as he led us into the IP.

After chute-opening, this was the most dangerous moment. If we were spotted from the ground we had no way to defend ourselves. It's impossible to operate a weapon when under a chute and still in the air. Jase had to get the landing just right, bringing us in so that we touched down into the wind, to help break our momentum and ease the impact. Plus the poor bastard had to get his passenger down safely, on top of everything else he was doing.

I checked my altimeter: 1600 feet to go. I reached forwards and pushed the two metal levers together on the bergen attachment system. I felt it drop away, as the pulleys let it fall to 80 feet below me. Like this the bergen would hit first, so taking its own weight. I concentrated on my steering, trimming the chute with the left and right toggles, to mirror Jason's line of approach.

I saw the dark terrain rushing towards me, and a moment later I heard the soft plop of the bergen hitting the ground. That was the signal to pull back hard on both toggles, which flared and slowed my chute. I hit the ground running, and did a few steps to keep pace with the chute and burn off the speed. I came to a halt and stepped to one side, the chute going past me and coming down like a bundle of washing.

I dropped down on one knee and scanned for Jason's position, then did a visual check that Dez wasn't coming in to land on top of me. Reassured that all was good, I unclipped myself out of my chest and leg harnesses and dropped the para-pack. I unslung my M16, grabbed a magazine out of my smock pocket, and slipped it into the weapon with a faint click. I cocked it, closed the dust cover, and I was locked and loaded. If we had been spotted by anyone I was good to fight.

I slipped my Silva compass out of my smock. I found north and lined it up with the dark silhouette of a distant mountain peak. I now had us oriented. From studying the maps I knew exactly in which direction was the nearest known threat. I grabbed my webbing and belt kit out of my bergen and slipped it on. I worked myself into my backpack, bundled up my parachute and made my way over to Jason's position.

Jase was our pre-arranged RV (Rendevous Point). By the time I got there he was still busy trying to sort out The Ghost, who was clearly in bits. We were in deadly earnest now and under huge time pressure to get to the target. With a 30-kilometre night march ahead of us we wouldn't use our NVG kit, for it'd be too much of a strain on the eyes. Our vision was well adjusted to the darkness, and there was just enough ambient light from the moon and stars by which to navigate.

As the lads came in to the RV they went into silent, all-around defence. I did a quick map check, then scanned the surrounding terrain. I detected a shallow ditch about 100 metres or so to the north. It was a good spot to stash the chutes.

'We're here,' I whispered, indicating our exact position on the map. 'We'll head out on a bearing of 060 degrees, heading northeast. We need to cache the chutes. Dez and Joe, go check out that ditch.'

Without a word the two guys disappeared into the gloom. I felt around inside my bergen and pulled out the smooth steel form of my SOPHIE thermal imaging system. The SOPHIE was an outstanding piece of kit. Via its optics any warm object would appear as The Predator sees it in the movies, outlined by its heat signature. A fire, a warm vehicle engine, or a living being would appear as a distinctive hot white heat blob.

I grabbed the SOPHIE, switched it to 'on', and started a 360-degree scan of the terrain. Apart from the rhythmic chirruping of the crickets in the dark bush, it was utterly silent out there. My sixth sense told me that our landing hadn't been observed, but one sweep with the SOPHIE would prove it either way.

I'd completed about half the sweep when I stopped dead. There was the distinctive form of a standing figure due east, and it appeared to be looking directly at us. For an instant it shifted, and I froze. Then it went down on all fours, took a few bounds across the earth, and stood again. I knew from the intel briefing what the main big game animals were, here in the mountains: gazelle, leopards, baboons. No guessing which this was then.

I finished the scan. Nothing.

'It's all clear,' I whispered.

Dez and Joe were done stashing the chutes, and Jase had got The Ghost pretty much sorted. I checked the map again. 'Our grid is 457395. Repeat: 457395.'

I glanced around at the faces before me, making sure everyone had got it. We knew in what order we'd start the march.

'Okay, let's go.'

We moved out, heading into the hostile darkness and the unknown.

CHAPTER ONE

We'd deployed to Kuwait sanitised. We wore no insignia or marks of rank – nothing to betray what unit we were from or who was in command, and nothing from which the enemy could gain the slightest advantage if we were captured or killed. Prior to crossing the border into Iraq we had to sanitise ourselves still further – removing all family photos, wallets, keys, tearing out any notes from notebooks, removing any marked-up maps, and snipping out manufacturer's labels from our clothing.

We couldn't afford even to miss a brand name. If we got captured and one of us had a Berghaus label in his jacket, it would give the enemy a clue, an edge. It would give them the nod that we were most likely Brits, and that would give them the chance to get inside our heads and break us. Do that and they could extract vital information, and that could compromise any of our unit still going forward to achieve the mission. That in turn would impact upon the wider war effort, jeopardising the ability of the British and US forces to bring about a quick and decisive end to this conflict.

It was March 2003, and some eighteen months since I'd had to pull my reserve whilst HALOing into the night-dark African bush. Now, we Pathfinders were the first British boots on the ground in what was to become known as the Iraq War. We had jetted into the gleaming, space-age terminal of Kuwait International Airport in an ageing RAF Tristar, a fleet of which operates out of RAF Brize

Norton. It said a lot about the British military's can-do, make-do attitude that its airmobile vanguard was sent to war in a converted Pan Am passenger airliner dating from the 1980s.

We were here as part of 16 Air Assault Brigade. The Brigade consists of 1, 2 and 3 PARA, 1 Royal Irish Regiment (1 RIR), 13 Close Support Regiment (Loggies), Army Air Corps, 9 Squadron Royal Engineers, 23 Engineer Recce Squadron, 5 Battalion REME (Royal Electrical and Mechanical Engineers), a Javelin Battery (hand-launched missile operators) and a few other bits and pieces tacked on.

16 Air Assault Brigade was the airmobile hammer of Britain's armed forces, one that was scheduled to spearhead the push into Iraq. All told, it consisted of some 5000 men and women at arms, and it was us – the Pathfinders – who were to be the eyes, ears and cutting edge of that force.

Twelve years earlier, in January 1991, a coalition of thirty-four nations backed by a UN mandate had gone to war against Saddam Hussein's forces, to drive them out of oil-rich Kuwait. The Iraqi military had invaded Kuwait on Saddam's orders. The First Gulf War had been a race to liberate Kuwait, then 'home for tea and medals', as we say in the Pathfinders. Mostly, there was an expectation that this conflict – the 2003 Iraq War – would go likewise. The Iraqis were expected to surrender in their droves, leaving us little chance of getting any trigger time.

But my gut instinct told me otherwise. This war was a wholly different prospect from its predecessor. Firstly, we would be invading the Iraqis' territory proper, not driving them out of a foreign country like Kuwait. Second, the case for doing so – that Iraq had weapons of mass destruction that threatened global security – was far from cut and dried. If we were sent across the border, we'd be going deep inside Iraqi territory on either reconnaissance (recce) or sabotage missions. That's why the Pathfinders exist, and those are the kind of tasks that we live and breathe for. And somehow, I reckoned there was going to be real war-fighting to be done out there.

The Pathfinders is an incredibly tight-knit unit. It consists of six patrols, each containing six men – so thirty-six fighting men in all. Each patrol has two vehicles – open-topped Land Rovers specially adapted for PF (Pathfinder) operations. Together with support staff – engineers, signallers and the like – that makes ours a sixty-strong unit.

Whilst we may be small, we're perfectly formed. Pathfinders are widely regarded as the most highly-trained and specialist mobility troops in the world. Unlike the SAS (Special Air Service) and the SBS (Special Boat Service), who are trained in all facets of anti-terrorism, anti-insurgency and irregular and regular warfare, we train relentlessly for one thing only: insertion deep behind enemy lines on recce, capture, demolition and kill missions.

We are experts at HALO (High Altitude Low Opening) and HAHO (High Altitude High Opening) parachute jumping, our usual means of ultra-covert deep penetration airborne insertion. HAHO enables us to open our chutes at extreme high altitude and drift for many miles silently towards target. HALO and HAHO are the bread and butter of what we do, and it's what we're renowned for. But we're equally highly trained for insertions via foot or vehicle far into hostile terrain.

We'd been warned that the British press would be waiting at Kuwait airport, to get the first photos of 'our boys' arriving in theatre. We'd been asked to tone it down as much as possible. Apart from the long hair and beards, we were not to make like a bunch of Mad Max mercenaries in front of the British media, which is what we Pathfinders have a tendency to look like at times of war.

We were whisked past the press pack via the VIP Arrivals Area, then bussed out of Kuwait City heading north into the desert. Although we had our personal weapons and kit with us, we were yet to be issued with any ammo. We were here fully expecting the war to happen, but we had little idea what the road ahead would be like for our unit specifically.

As we headed north I gazed out of the air-conditioned cool of the coach. There was the baking heat of a flat, featureless desert outside, burning sands stretching either side of the tarmac to the shimmer-ing, pencil-thin horizon. Here and there we passed the odd mosque or dusty village, places peopled by men with sun-blackened skin, and wearing white desert robes and dun-coloured waistcoats. These were the Bedouin nomads of the desert – the same tribes that Lawrence of Arabia had galvanised into a fighting force to harass the enemy, dur-ing the First World War.

It struck me that whilst the camel-riding Bedouin might be able to move around this empty, billiard-table surface pretty much unno-ticed, we were going to have serious problems trying to do so. We just had to hope the terrain on the Iraqi side of the border was very different, and would offer us some cover and the chance to advance without being compromised. Or better still, we'd get to go in via HALO or HAHO parachute-drop, which is the Pathfinders' preferred means of insertion.

The Kuwait motorway petered out into an A-road, a B-road and finally a desert track heading into nowhere. Eventually, the track ran out completely, and the coach driver began crossing the open desert. He was clearly no Bedouin. Within minutes he'd lost his way, and we were driving around in circles. The other PF lads and I couldn't help but find this highly amusing: here we were, the vanguard of Britain's armed forces, and we were riding the road to nowhere with a clue-less Kuwaiti coach driver.

'Fucking typical,' Tricky piped up, from the seat next to me. 'Lost, even before we go to war!'

Tricky is an excellent bloke and an outstanding soldier, and he was one of the two real jokers on my patrol. I'd happily have followed him to the ends of the earth, and fought back-to-back with him when we got there. In fairness, the poor Kuwaiti coach driver was trying to find a blob of open, featureless rock and sand, amidst a world of such terrain. But an important lesson had been learned already: it was very, very easy to get lost here, even for the locals.

Eventually, the driver managed to locate a unit of US Marines set-ting up camp amongst the sand dunes. He stopped and asked for directions. I couldn't help noticing how different we looked from your average US marine. The younger grunts were these buzz-cut, clean-shaven clones. They were fresh out of the factory, and they kept wrestling each other and 'hoo-aah-ing', and 'yessir-ing' the whole time. Your average PF operator was older, and more wiry, grizzled and battle-worn.

This massive, barrel-chested Marine Corps sergeant pointed our coach driver in the direction of the British base. Half an hour later we reached 'Camp Tristar', as someone had affectionately nicknamed it. We dismounted and took a look around. There was absolutely nothing but rock, sand and more rock. We knew that the Iraqi border was just a few kilometres to the northeast, but there was nothing to mark where Kuwait ended and Iraq began, and certainly no noticeable change in terrain. It was a godforsaken flat and featureless desert in Iraq, just as it was here.

Over the coming days the Royal Engineers would use their giant bulldozers to construct massive sand berms all around Camp Tristar. They would provide a little protection against blast, should Saddam Hussein decide to start lobbing SCUD missiles our way. But right now we were some of the first on the ground here, and no one had so much as scooped out a bucket-load of sand.

We were allocated a patch of bare desert as Pathfinder Central. It was tucked away to the rear, adjacent to where the brigade commander would establish his headquarters. The Pathfinder Platoon would work to the brigade commander's orders direct, so he needed us close at hand. Invariably, we'd be tasked with sensitive and urgent missions, and Brigade HQ and our own unit would be quarantined off from the rest of the camp, to prevent any curious journalists from wandering our way.

It was a fact of life that media ops had become a part of any war effort, but we were one element of 16 Air Assault Brigade that wouldn't be having any journalists embedded in our unit. We could see why reporters needed access to the front line: the British public deserved to know exactly what our soldiers were doing when they were fighting wars far from home. But we couldn't risk a journalist going far behind enemy lines with a PF patrol, especially as our kind of missions were far too unsuited to the glare of publicity.

It was last light by the time we got our tent pitched. The entire sixty-strong PF Platoon was housed in a large, green canvas affair. The clever bastards amongst us had brought their own fold-up camp beds as part of their personal gear. As yet little of the Pathfinders' 'comfort kit' had been shipped into theatre, so the rest of us had to bed down on the hard desert. We'd been a good thirty-six hours deploying from our home base on the east coast of England, flying out from Brizers and then transiting across the Kuwaiti desert. We were dog-tired and we crashed out early, each of us quietly hoping that this time the Pathfinders really were going to war.

Whilst it may have looked pancake-flat from a coach window, one night's kip proved the desert to be rocky as hell. Come morning, there was a bunch of grumpy Pathfinders at Camp Tristar who hadn't slept that well. As second-in-command of PF I decided remedial action was required. There was one military force that always had all the kit you could ever wish for in theatre: the Americans. We needed to beg, borrow or steal some camp beds off the nearest friendly Yanks.

The Americans had a permanent base down in Kuwait City, dating from the First Gulf War. It came complete with a bowling alley, plus a Burger King and a Ben & Jerry's. But the nearest American base to Camp Tristar was several kilometres to the south of us, back where the Kuwaiti bus driver had asked for some directions.

The Americans proved to be as typically forthcoming towards their poor British allies as they always are. We managed to blag enough rugged canvas US military cots to sleep most of the Pathfinder Platoon, and with a good few left over – which only served to remind us what Gucci kit the Yanks always seemed to manage to bring to war.

We decided that as soon as we had a moment free we'd pay a visit to their PX store at their Kuwait City base, and stock up on cheap, subsidised American cigarettes and scoff. I just loved the little bottles of Tabasco sauce the US Army did to accompany their MRE (Meals

Ready to Eat) ration packs.

Whilst there, we'd also score a job lot of US Army T-shirts. They were far better than our British Army ones, which were thick winter-cotton issue, and totally unsuited to the Iraqi desert. As soon as we'd stepped off the air-conditioned coach we'd started to sweat bucket-loads. The thick cotton soaked up the sweat, and when the sun set and the desert turned freezing cold the sweat-soaked T-shirt chilled you to the bone. The US Army T-shirts were made of a thin, breathable fabric, one that wicked away the sweat.

The American PX store would also have racks of DVDs that were cheap as chips. Here in Camp Tristar we were feeling the lack of the Pathfinders' favourite movie: *Things to Do in Denver When You're Dead*. It's about a group of ex-cons, some of whom are ex-forces, who come together for one last job. The movie had achieved iconic status amongst the PF lads, but somehow in the mad rush to deploy it had been forgotten. So we were on a mission to go score a copy.

We were unsure as to when we might get the green light to pile across the border into Iraq, but by the time we did so we wanted to be fully tanned-up and bearded. When heading behind enemy lines – the core function of PF – we would make like locals. A full growth of facial hair, plus a deep tan, would help disguise the fact that we were a bunch of British soldiers not long out of rainy mother England.

The brigade commander intended to use us to scour the ground for the enemy, recce numbers, positions and strengths, and attack, seize or destroy vital terrain or installations. And like every man Jack in my platoon I sure hoped we'd get used. I say 'my' platoon, for I was the 2IC (second-in-command) of the Pathfinders, which as far as I was concerned was the best job in the world.

I'd come to the Pathfinders from 1 PARA via the murderous PF selection course. In the PARAs – itself a crack unit – I'd served in Northern Ireland, Kosovo and Sierra Leone. When on operations with 1 PARA I used to long to have my 'dream team' around me, men who were totally dedicated, exceptional soldiers, with the psychological strength to deal with whatever the enemy might throw at them. Now, in the Pathfinders, I'd got it. The problem was that there were those in the PF who didn't see me in quite the same way.

There was no tradition of military service in my family. Both my parents had been teachers, and I'd found my way into the Army by sheer chance. I'd been going badly off the rails at school when an Army careers officer had offered me a chance of a sponsored place at military college. It was the draw of the outdoor life and the adventure that had hooked me. With the Army paying my fees, I'd gone to Welbeck College and managed to stay the course. I'd done well in my A-levels, and gone on to do officer training at Sandhurst.

At the age of nineteen I'd been commissioned into the British Army, and at twenty-one I was made a captain, the youngest for decades. At the age of twenty-five I'd passed PF selection, and I was doubtless the youngest 2IC the Pathfinders had ever had. By contrast, many of the blokes had been in the PF for a decade or more and were 'rankers' – they'd worked their way up through the ranks. Once in, PF was often a job for life. You might move on to the SAS or the SBS, but most would choose to stay with the PF. Understandably enough, some of the old and the bold looked on newcomers like me as upstart officers they could well do without.

I'd been with the unit for fifteen months, and I loved what we were about. I wanted to spend the rest of my soldiering days in the PF, but Iraq was the first time that I'd taken the unit to war. I was commanding men who in many cases had years of elite soldiering on me. It was one hell of a challenge. The PF works on the basis that patrol command goes to the most suitable soldier, regardless of rank. It's a meritocracy.

I was on a massively steep learning curve, and there were those in the unit who were just waiting for me to fail.

CHAPTER TWO

Whilst John – it was all first name terms in the PF – our OC (Officer Commanding), would remain at Brigade Headquarters to command operations, as 2IC I'd get the best of both worlds. I'd be closely involved with mission planning, yet I'd get to go out on the ground leading my fighting patrol. As 2IC I had a specific role to fulfil on ground operations. Once all six patrols were out on taskings, my patrol would act as a forward HQ. That way, if we lost comms with Brigade Headquarters I could orchestrate missions in the field.

The old and the bold were hugely protective over the PF pedigree, and rightly so. The unit traced its lineage back to some of the most iconic units of the Second World War. If the Pathfinders have a predecessor, then it is the 21st Independent Parachute Company, the original Parachute Pathfinders. Formed in June 1942, the Parachute Pathfinders made up part of the British Army's 1st Airborne Division. One of their tasks was to land at the DZ (Drop Zone) some thirty minutes before their comrades, and to pinpoint it by means of a Eureka radio beacon. They were then to clear it of obstacles and beat off any counterattacks by the enemy, so the main drop could be made in relative safety.

As with the PF, the men were all volunteers and had passed exacting physical and psychological tests, which foreshadowed the current Pathfinder selection process. The original Parachute Pathfinders saw action in Algeria, Tunisia, Sicily, Italy, Norway, France and Holland, and finally Greece and Palestine, although Arnhem was the most testing operation in which they took part. On the night of 17 September 1944 they led what was then the largest airborne force ever into German-occupied Holland, as part of Operation Market Garden. The plan was to seize bridges across the Meuse River and two arms of the Rhine, so enabling the Allied forces to outflank the Germans and encircle the Ruhr, Germany's industrial heartland.

But at the Dutch town of Arnhem actual events proved the intel picture hopelessly wrong. The British 1st Airborne Division ran into far stronger German resistance than the intelligence suggested was present, and only one end of the Arnhem road bridge could be taken. On 21 September the small force holding the Allied end of the Arnhem bridge was overrun by German forces, the men fighting to the last bullet and beyond. The remainder of the Division was trapped in a small pocket to the west of the bridge, and had to be evacuated.

As a result of the failure of Market Garden, the Allies were unable to cross the Rhine in sufficient numbers to achieve the mission objective. That in turn ended the Allies' expectations of finishing the war by Christmas 1944, and the Rhine remained a barrier to their advance until ground offensives in March 1945. The Arnhem raid was immortalised in a book and a film, both entitled *A Bridge Too Far*.

The Parachute Pathfinders were seen to have accounted for themselves well in Market Garden. 'Your unit is unsurpassed by any other in the world,' wrote General Browning to their commanding officer, Major Wilson, after it was all over. General Alexander commented that the Parachute Pathfinders had shown 'all the true qualities of good soldiers – high morale, dash and fighting efficiency'. Bravery, *esprit de corps* and professionalism were the hallmarks of the unit, even when it was deployed on what was ultimately an abortive mission.

The main difference between the Parachute Pathfinders and us was that in addition to para-insertions, we were exhaustively trained in vehicle mobility operations, enabling us to drive vast distances behind enemy lines. That side of the PF pedigree was inherited from the LRDG (Long Range Desert Group) of the Second World War. From December 1940 until April 1943 the LRDG operated alongside David Stirling's SAS in the North African deserts, driving fleets of Chevrolet trucks and Willys Jeeps. Their function was deep penetration behind enemy lines on recce, capture and sabotage missions, hitting enemy supply lines, fuel dumps, airfields and ammunition stores.

During the seventeen months of the North African campaign there were reportedly just fifteen days when the LRDG weren't operating behind enemy lines. In September 1942 the LRDG undertook Operation Caravan, perhaps their best-known mission. Seventeen vehicles carrying forty-seven men travelled 1859 kilometres across the desert. On arrival at the Italian-held Libyan town of Barce the patrol split, one half attacking the Italian barracks, the other the airfield. During the airfield assault, some thirty-two aircraft – mainly Cant Z.1007bis three-engined bombers – were damaged or destroyed.

By the time the attack was done the LRDG had lost ten men, three trucks and a Jeep. But the epic withdrawal would cost the LRDG dear, because they were repeatedly hit from the air, losing all but two of their Jeeps and one Chevrolet truck. The surviving vehicles continued with the wounded, whilst different groups set out to escape on foot, most making it out of there alive and linking up with other LRDG patrols.

The Commander of the German Afrika Korps, Field Marshal Erwin Rommel, admitted that the LRDG caused his forces 'more damage than any other British unit of equal strength', during that war. The LRDG was disbanded in August 1945, when its function was supposedly amalgamated into the UK Special Forces. But somewhere within that amalgamation a lot of the specialist capabilities of the LRDG had been lost, and eventually that led to the founding of the Pathfinders.

The Pathfinder Platoon was formed in the 1980s to fulfil a very specific role – that of an air and land mobile recce and sabotage force, one seen as missing from the British Special Forces. It was the SAS blokes who first established the PF, and for many years its existence wasn't even formally recognised – hence our nickname, the 'Ghost Force'. As with the SAS in its early days, the men of the Pathfinders were pulled together from various units, so forming a small handful of specialist soldiers.

The Pathfinders became known informally as 'the bastard son of the SAS', and while on paper the men of the PF were still serving with their parent units, in reality they were members of this ghost force. We felt a close affinity with our fellow elite operators – the SAS, plus their sister regiment, the SBS. Our kit was begged, borrowed and stolen from wherever we could find it, but mostly it was passed to us by the SAS or the SBS on the QT (on the quiet). The Pathfinders had fought for many years to be properly equipped to do the jobs that they were tasked to do, a battle that was ongoing.

During my first week with the PF I sensed the difference with this unit and its men. From day one the Pathfinders felt like a pack to me – like a living, breathing organism rolling forward with its own life-force and free will. The guys were totally self-motivated. No one was sitting around waiting to be given orders or to be told what to do. They were busy refining skills and knowledge to improve themselves, and for the good of the entire unit. When not on formal training, they'd be sharing skill sets. Each PF soldier brought his own experience and expertise to the party, and the unit would let him grow into his ideal role.

At the end of my first week in the PF we'd gathered in the NAAFI for a Platoon Drinks Night. It was one of the lad's birthdays, and there was this PF bloke called Smudge on stage, microphone in hand and sporting a full Elvis rig. This wasn't cheap Elvis gear. He had a real-hair wig, glossy sideburns, thick, gold-framed Aviator sunglasses, white skin-tight flares, platform shoes, and a tight, open-chested shirt. The Pathfinder lads kept calling out Elvis and Neil Diamond numbers, whereupon Smudge would croon away like a good one.

This Platoon Drinks Night struck me as being pretty outrageous. These guys were way out left-field. I came direct from the PARAs and I was in at the deep end, getting my first taste of the über-confidence and individuality that the Pathfinders nurture. It was such a contrast to my previous life in the Regular Army. I can't sing for Adam, but the lads kept telling me that it was a sacrosanct PF tradition that the new guy – *that was me* – had to sing. They wanted me up on stage with Smudge, shirt unbuttoned to the waist, hips gyrating and crooning away.

I was fresh out of the trial by fire that was Pathfinder selection, but to me being forced to sing was far more daunting than any physical challenge. Singing and dancing are two of the things at which I am genuinely, utterly crap. During officer training at Sandhurst I'd been taught what to wear when at a casual function like a dance. The standard rig for an officer was red cords, pink-collared shirt and a blue blazer with brass or silver buttons. That, according to Sandhurst, was the acceptable dress code, and jeans were the 'devil's cloth'.

I never could go there, and thank fuck that at my first Pathfinder function I'd ignored the Sandhurst dress code. Early on in the evening a PF veteran called Jock came over to talk to me.

'I like your shirt, Dave,' he remarked. 'Where did ye get it?'

I was wearing this ill-fitting Levi's shirt, one that I'd picked up in town that day. I was happy to talk to Jock about pretty much anything, as long as it wasn't about me getting up on the stage to sing. We were five minutes into a conversation about my denim shirt – *Really Dave, is that right?* – and whether Jock should get one himself, when I realised that he was quietly ripping the piss out of his new 2IC.

Jock's verbal wind-up was a far more effective test than an arm-wrestling bout or a fist-fight would ever be. We ended up having a good laugh about it, and Jock figured I was all right as far as officers went. I'd passed that first major test, and I hadn't freaked out too much at the Elvis carry-on. And God was I relieved when it came to the end of the evening without me having to dance or sing. But it left me thinking what a bloody weird way this PF lot went about letting their hair down. It wasn't exactly 'normal' squaddie behaviour. I was more accustomed to the get-naked-and-drink-a-pint-of-piss-and-have-a-punch-up PARA way of partying.

My first few weeks in the PF continued to prove a total eye-opener. The unit had an entirely different way of operating. At that time John's predecessor, Lenny, was in command. One morning a female officer cycled over to our end of the base, to have words with him. She was based in the Regimental Administration Office, which provided admin support to the Pathfinders. A lot of the admin clerks were female, so Steve was forever volunteering to take the paperwork over there to get some face time with the office girls.

The lady officer explained to Lenny that she had a serious problem with the way the PF soldiers were behaving. They were failing to salute her, or to say 'Good morning, ma'am', as a junior rank should do. Lenny gave it to her straight: *They don't salute me, so they sure as hell aren't saluting you!* That lady officer had been in the Army for three years commanding a bunch of clerks. Many of the PF lads had been in for a decade or more, and were decorated combat veterans. It was hard for them to see why they should salute her: many believed the PF had no need for officers.

Camp Tristar was a flat, featureless moonscape of rock and sand, without a scrap of natural shade in any direction. It was burning hot, pushing 40 degrees centigrade. During the first few days we were ramming water laced with rehydration salts down our necks, in an effort to acclimatise as quickly as possible. Gradually, we started sweating less and then needing to drink less, as our bodies adjusted to metabolising at this kind of temperature.

We started building fitness training into our acclimatisation regime. We put together a home-made gym, using ammo boxes, jerry cans of water and scaffold poles as makeshift weights, plus we began running circuits around the base perimeter.

More of our kit started arriving. Big steel shipping containers were dumped at our end of the base, stuffed full of PF-essential gear, including our HALO and HAHO parachuting equipment. It was the dream of every PF operator that we'd get to do an airborne insertion behind enemy lines, and secretly we were all hoping that Iraq might offer us the chance to do so.

We established a logistics base and an armoury next to the accommodation tent, and started ticking off all the mission-essential kit, which included at least one full set of Elvis gear. It was SOP (Standard Operating Procedure) that Smudge's Elvis kit got deployed on all operations. It went everywhere we went, and for good reason: it was a crucial element of Pathfinder morale.

We'd also got issued with a new piece of kit, the L17A1 UGL (Under-slung Grenade Launcher), one that slotted on to the underside of our assault rifles. We rehearsed weapons drills with the 40 mm UGL, and as soon as the Camp Tristar ranges were up and running we'd be out there test-firing the weapon. We studied the maps of southern Iraq, and recced potential routes across the border and north towards the prize – Baghdad.

During all such activity, Steve was acutely aware that just across the sand from us was the Army Air Corps camp, which meant female pilots. Whenever he got a chance he'd have his top off and his shades on, and be out there catching some rays while posing in front of the girls. I'd have expected nothing less of Steve, but there was one member of my patrol who disliked him for it: Jason.

Jason was the Pathfinders' platoon sergeant and my second-in-command. He and Steve were like the proverbial chalk and cheese. I could feel the tension between them bubbling away just below the surface, plus I feared that Jason had issues with my command.

With only thirty-six fighting men in the Pathfinders we were an extraordinarily close, tight-knit unit. We knew each other intimately, even more so within each six-man patrol. As with all families, personality clashes could cause real problems. We were on the verge of going into Iraq, and my patrol absolutely needed to have its shit together. It was crucial that we started to function as one well-oiled, war-fighting machine. I feared that we were not, and that these kinds of tensions could end up tearing us apart.

We were a week into Kuwait and we'd tuned into our environment well. We'd acclimatised to the heat, and had grown seriously unshaven, dirty and hairy. It was obvious the war was going to happen now, and we were chomping at the bit to get across the border. We killed time doing intensive mobility training in the desert terrain around the base. This wasn't only about learning how best to use the vehicles and weapons in such a hostile environment: it was also about getting us working as a team in such conditions.

We headed out one evening for an extended stint of night driving. I flipped down the night vision goggles from my helmet-mount, until the twin leather cups were resting on my eye-sockets. The NVG resembled a small pair of binoculars, and they weighed about the same. They worked by amplifying ambient light from the moon and the stars. That night there was little or no cloud cover and the sky was star-bright above us. The NVG functioned exceptionally well under such conditions. Every way I looked they painted the desert in this weird, foggy-green glow, which was almost as good as driving in daylight.

But with the NVG down it was impossible to wear sand goggles – plastic safety glasses similar to those a welder uses, which are designed to protect your eyes during sandstorms. You couldn't fit them over the NVG. The weather in Kuwait had been pretty much the same every day: blistering hot during the daylight hours and bitterly cold at night, plus a good number of sandstorms. Some were minor flurries that you could drive through. Others were monsters, piling up like dark thunderclouds on the horizon and dumping half the desert on your head.

The only choice when you were hit by one of those storms was to go firm, which meant searching for some suitable cover. Our standard operating procedure was for Jason's vehicle to take the lead, and for us to follow him to whatever LUP (Lying-Up Point) he could find. We'd remain in the LUP until the storm had blown over, at which point the air would clear and we could see to navigate once more. But on night mobility exercises we didn't have the luxury of being able to use the sand goggles.

We'd been driving for a couple of hours when a storm hit. It wasn't a monster and I figured that we could keep going. Then I felt something hammer itself into my eye. I could sense my eye starting to close up, and then it began to weep liquid into the shemagh – the Arab headscarf – that I had wrapped around my face. We followed Jason's lead into a patch of undulating terrain and went firm. By now I could only see out of the one good eye, and I was losing my spatial awareness – my ability to judge distances and bearing by sight.

I was dead worried. If the injury proved to be at all permanent, then that would be me out of action for the coming war. It was also a sharp reminder of how vulnerable we were. Pathfinder or not, I'd suddenly become a liability to my team. Worse still, it was my trigger eye that had been damaged. There was no way that I could fire a weapon, or go to war, in this state.

Steve was the patrol medic, which meant that he'd done advanced first aid training, and was also responsible for the medical kit that each vehicle carried. He'd volunteered for the role, because it provided ample scope for liaising with medical staff wherever we might be – *and that meant nurses*.

He took a look at my eye, but he couldn't see much in the dark. Then he grabbed a bottle of eye-drops from the medical kit and squeezed a few drops into my damaged eye, but I still couldn't get it to open. There was an American field hospital not so far away, and Steve suggested we navigate our way there to seek help. But Jason started pulling a face like a dog pissing on a patch of thistles. He clearly thought it was all a lot of fuss over nothing.

'It's only some bloody grit in his eye,' he started muttering. 'We should bloody well crack on.'

In truth, I did feel like something of a big girl's blouse, with my hand clutching my eye and tears weeping out of it. Being the patrol medic Steve overruled Jason, and we headed for the field hospital. After a short drive we reached the American base. Whilst I waited to be seen by the doctor, Steve was doing his thing with the American nurses, so no surprises there.

The doctor gave my eye a good sluicing out with an eye bath, and a desert-load of sand came out. He inspected the eyeball, and told me that it was badly scratched. He gave me some prescription eye drops, and told me to keep treating it hourly with those. Do that and avoid any more sandstorms, and it should recover, he told me. But if I didn't look after it, it would turn septic, and that would be the end of me going to war in Iraq.

Steve wasn't the hottest medic in the Pathfinders, but he'd done all right by my injured eye. When push came to shove, he'd delivered. It had been Jason who to my mind had wanted to ignore it and 'crack on'. Yet I knew that Jason had a unique set of skills to contribute to the team, and we had to try to make it work. A lot of life was like that, trying to pull teams together, trying to make them work. The difference was that when you were in the Pathfinders you were in a pressure cooker, being in such close proximity to each other 24/7.

Plus we had the added stress of fatigue, dehydration, exhaustion and war-fighting to come.

CHAPTER THREE

Jason 'Jase' Dickins was a squat, short, compact kind of soldier. He was around five foot seven, and at some stage he'd had his two front teeth knocked out whilst playing rugby. He was supposed to wear a plastic plate with two false teeth in it, but he rarely did. As a result, he looked like a Bedouin version of Popeye the Sailor when he was all done up in his desert warfare gear. He also had this Popeye high-pitched strangled-chicken chuckle, which I figured the blokes found fucking annoying, as I did.

He had sandy hair, which was receding, and he was somewhat awkward-looking – hardly one for the ladies. But he was a battle-hardened operator, and he was possessed of a blind, brute strength and courage that demanded respect. He was also an extremely capable sergeant, with widespread demolitions and other specialist experience. He'd been in the PF for nine years, for many of which he'd commanded his own patrol. It was hardly surprising that he didn't exactly love it when he was put under my command in Kuwait. I was several years his junior and a relative newcomer to the PF, and I knew that Jason would far rather be leading his own patrol into Iraq.

Jason was the only married member of our six-man patrol, and Steve's suave, womanising ways really wound him up. Steve would taunt Jason about it, just to wind him up still further. But Jason couldn't seem to nail anything on Steve in terms of wrongdoing, and as far as I was concerned we were all big boys, so I was hardly going to intervene. Jason was big enough and ugly enough to fight his own battles.

No one could fail to respect Jason's military experience and expertise. As a tandem master, he had reached the ultimate in military parachuting. He could HALO from extreme high altitude with a fellow jumper strapped to his body. There are only a handful of soldiers in the world who are that jump-capable. There are very few tandem masters in the entire British military, and Pathfinders boasts a good number of them.

Jason could carry a non-parachutist – an intelligence officer, or an electronic-warfare or language specialist – deep behind enemy lines on operations. He could do the same with specialist stores – sensitive electronic-warfare devices for example – the kind of delicate kit that needs a human jumper to shepherd it to earth. Jumping at extreme high altitude strapped to another person, or a massive tube of stores, is extremely physically demanding.

The training was so intensive that you'd only ever get selected to do it if you were staying in the Pathfinders for several years, so the unit could reap the long-term benefits. Jason certainly wasn't going anywhere outside of the PF any time soon. He loved the unit, and I guessed that was the one thing that united us – Jason, Steve and me. We were Pathfinders, and we were intensely loyal to the PF family.

Of all the lads in my patrol I was closest to Will 'Tricky' Arnold. Tricky rode in my vehicle as the rear gunner, manning the 50-calibre heavy machine gun, our punchiest weapon. He was in charge of Pathfinder communications, and he was also the Platoon's most senior JTAC (Joint Terminal Attack Controller), the soldier who calls in the battle-winning air power. With Tricky embedded in my team we could act as a normal PF fighting patrol, but switch to being a forwards HQ element as needed, orchestrating comms between all patrols and conducting air strikes.

The nickname 'Tricky' suited him perfectly. It had a non-aggressive, cartoon character kind of ring to it. Whilst he smoked forty tabs a day, Tricky was still one of the fittest and hardest men in the entire unit. As with all truly handy blokes, he rarely had to show it. Tricky was like Jason Statham in looks and build, but he was a calmer, surfer-bum version, and more raggedy and battle-worn. He'd be well at home on a Californian beach, but he'd have a look in his blue-grey eyes that told you that if he levelled it at you in a beach bar, you wouldn't want to challenge him.

Tricky was three years my senior and was the living, breathing example of what a PF soldier should be. Whatever shit we might get into, I knew I could rely on him to keep cracking the jokes and cracking on. Nothing ruffled him. He didn't tend to love the 'officer class', but he and I had a special bond. He'd been my DS (Directing Staff) – akin to an instructor-cum-examiner – on Pathfinder selection, so he'd brought me into the PF. He was well aware that Iraq was the first time I'd be leading my patrol into action, and he was hugely supportive of me.

Tricky had come to the PF from the Royal Signals, which meant he'd spent a lot of time around headquarters and officer types. He was best placed to judge a relative newcomer like me. It didn't matter if you had all the ability in the world: in the Pathfinders, if you didn't get your hands dirty you wouldn't win respect. That was what Tricky saw in me, that I was a doer and a trier.

It was working in a Signals Squadron headquarters that had given Tricky such an in-depth understanding of warfare: the people who fight it, the command structures, the interpersonal relations, and the situational awareness that is needed if you are to make sense of a fast-moving battlefield. He commanded universal respect from the men, and in many ways he was ideally placed to be the Pathfinders' platoon sergeant. That position had fallen to Jason by virtue of his seniority, and because it was seen as more suitable for a PARA Regiment bloke, but I'd have preferred Tricky as my second-in-command any day. He was no sheep. He could be challenging at times. Yet from day one he and I had gelled.

Tricky had this smooth Edinburgh burr, which was soft and gentle on the ear. He used that – plus his looks – to devastating effect with the ladies. It was another point of bonding between us. Whether we were HALO jumping in California or doing vehicle mobility training in Sweden, 'The Findermen' – as the PF are known – worked together when on the pull. As long as you were fit for duty the next morning all was good, and we were none of us greedy. My PF nickname was 'Dave The Face', and the lads used to rip the piss out of me for what they said were my 'chiselled good looks'. Whenever we were out in a bar it was always: 'Let Dave The Face go first.' I was the eye candy. The lads would order me forwards, with the instruction to act gorgeous and shut the fuck up ringing in my ears. Once the women were in tow I had to let Tricky or Steve take over. Let me open my mouth, they said, and it'd all be over.

Steve was the bloke in the patrol that I was next closest to. He and I had soldiered together in A Company, 1 PARA. I may have been an officer, but I was still one of the fittest men in the company and I'd led by example. I'd earned Steve's respect back then and he hadn't forgotten. Steve wasn't an 'officer hater'. In fact, Steve didn't hate anyone. It was love – particularly the love of women – that was his major undoing.

A Scouser, Steve had toned down his accent because he'd figured out that the women preferred it that way. Whenever we were out on the town there was a touch of Enrique Iglesias about him. He'd wear a black shirt, sleeves rolled up past the elbows, and buttons undone to show off a bit of chest hair, plus lashings of aftershave. He was classically handsome in the dark-haired, dark-eyed Italian way, and he was forever telling the women that his family hailed from Italy, which was complete bullshit. That epitomised Steve: never one to let the truth get in the way of a good story.

As the Pathfinders' armourer, Steve got every chance to indulge his love of weaponry. Back at our base in the UK we had a purpose-built, impregnable underground armoury, equipped with a state-of-the-art alarm system. That was Steve's domain. It would take time to oil, issue and make an inventory of all the Pathfinder weaponry, and Steve had it down to a fine art. He'd stretch a two-day job into seven, and all the while he'd be down there in the Kingdom of Steve, his laptop hooked up to the Internet, surfing cyberspace for chicks.

If there was a training job going down with Jason in charge, Steve would suddenly discover a shed-load of armourer's duty that needed doing. He'd find a dozen 50-cals requiring urgent maintenance. No one was going to argue with the armourer, because your weapons were key to your survival.

Being PF armourer was about as much responsibility as Steve ever wanted in life. Some saw him as a shirker, but whilst I knew he'd take the easy path he'd never do so at another patrol member's expense. He was bird happy in the PF, and didn't give a fuck about progressing his career or sucking up to anyone. He was an excellent soldier, and I liked his calm, chilled exterior, and the fact that he was always – *always* – talking about women. Steve was the driver on my vehicle, and no matter where we were he'd turn to me and start philosophising about the fairer sex. He was a thirty-year-old, single, smooth-talking, chilled Scouser, and a total Casanova.

Dezmond 'Dez' Vincent was the fourth member of my patrol. He was a sergeant, but he'd been with the PF less than a year, and he hailed from the Engineers, so he had little infantry experience. As a REME (Royal Electrical Mechanical Engineers), he'd deployed to the First Gulf War, but he'd spent his time fixing tanks. He'd decided to go for PF selection because he'd been in the Army for years and had never seen any combat. He was bored, and wanted to be truly tested.

You can go for PF selection from any unit in the British military. There are only two rules: one – to Steve's eternal regret – you can't be a woman; two, you have to have served at least three years in the armed forces. Coming from the REMEs, Dez loved his wagons and he was a vehicle mechanic par excellence. He was a great asset for a unit like ours that relied on vehicle mobility much of the time.

When planning ops the blokes were always saying: 'Dez, just worry about the Pinkies, mate.' Ever since David Stirling's SAS ran riot amongst German commander Erwin Rommel's forces, during the North Africa campaign of the Second World War, pink has been the colour of choice for British Special Forces desert vehicles. Pale pink was found to be the colour that best blended in with the desert sands, and – no doubt about it – Dez loved looking after our Pinkies.

The Army was Dez's life, and he was covered in tattoos from the various units that he'd served with. He'd got a Commando REME tattoo; another with a dagger-type motif; and a REME cap-badge tattoo depicting a horse. Directly before coming to the Pathfinders Dez had been attached to the Royal Marines and spent a lot of time at sea. Marines are known for washing themselves the whole time, and Dez had got into the cleanliness habit big time. In the closed confines of a ship cleanliness was crucial, for disease could quickly spread, but in the PF this was anathema.

Long before deploying to Iraq we'd have stopped washing completely. There was no point going sneaky-beaky far behind enemy lines, if the scent of soap or deodorant gave you away to the local stray dogs. There are strays everywhere in Iraq, roaming the night in packs of a dozen or so. The more you smelled like a clean human, freshly bathed in shower gel, the more alien your scent would be to the dog packs, and the more likely they would be to raise the alarm. Conversely, the more you smelled like an animal, after taking on the odour of your environment, the less likely you were to be detected.

Once we had crossed the Iraqi border we were also fully expecting to be hunted by their military. Whereas the US Marine Corps and most of 16 Air Assault Brigade would be taking on the Iraqi forces in open warfare, our role would be to penetrate the enemy lines undetected. Just as soon as the Iraqi forces suspected we were there they would try to track us. They'd do so from the air, using surveillance and spotter aircraft. They'd do so from the ground, using EW (Electronic Warfare) devices that tracked our radio and satphone signals – and we knew that the Iraqi military had a fine EW capability. They'd do so by sight, using night-vision and thermal imaging kit to pick up human body heat. And they'd do so using tracker dogs trained to pick up the human scent, which was perhaps the single most difficult thing for an elite force like ours to evade.

Since reaching Camp Tristar we'd stopped shaving completely. Shaving wastes precious water and can cause infections. We wouldn't be washing on operations, so our skin would be dirty and smeared in old camo cream. Shaving causes cuts, which lets the dirt and gunk leak into the bloodstream. It also produces waste water full of human hair and soap, the scent of which is a dead giveaway. We needed to blend in with our environment as much as possible, looking and smelling like the wild.

We also needed to tune in mentally to that environment. If you were trying to move through the Iraqi positions, but you were worried about getting your hands or your uniform dirty, you'd never make it. We needed to fuse with our environment, becoming at one with it. Dez found all of that a bit of a challenge.

Whilst out on ops we'd be on hard routine, shitting into plastic bags and carrying it with us. If you left any behind it was easy for a search dog to detect, and then it could pick up your scent and track you. Shit could also provide vital intel to the enemy. If you'd been in a hidden OP (Observation Post) behind enemy lines, and you left six turds in six holes, the enemy could figure out there were six on your team. If you were compromised and forced to go on the run, the enemy would know how many they were hunting.

They could count the number of craps you'd had, and estimate the number of days you'd been there. From that, they could make a good guess as to whether you'd secured the intel that you came for. There may have been a SCUD missile delivery four days back, and your shits might indicate if you'd been in position long enough to have witnessed it.

Being on hard routine was brutal, and it could lead to some horrendous problems. Prior to deploying to Iraq we'd been on an exercise on Salisbury Plain. Inserted by Chinook helicopter, we'd been tasked with a night march to an objective where we'd carry out a close target recce. As soon as we hit the ground Leo, one of the most senior blokes on the patrol, had run into problems. He'd got the shits real bad. He hadn't been ill beforehand. It had just hit him from out of the blue.

All of a sudden we had to stop every fifteen minutes, so Leo could squirt into a plastic bag. It's quicker and easier if your mate holds the bag for you, but Leo's problem was proving so bad that it needed a plastic bag *and* some cling film. Each time he needed to crap we had to go firm in some kind of cover, whilst Leo struggled out of his massively heavy pack and dropped his trousers. We were under huge time pressure to recce the enemy position and report back to HQ, but we had to keep ripping off the cling film so Leo could let rip.

If we didn't keep catching and carrying his crap, we'd make ourselves a piss-easy target to track. We were stopping every five minutes by now, so this was seriously slowing us down. Taking his bergen on and off repeatedly was proving exhausting for Leo, and he was getting seriously dehydrated from all the shitting. Eventually, we took Leo's heaviest kit and shared it around our own bergens. That done Jason took point, and set a blistering pace to try to make up time. But we were bent in two by our loads, as we tried to move fast at night across punishing terrain, so our knees and ankles were getting hammered.

We were doing a forced march that was tougher and faster than PF selection, and one of our blokes was seriously ill with the shits. In spite of the cold the pace got us sweating, but each time we had to halt so Leo could crap we'd quickly freeze. We were hot-cold-stop-go for hours on end, but Jason never let the pace waver. I thought about how he'd come last on a PF training run at the start of the week, but out here on the moors and under a punishing load he was unstoppable.

We helped Leo as best we could, and we each knew that if we'd been in Leo's sorry position the lads would have done the same for us. We made up the time and managed to recce the objective, but by then we were plastered in Leo's shit. And all of this really wasn't Dez.

At Camp Tristar water was supposedly strictly rationed, but Dez was forever in the showers. He was full of nervous energy and permanently jiggling and jumping about. He was either running and doing press-ups, or in the showers scrubbing away at the sweat and the dust. There was the equivalent of a giant paddling pool on the roof, one that fed sun-warmed water into the showerheads. The showers were open plywood boxes, which left the head and shoulders free.

Tricky took the piss the whole time. 'Dez, what're you doing now, mate?'

Dez would worry that he'd done something wrong. 'I'm just having a wash, aren't I?' he'd answer, defensively.

Tricky would raise one eyebrow. 'But you had one this morning, mate.'

'Yeah, but I just did some more phys, so I'm sweaty again.'

'Dez, there's nothing wrong with being sweaty. You're not with the Marines now mate. You're with the PF.'

'Yeah, I know, mate, but it's hard to break the habit, and I have been in the Army for thirteen years, and I just like to keep in shape and keep clean.'

Tricky would exhale a long plume of cigarette smoke. 'Dez, take it easy. Once we're across the border there'll be no washing for weeks on end.'

I figured Dez was a bit of a misfit in the Pathfinders, but deep down the blokes liked him. He'd joined the Army at sixteen and worked his way up to being a REME sergeant. He'd thrown away any chances of further promotion, and all the pay and perks that went with it, because being a PF operator was the one thing that he hungered for. He didn't want to be in charge of a hundred engineers fixing tanks. He wanted to be part of a six-man patrol on operations behind enemy lines. Dez wasn't particularly bothered that he had the least combat experience in our team. He'd do any job asked of him and was keen to learn, and that demanded real respect from the rest of us.

The last man in the patrol was Joe Hamilton. Joe was twenty-one years old and he'd been in the Army for barely three years, which made him the runt of the pack. He sounded as if he hailed from the southeast of England. Like Tricky he had transferred from the Royal Signals, so Tricky had become like a big brother to him, which made him pretty much untouchable. Joe was keen and hyper-fit, but very, very quiet. He knew he was here to listen and to learn. He was skinny and boyish-looking, with wide blue-green eyes and brown spiky hair. On top of that he was puppyish, with gangly, bandy legs, and there was something slightly Fraggle-ish about him.

Whereas Steve could chat up anyone, Joe would be totally tongue-tied with the ladies. Like Tricky, he smoked like a chimney, and by rights he shouldn't have been as fit as he was. Joe and school hadn't worked out, but he was actually incredibly sharp. The Pathfinders was the alternative school in which he'd truly started to spark and come alive. The teachers here were people like Tricky and Jason, blokes he respected enormously, and he had no choice but to learn, for our lives depended upon it.

My guess was that Joe came from a tough home background. Something about him told me that, but we rarely got to learn each other's personal stories. The past was the past in the Pathfinders, and blokes generally didn't bleat about it. He'd passed the rigours of selection and completed the basics of PF training, and he was about to go behind enemy lines as the machine-gunner on one of the wagons in our patrol. We were Joe's family now.

Still, there was a part of me that was concerned about Joe. He was the youngest and the least experienced on our patrol, and if we had a weakest link I figured Joe was it. Technically, we were unsure if he had done enough time to qualify for PF. A soldier had to have served a minimum of three years in the military, and he was unlikely to get in without having served closer to six.

Still, we were in Kuwait and about to go on combat ops, so no one gave a toss about that now. We needed every man we'd got.

CHAPTER FOUR

Tricky was the guy that I'd choose to go back-to-back with if we were on the run behind enemy lines. Dez could out-bench press and out-run Tricky, but it was mental hardness that mattered most when on PF operations, and Tricky's psychological stamina was second to none. He'd keep going no matter what had happened and what parts of him were blown off and missing. Tricky would share his last mouthful of water with you, but he'd also be able to outwit the enemy.

After Tricky, I'd choose Jason as the guy to go on the run with, because of his experience and his solidity under fire. Jason would get you out of there, but it'd be less personal. After Jason, I'd choose Steve. You'd have a laugh with Steve even when you were dying: 'What d'you reckon those Army Air Corps chicks wear beneath their flight suits, Dave? I always was a lover not a fighter, mate!'

Next, I'd go for Dez. If you told Dez to go and attack an enemy position with his bare hands, he'd do so without hesitation, and regardless of whether it was the right or the wrong decision. He was a fearless military machine. And finally, I'd go for Joe. Joe would look to me to lead any decision-making, because my experience and skills were better than his. But I was certain that even young Joe wouldn't be found wanting if and when the shit hit the fan.

Breaking down the six of us between the two Pinkies was a bit like picking a football team at school. Tricky came with me automatically, for he was the platoon signaller, and he had the TACSAT comms system with which I could talk to PF headquarters.

Dez volunteered to be Jason's driver, because the two of them were real close. Steve jumped at being mine, and I figured there was no way that he and Jase could be in the same vehicle. That would be utter misery for the two of them, and could spell disaster for the patrol.

It was young Joe who drew the short straw. He got lumped with the last available place, on Jason's wagon as his rear gunner. He'd have been far happier on our vehicle. He'd have been with his mentor, Tricky, and no one would speak down to him. Steve would have made him laugh his tits off, and I'd have been able to keep a close eye. But there was no other way to configure the patrol to make it work.

When not practising night driving we've been doing mobility exercises by day, using the mark one eyeball. We've moved from point to point navigating across the open desert using compass and maps, and relying on the GPS only as backup. In the Pathfinders we only use our GPS as an emergency navigational aid, for it can and does fail. Batteries get drained in the blistering heat; desert-blown dust works its way inside; electronic circuits malfunction and go down. Navigating on GPS also tends to make you horribly disorientated. It gives you no sense of your geographical position or what the surrounding terrain is like, and you don't know where to run if you're compromised. We never use a GPS close to a target, or a recce tasking, for the glow from the screen could give your position away.

We practised desert driving and contact drills relentlessly, but we had to move carefully, especially when ramping the Pinkies across the Kuwaiti sand dunes. The wagons are top-heavy when loaded up with ammo, water and fuel, and they're vulnerable to rolling. During my days in the Parachute Regiment I'd had one of my best mates roll one. He'd been doing contact drills and had been turning across a slope when the wagon had flipped. He was a monster of a bloke, but still the accident had ripped his shoulder apart. He was very lucky to have survived.

At times we'd been taking a break from our Kuwaiti mobility train-ing and having a brew, and Steve would be slouched against our Pinkie, lost to the world. To the casual observer he'd look like he was sunbathing or half-asleep. Jason would get so wound up by it, he'd practically have steam coming out of his ears. But what could he say? He couldn't exactly have a go at Steve because he was too chilled out.

Over the brews Tricky and Steve would share a ciggie between them. Just as soon as he got the faintest whiff of smoke, Dez would stagger back like he'd been punched in the face.

'Fucking smokers,' he'd mutter. 'Don't you know how bad it is for you? It takes three weeks to get one cigarette out of your system. D'you know how many people die of smoking every year?'

That I guess was the divide between the two teams in our patrol: the chilled, and the distinctly un-chilled. As we trained relentlessly for going across the border, I wondered just how we were going to pull together once we were deep inside Iraq and under fire.

One thing became crystal clear as a result of all the mobility work: we needed run-flat tyres. We were using standard cross-country tyres complete with inner tubes, for they were easier to repair if punctured. We hadn't opted to fit specialised sand-tyres – which have a special tread pattern and run at a pressure designed to float across dunes – for we expected to be operating across a mixed terrain: tarmac road, dirt track, hard plateau, and trackless rock and sand.

But driving un-armoured Land Rovers like we were, all the Iraqis had to do was shoot out our tyres and we'd be well and truly buggered. I put an urgent request through to our UK headquarters for twelve sets of run-flats. With run-flats you could keep driving, even when they'd been shot out by small-arms fire. But right now any number of Brit-ish soldiers in Kuwait didn't even have body armour, they were that under-equipped, and it came as no great surprise when the request for run-flats was denied. We'd just have to make do with what we'd got, and hope the Iraqis couldn't bloody shoot straight.

There was only so much training we could do in the heat and dust of Camp Tristar. Frustration was on the rise as we waited to go to war. Sand seemed to work its way into every crevice, and it stuck to every sweat patch. We worked off some of our pent-up tension by sparring with each other. Tricky trained with his mate Lance, the champion bare-knuckle boxer. He would hold the pads as Lance smashed the fuck out of them, and then they'd swop around, each egging the other on.

There was nothing cosmetic about the six-packs, or the neck and arm muscles on these guys. They were the real deal: highly trained and carefully honed fighting and killing machines. They weren't like most guys you'd see in the gym, where appearance meant so much. With Tricky and Lance, every ounce of muscle was there for functionality. They could run over long distances carrying serious amounts of weight, even in arduous conditions like the Kuwaiti desert, and at the end of it they would still be ready to fight relentlessly hard.

As for me, I was spending more and more of my time with John McCall, the Pathfinders' OC, dealing with the planning side of things. I'd rather be training, or better still out on ops, but the command side was crucial to what I did in the Pathfinders, and I had never wanted anything more than to be 2IC of this unit. I didn't want to get promoted, for then I wouldn't be doing HALO jumps from the roof of the world as part of a six-man patrol. I didn't want to get my major or colonel, for then I'd have hundreds of lads under me fresh out of the factory, and I'd be dealing with red tape, court cases and all that crap. I wanted to remain as 2IC of the Pathfinders, and to enjoy it and do it well, for it could never get any better than this.

But all work and no play makes Jack a dull boy, and we all needed some downtime at Camp Tristar. Music plays a big role in the Pathfinders' unique *esprit de corps*. A mixture of timeless sounds had become associated with the Platoon: Johnny Cash, Neil Diamond, Kenny Rogers, and AC/DC for when we were about to jump off the rear ramp of a Hercules. New blokes picked up the classic tunes as the veterans faded into the dying light. Often you'd hear Kenny Rogers' 'The Gambler' blaring out on someone's speakers, before the whole Platoon would start to sing along.

Recently, Tricky had broken the mould a bit and got big into Pink, and he kept blaring out her girly, punky rock tunes. Anyone else in PF would get real stick for playing Pink, but no one was going to tackle Tricky. That all changed when the American SOF (Special Operations Forces) pitched up at our end of camp.

We were three weeks into Kuwait, and going stir crazy waiting to go to war, so it was a welcome distraction when the American SOF guys came along hoping to do some joint training with us. But it seemed that a bunch of unwashed, hairy, bearded, scruffy weirdoes blaring out Pink at top volume wasn't quite what they'd been expecting from this infamous Pathfinder ghost force.

In the PF it's every soldier's choice what gear he wears, and we'd culled bits of kit from just about every armed force in the world. Almost no one wore standard British Army issue gear. The British Army's desert boots had a hopelessly flimsy sole, and we knew that if we went in on foot we'd be man-carrying ridiculous amounts of kit for days on end. Instead, most Pathfinders wore Alt-Berg desert footwear. Alt-Bergs have a proper, mountain-wear Vibram sole, and they're made of a light and breathable material, which wicks perspiration away from the foot and into the desert air.

Alt-Bergs are manufactured by a tiny, specialist factory in Richmond, Yorkshire. That factory just happens to be next door to Catterick, where selection takes place for the Parachute Regiment. With PARAs fast wearing their boots out on selection, business at the Alt-Berg factory had boomed, and it was PARAs coming into our outfit that had brought Alt-Bergs to the Pathfinders. Steve just happened to know one of the girls who worked on reception at the factory, and just as soon as we'd heard we were off to Kuwait he'd got her to fast-track a bulk order.

A lot of the lads had brought a windproof smock with them. They were made of rip-stop cotton, and provided a shield from the cold desert night. We'd got them oversized, so we could wear a down jacket underneath, and so that the smock didn't ride up when marching under a heavy load. A few of the die-hard ex-PARA blokes insisted on wearing a PARA smock – a slightly more modern version of those worn by the Regiment at Arnhem. I wasn't one of them. In my view the windproof smocks were far superior.

As with boots, webbing was a deeply personal choice as a piece of kit. If we were forced to go on the run, we'd be living out of our belt or webbing kit, and blokes had that down to a fine art. A normal, rucksack-style belt clip makes a sharp click when opened or closed. It can even open by accident when crawling on your stomach. Instead, the PF lads used an old-fashioned roll-pin belt made out of canvas. Once it was pulled tight it wouldn't come undone, and it was silent to fasten or remove. On to that was sewn whatever tried-and-tested collection of pouches each bloke favoured. The priorities were ease of use and access, and making sure that nothing in your belt clip rattled when you were moving fast on foot.

Some guys preferred chest webbing, so they wouldn't be sitting on their belt kits when in the vehicles. Some had SADF (South African Defence Force) webbing, which was a hybrid belt-and-chest kit. The SADF had masses of combat experience, and their kit was generally first class.

Jason was a belt kit man, as was Tricky, and theirs was more battered and seasoned than most. I was also a belt kit bloke, but I combined it with a compact set of Soviet Army chest webbing, which gave me the best of both worlds. Dez was a chest-webbing guy. He'd often be lying on his back tinkering away under the vehicles, and he could do so in comfort with his chest kit on. Joe wore chest kit because that's what he had done in the Royal Signals, and Steve had SADF webbing because it was a damn good pose.

Every piece of kit was tailored and modified to suit a bloke's personal experience on the ranges and in combat. It was also heavily worn-in. Pouches had been flipped open a thousand times to grab magazines; pistol holsters had been sprayed with DPM (Disrupted Pattern Material) paint, to better camouflage them; combats were patched, faded and worn. As a result, we tended to resemble a bunch of action-figure hobos.

Just prior to deploying to Kuwait we'd been on a training exercise in Scotland, doing a high-altitude para-insertion. On the drive back we'd called in at a motorway service station. We were dressed in our usual motley selection of gear, and we had long matted hair and greasy beards from being out on exercises for days on end. Not a pretty sight.

A little kid was passing with his mum, who was really quite tasty. The kid pointed to us and yelled excitedly: 'Look, mum, cowboys!'

Tricky kind of let out this half-grunt, half-laugh: 'You dunno how right you are, lad.'

We had that same kind of look when the US Special Ops guys pitched up at Camp Tristar. For the Americans there was already something odd about the lack of any insignia that marked us out as being something *special*, but then Smudge came out wearing his Elvis wig just to wind them up, and there was Tricky singing along to Pink at top volume. The American Spec Ops guys didn't seem to know what to make of us. The more macho amongst them were giving us these looks like we were all gay, or mad or both.

'Say, pal, d'you mind turning down the music?' one of them remarked to Tricky. Tricky lowered the volume a fraction, but upped his singing to compensate. 'So, how much can you bench press?' the guy asked him.

Tricky stared at the bloke for a long second, wondering how to respond to such a bone question. 'How many ciggies can you smoke in one day?' Tricky finally countered.

'I don't smoke,' the guy replied. 'And I can bench press 150 kilos.'

'Well I smoke forty tabs before breakfast,' said Tricky, 'and I'm not even trying.'

'So how many press-ups can *you* do then, mate?' Steve chipped in.

The Spec-Op guy took the bait. '*Man, press ups?* I hold our unit's record for press-ups done in one day: *4,500*. I do them knuckles on the deck, 'cause it's harder and it works the wrists and fists too …'

It was now that Bryan Budd, ones of Steve's best mates from a sister PF patrol, pitched up. He pulled this mock, but extremely snappy and formal-looking salute, and the Spec-Ops guys stiffened their backs and pulled salutes in return. 'Sir!'

'To all of you who've done well, well done,' Bryan announced, in this perfect impersonation of a stiff, plum-in-the-mouth English officer's accent. 'And to all of you who've not done so well, well… well done anyway!'

The Spec-Ops guys were staring at him like he was cracked. He had no rank insignia, so for all they knew he could be a general. As for the rest of us, we were trying desperately not to laugh. In an effort to avoid the weird General Bryan Budd, one of the Spec-Ops blokes turned to have words with me.

'So, man, like where d'you come from in the UK?'

'London,' I told him. 'Have you heard of it?'

'Yeah, man, I know London,' he enthused, completely missing my sarcasm. 'I've been there once and don't you just love Leicester Square?'

He pronounced it 'Li-ces-ter', and before I could reply Steve cut in again.

'Yeah, I love Li-ces-ter Square. Next time you visit London go to this bar there – it's full of these chicks and they'll just love you American guys with all your muscles. It's called The Shadow Lounge.'

I had to kick myself to stop the laughter. The Shadow Lounge is London's number one gay bar. Me and a couple of the PF lads had stumbled in there one evening, after a 'Leo Sayer' – an all-dayer drinking session. As far as party atmospheres went, The Shadow Lounge rocked. We figured if you could survive a night as a straight bloke in there, you could survive just about anywhere.

The chest-puffing from the Spec-Ops guys and the piss-taking from us was over pretty quickly, and they asked us if we'd be willing to do some cross-training. They figured we had things we could teach them, and vice versa, plus it would break up the monotony of waiting to go to war. We headed for the ranges to have a go on their M4 carbines, whilst leaving them to try to figure out how to use our SA80s.

Recently, we'd been forced to give up our favoured weapon, the superlative M16A2 assault rifle. The M16s we'd been using were old and combat-worn, and we'd lost the battle to get replacements. Instead, we'd had the SA80 foisted on us, and we hated it. The M4 being used by the Spec-Ops guys was a fine weapon, being a lighter and more versatile version of the original M16 assault rifle.

We slammed through a few mags of ammo on the Camp Tristar ranges, putting the M4 through its paces. It was clearly well engineered, reliable, accurate and easy to clean and reassemble. It was also simpler to use, lighter and less prone to stoppages than the SA80, and you didn't have to reach one arm over the other to cock it. We wished we had the M4, and from the looks on the American operators' faces we could tell what they thought of our SA80s!

The guys were keen to show us what their Humvees could do. Like everything American they were massive – like a 4x4 jeep on steroids. They were better across country than the Pinkies, and they were up-armoured, providing far greater protection for the vehicle's occupants. By comparison, our wagons were Mad Max dunemobiles with the tops open to the sun and the air. But we still preferred them: they had better all-round vision, and vastly superior arcs of fire. They weren't low, claustrophobic and cramped, which was how the interior of a Humvee felt. Plus the Pinkies were easy on the gas, which meant they had a far greater range.In contrast to the SA80, which was a shit piece of engineering, we were proud of the Pinkies. The Spec-Ops guys could tell it, too. They were more than a little intrigued as to why we were so attached to vehicles that clearly offered so little protection from fire. They kept expecting us to show them a secret lever, which when pulled changed the Pinkie into something entirely more James Bond-like.

'Keep it quiet, lads,' Steve told them eventually, lowering his voice to a whisper. He pointed out the bonnet release catch. 'When the going gets tough – but only *real tough* mind – that is the special button you have to press, and hey presto! Of course, I can't tell you exactly what it does, 'cause it's classified.'

The guys were lapping it up. They didn't know that the Pinkies were basically the same piece of kit that the LRDG had taken to war some sixty years earlier.

CHAPTER FIVE

I t was during the aftermath of the Second World War that the Land Rover was conceived by the late lamented Rover Company. Rover's Coventry car plant had been destroyed by German bombing, and it had been forced to move production to a 'shadow factory', where it was only able to make cheap and simple vehicles. The original Land Rover concept fitted the bill completely: it was basically a cross between a light truck and a tractor.

The first Land Rovers were built on a Willys Jeep chassis, using the engine and gearbox from a Rover P3 saloon car. The bodywork was handmade from an aluminium–magnesium alloy called Birmabright to save on steel, which was closely rationed after the war. The Land Rover was designed to be in production for only two or three years, in order to gain some cash flow for the Rover Company, which would enable it to restart car production.

But the Land Rover proved so wildly successful that it outsold Rover's cars, so leading to the birth of the iconic brand that the British Army would come to rely on so heavily. The Pinkies that we were showing off to the Spec-Ops guys in Kuwait were based upon the sturdy box-section chassis of the original 1947 design, with the same flat, lightweight alloy body panels that were used then. Compared to the HUMVEE the Pinkie was an arcane piece of kit, but we in the PF loved 'em.

Of course, we knew this was an American-led war, and that we were here as the Yanks' poor cousins. The US Marine Expeditionary Force had a full division – that's 10,000 marines, plus warplanes and heavy and light armour – poised to punch across the border. There were tens of thousands more marines here to back them up, plus massive teams of SOF (Special Operations Forces). The American SF community was somewhat different from our own: for a start, there were some 60,000 active duty and reserve SOF in the US armed forces. There were no more than a few thousand Special Forces troops – active and reserves – in the entire British military. The relative level of training, and the calibre of the recruits, was reflected in those numbers.

Yet we in the Pathfinders dug the US military. Big time. They had all the Gucci kit you could ever wish for, and they were hugely generous with it. Plus they seemed to love poorly-resourced, yet exceptionally highly-trained and resourceful, British Army blokes like us. Once we were done showing the guys the non-existent secret weapons systems on the Pinkies, we headed off to the ranges to fire their Javelin missiles, which at $40,000-a-pop was absolutely fabulous.

The Javelin is a man-portable system, and all you basically had to do with the thing was load a rocket into the launcher, crouch with it on your shoulder, aim and fire. After it had been ejected from the tube, the missile travelled a good distance before the rocket motor ignited, so there was less chance of the launch team's position being spotted by the enemy, and less danger from the back-blast. A fire-and-forget missile, it would lock on to the target prior to launch, and use an automatic self-guidance system to home in. It was a compact, simple and highly effective tank-killing weapon.

We in turn initiated the Americans into the joys of the LAW-90 (Light Anti-tank Weapon-90), which was the nearest equivalent we had. The LAW-90 was British-made and supposedly man-portable, but at 2 metres long in the unarmed position it was like lugging a roll of carpet around the battlefield. If you were on foot, the only way to carry it was strapped crossways to the top of your bergen, which was a Laurel and Hardy-esque way of going to war if ever there was one.

Whilst carrying a LAW-90, there was every chance you'd turn around and knock someone out with it, or get stuck fast when tabbing through thick bush. When you're first taught to use the weapon, you have six sessions in the classroom before being allowed to try one out on the ranges. Here at Camp Tristar, Steve offered the Yanks a bit of background and a quick lesson on the weapon's capabilities, with me doing the demo of how you operated the thing.

'The LAW-90 was designed in the late '80s by a British Army engineer called Sid Vicious,' Steve began. He just couldn't resist slipping a couple of priceless wind-ups into the lesson. 'It's got a range of 500 metres to effect a mobility kill, and 300 metres to stop enemy armour dead. It's a short-range weapon, so it's best to engage an enemy target that isn't driving directly towards you.'

A 'mobility kill' means immobilising enemy armour, as opposed to destroying it. Steve explained the series of moves required to get the LAW-90 armed, whilst I demonstrated with the weapon at hand.

'It takes ten separate operations to arm the LAW-90,' Steve announced. 'Watch carefully as Dave demonstrates, for I am not about to repeat myself. First, remove your tube ends …'

I removed the hard black protective covers from either end of the 2-metre tube.

'Second, extend the tube.'

I tried concertinaing the thinner tube out of the thicker one, but predictably it was jammed. From experience I knew that only brute strength would shift it. I got the LAW-90 vertical, with one foot on the bottom end of the tube, and yanked hard. The top end shot upwards, until I had it extended to about 4 metres in length. The lads were in fits of laughter, as they imagined me doing this with a Soviet tank charging towards us, which was the kind of target the LAW-90 was originally designed to kill.

'As you can see, the LAW-90 is a perfect low-profile and concealment weapon,' Steve quipped. 'Now, Dave, slide forward the pop-up sight please …'

I flicked the slide and up popped the sight. On Steve's instructions

I folded a lever around to activate the trigger, dropped the safety catch to off, mounted the tube on to my shoulder, and checked the area to my rear, for anyone up to 30 metres behind me would get badly burned by the back-blast.

'Now, what crucial move has Captain Blakeley forgotten?' Steve queried.

The Spec-Ops guys gave a collective shrug: *How the hell would we know?*

'Oooh! Oooh! I know! I know!' Dez was jumping around and eager to dump on me from a great height.

'Okay, Captain Blakeley, what have you forgotten to do in order to fire your LAW-90?'

'Well, Steve, I need to fire a spotter round from the magazine before switching to main armament.'

Steve set about explaining to the guys the incredibly long-winded process of getting the LAW to make a kill. You had to select a target, then fire a spotter, a small tracer round that once fired would show you if your aim was true. After firing between one and five spotter rounds, you shifted to a main charge and prepared for the big blast.

'This is all very well in theory,' Steve continued, 'but with a moving target who can tell me the disadvantages of using a spotter round? Americans only to answer, please.'

'Well, seems kind of dumb to me,' one of the Spec-Ops guys volunteered. 'By the time you've hit the target with the spotter round, the damn thing will have moved!'

'Bravo!' said Steve. 'Anyhow, you try to keep yourself cool under pressure having just given your position away by firing the spotter round, and then you unleash the main charge. Now, have you all got that? Who wants a go?'

Two of the Spec-Ops guys volunteered to have a try firing the LAW-90. I figured they were true sports. It seemed to me we'd been ripping the piss out of the Americans' hospitality something chronic: first we'd blagged a load of their camp beds; then we'd fired off a shedload of their missiles and ammo; and now we were going to make them look like complete idiots with the LAW.

Steve pointed out a couple of wrecked trucks lying towards the end of the ranges. The first guy took up his firing position, sighted the weapon and let rip with the spotter round. It was bang on target. He flicked the magazine over to the main charge, and sighted again. He had to know that every one of us – PF and Spec-Ops alike – was dying for him to miss, so we could give him the biggest ever slagging. He pulled the trigger, a massive jet of flame spurted out of the launcher's rear, and a moment later the truck was engulfed in a powerful explosion.

He'd hit it first time, having had only a five-minute Monty Python-esque demo from Steve and me. It was some shooting. His buddy followed and did a repeat performance. Two shots with the LAW-90: two kills. Those guys had years of soldiering behind them, and that cumulative experience gave them the confidence and aptitude to fire even our most eccentric of weapons. All credit to them.

The LAW-90 was a heavy piece of firepower, but we'd have far preferred the Soviet-designed RPG (Rocket-Propelled Grenade). With the average speed of a tank over rough terrain being around 30 kph, the key qualities you wanted in a man-portable tank-killing weapon were light weight, plus speed and ease of operation. The RPG had those qualities in bucket-loads.

By contrast, the LAW-90 was a seriously inept piece of weaponry, but it was all we had and we'd never refuse the opportunity to take such firepower into the field. If nothing else, unleashing a few LAWs might buy us the time to extract from battle, if we were facing serious amounts of enemy armour. But what we wouldn't have given to be able to take a handful of the American Javelins to war.

Together with the Spec-Ops guys we burned through over a million dollars' worth of rockets, missiles and grenades on the Camp Tristar ranges. There was no doubt in our minds that we were going to war now. If we weren't, we'd never have been allowed to have so much fun at the expense of the British and American taxpayers.

Before heading back to their desert camp, the Americans suggested we trade some of the food in our ration packs with theirs. We jumped at the chance. We managed to offload a bulk load of stodgy treacle pudding in exchange for several dozen bottles of Tabasco sauce. None of the Yank operators had a clue what treacle pudding was, so we managed to convince them that it was ideal hot weather food.

All day every day there had been US aircraft howling through the skies above Camp Tristar. An endless series of UAVs (Predator Unmanned Aerial Vehicles) – a pilotless drone – would go buzzing overhead, flying recce missions into southern Iraq. Recently, we'd got news that two Predators had been shot down by Iraqi ground-to-air missiles, the first concrete sign of the looming war. That had been followed by the first wave of SCUD missile launches. Early one morning we'd heard this enormous rushing roar, like a tidal wave going over our heads. As a series of SCUDs streaked across the sky, we saw the US fast jets screaming overhead in an attempt to find and hit the launchers. There were scores of US and British bases here in the Kuwaiti desert, so one lucky shot by an Iraqi SCUD could cause carnage.

When he wasn't listening to Pink, Tricky had his radio tuned to the BBC World Service. It was a great source of information in this weird bubble that we were living in. The BBC reported that the UN was still trying to get Saddam to comply with its resolutions, in an effort to prevent war, but we knew Saddam wasn't about to do so and that we were going in. We heard news that the Iraqi commander nick-named 'Chemical Ali' had moved down to Basra. Chemical Ali was responsible for gassing the Iraqi Kurds, back around the time of the First Gulf War, and he was the architect of Iraq's chemical warfare programme. His arrival in Basra put him 50 kilometres or so from us, so well within SCUD range.

We started practising our NBC (Nuclear, Biological & Chemical) warfare drills, donning NBC suits, gloves and respirators as soon as the NBC alarm sounded around Camp Tristar. But pretty quickly it became clear that it was impossible to wear all the NBC kit and oper-ate properly as a Pathfinder. No way could we recce enemy positions and remain covert and functional when dressed in full NBC gear. We'd just have to hope that Chemical Ali's cartoon-character bad-guy name reflected the cut of the man, and when it came to it he'd baulk at unleashing any mustard gas or sarin on us.

As the drums of war upped their tempo, I was given the task of drawing up our EPs (Emergency Procedures), should we get compromised in Iraq. I picked Jason to help me do so, in an effort to give him some of the responsibility that he craved, and to try to forge a better bond between us. We went to visit the Army Air Corps, who were marked down to fly Lynx and Gazelle helicopters in CSAR (Combat Search and Rescue) missions on behalf of 16 Air Assault Brigade.

The Lynx is a British aircraft manufactured by Westland Helicopters. It is agile and fast – a Lynx broke the helicopter speed record back in 1986, flying at 249.1 mph. It's operated by a pilot and a co-pilot/navigator, and it can carry nine fully-equipped troops in the rear. That made it more than large enough to accommodate a PF patrol. But the AAC pilots were pretty blunt about the Lynx's capabilities out here in the desert. In the burning heat of the day its engines threatened to overheat, which basically meant it was unable to fly except at night.

In addition to the Lynx they also had a handful of Gazelles in theatre. Manufactured by the French company Aérospatiale, and in the UK under licence by Westland, this light helicopter was designed chiefly as an anti-tank gunship. Unfortunately, it's only capable of carrying five people, including aircrew, so it would take two Gazelles at least to rescue one PF patrol. The AAC lads had to keep cannibalising the few Gazelles they had in theatre, in order to keep a bare minimum operational, and there were no guarantees as to how many they'd have flying if and when we might need rescue.

In short, the Army Air Corps didn't have the spares or the supply chain to keep the right airframes reliably airborne. They promised to do their best to get us out if we did have to go on the run in Iraq, but there were no guarentees. It was hugely frustrating being in a so-called 'Air Assault' Brigade that didn't have the bare minimum of air assets, especially when those few airframes that we did have were dodgy as fuck.

We didn't have anywhere near the air assault capability the American military had had during the Vietnam War, and that was over thirty years ago. But you always want more and better kit in theatre, and there always comes a time when you just have to crack on. The selection and training we did in the Pathfinders were all about self-reliance: it was about depending on yourself and your small team to get you out of the shit, no matter what.

As we couldn't rely on the Brigade's own air assets for CSAR, Jason and I looked at other options. On our TACSAT comms systems there were two main nets: one was the British ground forces net, the other the air net. The air net was monitored by US AWACS (Airborne Warning and Control System) aircraft, which meant that US air assets should be able to pick up an emergency call from a PF patrol. The American military had a massive CSAR capability, and the potential to get lifted out by them was very real.

The Americans operated the Sikorsky MH-53 Pave Low, a state of the art CSAR helicopter. It had been designed to fly by day or by night, in all weathers and over all terrain, with unrivalled navigational aids and armour. It also boasted an in-flight refuelling probe, external long-range fuel tanks, a rescue hoist, and three gun mounts, equipped with two 7.62 mm six-barrel Gatling-type machine guns, and a single Browning 50-calibre heavy machine gun. If you had to be rescued, that was the boy you wanted flying in to pluck you out of harm's way.

Our default CSAR procedure would be to rely on our own forces – the Army Air Corps boys. But we also drew up plans for two RAF Chinooks to fly in a company of PARAs trained in CSAR techniques. We'd be at a designated HLS (Helicopter Landing Site), fighting off whatever force was pursuing us, as the PARAs hosed down the enemy and lifted us out. And as a third option we'd use our TACSATs to call up the American AWACS, and get patched through to one of their shit-hot CSAR teams.

We briefed the Army Air Corps lads, the American AWACS and the RAF aircrew on our call-signs, just in case we needed to speak to each other. The Pathfinder call-sign was *Mayhem*. My patrol had the specific call-sign *Mayhem Three Zero*. The AWACS aircraft were call-sign *Magic*, the British Chinooks were call-sign *Lifter,* and the Army Air Corps were call-sign *Rookie.*

At least we now knew how to talk to each other.

CHAPTER SIX

J ason liked getting involved in all of this big picture stuff, but at the same time he struck me as being a little out of his depth. We were liaising at officer level with the RAF, and with senior American aircrew. This required a bit of charm and diplomacy, and Jason's rough-and-tough soldier ways didn't always cut it. I figured he was starting to see a bit of the value-added of having an officer around. We weren't surrounded by the blokes here, so Jason could drop his anti-officer façade, and I was seeing a different and far more likeable side of him.

We'd been in Kuwait for the best part of a month, when finally we got the orders that we'd been waiting for. We were out in the desert doing mobility training, with a temporary field headquarters tent pitched amongst the dunes. John, the OC, would call for his patrol commanders whenever there was an important briefing. Jason, being an ex-patrol commander and now 2IC of HQ patrol, normally got included. But this time, when John called us in by name – 'David, Geordie, Lance, Gall ...' – there was no request for Jason.

We gathered in the ops tent and were given the H-Hour, the time to cross the border into Iraq. We were making an 'Army move', with the whole of 16 Air Assault Brigade plus the 10,000 warriors of the US Marine Expeditionary Force moving through. All times were calculated down to the last minute, or else we'd fuck up the roll-through. Pathfinder Platoon would cross the border at 0300 on 16 March, and make for a FOB (Forwards Operating Base) deep in the Iraqi desert.

This meant that we had little more than twenty-four hours to get ourselves fully sanitised, get our shit together, and get the vehicles packed and mobile. And there was a shedload of stuff to do before then. I returned to where our patrol vehicles were gathered in the desert, to give the lads the good news. We'd parked in a shallow wadi – a dry riverbed that would only run with water when it rained – which provided the only scrap of cover for miles around.

As I descended down the rough, rocky slope, I could see the distinctive forms of our wagons parked up in the sliver of shade provided by the wadi's side. The heavy 50-calibre machine guns were sunk back on their mounts, the muzzles pointing skywards like the necks of some fearsome birds of prey. I came out from behind our Pinkie and Jason was holding forth. He'd got his back to me, and I was just about to interrupt when I heard what he was saying.

'Fucking Dave The Face!' Jason spat out. 'He's just passed his 21st birthday and thinks he knows …'

I didn't catch the rest, but I could see by the looks on the blokes' faces that Jason had been gobbing off. Steve, Tricky and Joe were facing me, and their expressions said it all. They knew that I'd just caught Jason backstabbing me, and Jason had twigged from the looks on everyone's faces that I was right behind him.

I figured I had to do something immediate and decisive, or I'd be seen as being weak. But I also knew that I couldn't lose my rag or tear him apart verbally. That would only serve to belittle him and make his resentment fester. The lads knew I wasn't some wimpy officer type who'd never been in a scrap. Prior to the Pathfinders I'd spent six years in the PARAs, before which I'd been in the boxing team at Sandhurst. Even so, I had to kill this now, before it blew up big time.

I spoke into the silence: 'Jase, let's go have a private chat.'

He turned slowly and rose to his feet. I led the way into the open desert, heading for an area where we wouldn't be overheard. I was keeping my pace slow and even, and Jason was following me in a tense silence. He knew he'd been caught red-handed. He knew he was in the wrong. He knew I'd never have done the same to him. I'd read all of that in the quick, guilty flash of his eyes as he'd turned to follow me.

As we walked the two hundred yards or so I was rehearsing what I was going to say in my head. In the past I'd had PARA corporals and others be difficult under my command, but I'd always made it work. The difference was we were about to go to war, and Pathfinders like Jason were as strong-willed as they came.

I stopped, Jason stopped and we turned to face each other. In a way, we were polar opposites. I was tall and wiry whilst Jason was squat, solid and meaty.

'Tell me, Jase, what's the problem?' I asked.

He paused. He was quiet, staring at the sand for a long moment.

Then: 'Dave, you just got to know there's a lot of senior blokes here in the patrol, and I'd just like you to know to use the blokes … Just use the blokes, that's all …'

I was in no rush to reply. I knew he'd lost face on this one. I had to try to be magnanimous here, and give Jason a way out of the confrontation that he'd got himself into. I offered him a simple route out of there.

'Jase, if you've got any more problems or issues with me, I want you to come and speak to me first, and be direct about it. Don't let it fester amongst the lads, okay?'

Jason nodded: 'Okay. Fair enough.'

There was no shaking of hands. No man hugs. Nothing corny like that. It was just a few stark words spoken in the open desert, and we were done. I hoped we'd got it sorted. We were about to go to war, and it was high time we buried such rivalries.

Jason was 'a ranker' – he'd worked his way up through the ranks – and I was sure that he saw me as typical 'officer class'. He figured I was from a posh, moneyed background and here by dint of privilege. He saw me as baggage that he'd have to carry, and rules that he didn't need. He was wrong on several counts. First, *no one* gets into the PF without passing the gruelling selection. *No one.* Second, I was brought up in Middlewich, a town on the outskirts of Manchester and I grew up on a boring 1970s housing estate.

My dad taught kids with learning difficulties and behavioural problems, many of whom came from troubled backgrounds. He had the patience of a saint with those who had been written off by the system. He managed to listen to them and treat them as human beings, and he turned many of their lives around. A few of those lads went on to join the Army, and on their first leave they'd come back to visit, and they'd thank him for what he'd done for them. I didn't think I could do what he did, and certainly not with the same kindness or effect, and I looked up to him enormously.

I'd gone to St Nicholas's, the local state school, and it was an accident of fate that got me into Sandhurst. I'd started to mess around at school, and at the age of sixteen I'd signed up to join the Army on a whim. When a visiting Army recruiter had noticed the grades that I'd been getting, he suggested I try for a sponsored place at Welbeck College. I'd go to Welbeck to do my A-levels, and if I stayed the course I'd go on to do officer training.

Welbeck is this top-notch private school, set in the magnificent former home of the 5th Duke of Portland. As far as my parents were concerned, this was a golden opportunity to get me a private boarding school education, one subsidised by the Army. It was something they could never have afforded. They were concerned that I was going rogue, and about to follow in the footsteps of some of my mates, who were getting banged up for dealing drugs and other crap.

The nearest we came to having any military tradition in the family was one of my grandfathers, who'd been conscripted into the Second World War. On my first day at Welbeck we had to do a 1.5 mile run. It was the longest distance that I'd ever run, and I came in second from last. I didn't like being at the back of the pack. I did well at Welbeck and by the time I made it into Sandhurst I'd turned my life around. I was one of the fittest officer cadets, and I was recruited into the Sandhurst boxing team.

But the one thing I couldn't abide was all the pomp and snobbery that seemed to go with being 'officer class'. My closest mate was a guy called Matt Bacon. He was ex-Army Air Corps and he'd served in the First Gulf War. He was also a corporal who'd worked his way up through the ranks. Matt organised a secret birthday party for me, which epitomised our time at Sandhurst and how we went against the grain. We had 200 blokes there. James Blunt – then an officer cadet himself – played guitar and sang, and Matt smuggled in a bunch of strippers.

It was definitely not 'officer class behaviour', and it was the kind of thing we would have got kicked out of Sandhurst for, if anyone had caught us. Matt was the oldest recruit in our year and I was the youngest. A lot of officer cadets would cruise into easy placements, ones that their schooling and family background somehow 'qualified' them for. Matt and I were the opposite. We kept ourselves at the same level of ultra-fitness and we trained together relentlessly.

It was Matt who encouraged me to go against the Army's intentions, which were to make me an officer in the Royal Engineers. I had zero interest in being left in the rear with all the gear. Instead, I opted to try for PARA selection. I saw the PARAs as a classless regiment where I could properly fit in.

In due course it was Matt who would encourage me to try for selection into the one unit that eschewed all the status-obsessed Army bullshit – the Pathfinders. Many of the blokes came to the PF to get away from the rules and regulations of the Regular Army. I was one of them.

One of my favourite movies is *The Wild Geese*, in which a group of veteran soldiers get recruited to carry out a crazed do-or-die African coup. I saw the Pathfinders as a similarly maverick force, a bunch of rebel warriors going behind enemy lines to spread mayhem and carnage. As with *The Wild Geese*, we were a small group of very determined men setting out to achieve the seemingly impossible.

The Wild Geese includes a HALO jump, which very few movies do, another reason why blokes in the Pathfinders rated it. We also rated *Heat*, the Robert De Niro bank heist movie. Again, the guys in

Heat were a small team working together as a band of brothers. The common theme of an unbreakable bond coupled with the honour of thieves – the one last job – ran through much of the PF.

It was another reason why the press has to be kept away from us. A PF bloke had once been asked by a reporter if he could ever see himself working in a bank.

His reply: 'Yeah, maybe with a balaclava and a shotgun.'

It didn't matter – or shouldn't matter – what your background was, especially in the Pathfinders. In my rulebook, you treated everyone as a human being and you didn't seek popularity at the expense of others. I appreciated Jason's soldiering skills, and his dedication to the PF was unquestionable. But I was buggered if I was going to start justifying myself to him. I wasn't about to start jumping through any hoops for Jason, or anyone.

As we made our way back to the Pinkies, I resolved to do something more to bring him onside. Jason had commanded his own PF patrol, so I'd been expecting a power struggle. I'd seen him chomping at the bit for more responsibility, so I decided to give it to him. I was going to hold out the hand of friendship and show him that I valued him. It was the counter-intuitive thing to do: after being caught slagging me Jason expected to get punished. But from past experience I'd learned that coming up with the unexpected could have an amazing effect on difficult blokes under my command.

In Sandhurst I was taught to lead by authority. 'You might run with the hounds, but you should never *be* a hound' was one general's view. Familiarity breeds contempt, I was told. You had to keep yourself apart. It didn't make a lot of sense to me back then, and it made even less in the PF. John Keegan, the head of leadership studies at Sandhurst, had written a book called *The Mask of Command*. It studied the ways of Alexander, Wellington, Grant and Hitler, and broke command down into a scientific kind of formula. But command wasn't that: it was human, personal, individual and instinctive.

In fact, leadership was largely intuitive. And a study that dealt with four such towering commanders and generals dealt with men whose very position meant that they would rarely, if ever, be disobeyed. They were commanders by right, not true leaders. I was far more interested in how a lance corporal managed to get his men to follow him over the top, in order to assault a German bunker during the Second World War. How did he get his men to follow when leading a charge to almost certain death? And how did a private take over command, when all the senior ranks around him had been put out of action?

Those were the true marks of leadership, for only via such a man's instinct, character and example would he get his men to follow him. One of the best things I ever learned at Sandhurst came from the writings of one of the most gifted, yet underrated generals of the Second World War. Field Marshal Bill Slim masterminded the brilliant Burma Campaign, leading a multilingual army composed of many races, and turning defeat into victory against the Japanese. He was fearless in combat, plus daring and maverick in designing missions that often struck deep behind enemy lines. He was also universally loved by his men.

Slim wrote: 'Leadership is simple – it's just plain being you.'

I'd never forgotten those words. If I had tried to adopt *The Mask of Command* here in the PF I wouldn't have lasted five minutes. The blokes would have quickly seen through the façade. With the PF I had to lead by instinct and example, and use the lads to help me do so.

I'd not tried to pull on 'The Mask of Command' to upbraid Jason. Instead, I'd talked to him man-to-man. I'd made it clear that everyone's experience counts, as did their opinion. As Slim advised, I'd just plain been me. I hoped Jason recognised that, and that he would react to it accordingly, and help me lead my patrol and the platoon into war.

I gathered the lads, and explained the game plan that John had briefed me on. We'd cross the border and establish an FOB inside southern Iraq. From there we'd be airlifted deeper inside the country, to seize targets of vital strategic value. We'd not been briefed on those targets yet, for it was all done on a need-to-know basis. But our deep penetration missions would be backed by 16 Air Assault Brigade, with crack units like the PARAs and the Royal Irish Rangers flying in to capture terrain that we'd recced, secured and marked on the ground.

The battle plan was designed to enable the US Marine Corps to outmanoeuvre and outflank the Iraqi forces. A series of lightning air assault and airborne advances would leapfrog the Iraqi positions, in a wave of *Apocalypse Now*-type strikes. We'd render the Iraqi front lines redundant via our speed and our reach. Or at least, that was the plan.

There had been a great deal of talk about doing parachute drops. It made perfect sense, for there were so few airframes available to put troops on the ground. We just didn't have the Chinooks to move an entire Brigade forwards, but we did have the C130 Hercules aircraft to do a series of massive air-drops.

A single battle group – 16 Air Assault Brigade consists of four battle groups – requires fifteen C130s (a 'fifteen ship') flying in formation, to air-drop into theatre. That's ninety men per aircraft, so 1350 men in all. I couldn't wait to be at the spearhead of that force, as the PF parachuted in behind enemy lines to find the way.

We broke down the planning for the move into Iraq, so each man got a sense of ownership. Tricky did the air plan (how to use any airpower we had on hand to support us); Joe did the comms plan; Steve and Dez used the maps to recce the route across the border. In spite of our altercation in the desert, I gave Jason responsibility for 'actions on' – the patrol's set procedures should the mission go pear-shaped at any stage – a vital tasking. I knew he was hungry to be valued, and I figured that would bring him onside.

When I was a kid my mother realised her lifelong dream of owning and riding horses. She'd grown up in Liverpool, where the only way she ever got a chance to ride was by looking after the steeds of wealthy people. She was determined that horses would be a part of our family life, so she and my dad scrimped and saved to make that dream a reality.

I was six years old when she'd first given me the chance to learn to ride, and I took to it like a fish to water. I learned that when you were riding a particularly troublesome steed, it was often better to do the counter-intuitive thing and loosen the reins. The horse realised it could have its head, and it would be more responsive and faster. That was my philosophy with Jason: give him some rope.

It was a gamble, but time was short and it was all I'd got.

CHAPTER SEVEN

Finally, 16 Air Assault Brigade's commanding officers were getting their men keyed up for the move across the border. In front of the massed ranks of 1 Royal Irish Rangers, Colonel Tim Collins did his epic 'We go to liberate, not to conquer' speech, the one that the then American president, George Bush, would hang on his wall in the White House.

The media were there in their droves, so we kept our distance and listened in from the sidelines. Colonel Collins was ex-SAS, and we had a great deal of respect for him. We'd been bumming around in Kuwait for approaching a month now, and Colonel Collins' speech reinforced the sense of anticipation we felt. We were going in.

The BBC reported that the speech had gone down a storm at home and in the States. We figured it was no bad thing that the American leadership knew and appreciated that we Brits were here alongside them, ready to get our hands dirty. After all, we pretty much depended on them for air logistics and air power, not to mention camp beds!

We checked and rechecked our wagons in preparation for the move. The pinkish paint of our vehicles was specially engineered to reduce the vehicle's thermal signature. The Pinkies were open to the elements, so the interior dash units were sealed and ruggedised. The seats were made of a tough plastic, with a gap between the back and the bottom where water could drain through.

Our ethos in the Pathfinders was that 'skin is waterproof'. It was better to have an open-topped wagon and risk getting wet, than do without all-round firepower. When moving at speed in the driving rain we'd put goggles on, and we had shemaghs to protect our faces, although we didn't exactly expect such problems when moving into the blistering heat of the Iraqi desert.

Each Pinkie had a GPMG (General Purpose Machine Gun) on the front passenger side – my side – mounted on an arm, so we could swivel the weapon around. The pivot was well balanced and manoeuvrable, and had a gliding, *Star Wars* kind of feel to it. It basically took all the weight of the weapon, leaving the gunner free to control, aim and fire. Once practised, we could fire accurately, even at high speed. The GPMG gave a 180-degree arc of fire – so from Steve's head in the driver's seat around to Tricky, stood at the 50-cal behind. With Tricky's 50-cal being in a raised turret, it had a 360-degree arc of fire.

Strapped to the roll bar behind me were three bergens, each packed with sleeping bags, bivvie bags and specialist clothing, plus water and rations for ten days. Most Pathfinders used the standard British Army short-backed bergen, as it sat better on your webbing, with extra pouches sewn on for quick access to ammo. But a few of the old and the bold used ancient SAS-issue bergens, complete with metal frames.

Under the straps of the bergen you stuffed your grab bag. If you were compromised and you had to go on the run the bergen could be ditched, and you could leg it just with your grab bag. Each bergen could hold 80-plus litres, and weighed in the region of 30 kg when fully loaded. When on foot we'd be carrying all of that, plus our webbing kit and our personal weapons.

Ammo tins were piled between the front passenger and driver seats, including six 200-round boxes for the GPMG, so 1200 rounds in all. Each box was stacked the same way around, rounds facing forwards, and with the seals broken. That way if I needed to change an ammo belt I simply lifted the breach on the weapon, flicked open an ammo tin, flipped the belt across, closed the breach, pulled back the cocking handle and I was good to go. I'd drilled so heavily for it I could do it in two seconds at night and working simply by feel.

Stacked in the vehicle's rear were 1000 rounds for the 50-cal. There was an SP-GPRS – a specialised military GPS unit – fitted into the dash of the Pinkie. The SP-GPRS is encrypted, so that the enemy can't trace the GPS signal. It works to the military's dedicated satellite network, as opposed to the civilian network that normal GPS systems use. The Americans are able to shut down the civilian network, which they might do if the enemy were using the civvie network to target them. The military satellite network would always be kept open.

To the front, on the bonnet, we had a couple of the cumbersome LAW-90s strapped crossways, right in front of the dash. A bundle of camo netting was strapped on top of the LAWs, with the camo poles wrapped inside. Once we were out on the ground in hostile territory, we'd erect the camo nets in such a way that we could drive the Pinkies into and out of their hides.

A couple of the vehicles had machetes in them. The lads would use the big knives to clear vegetation, or to make camp. We weren't Samurai and they weren't for fighting. If you saw a soldier with a huge knife strapped to his waist then generally you knew to give him a wide berth. We had a standing joke in the PF if ever we saw a guy dressed like that: *Yeah, but what's he like in a dark room with a knife?* It was a piss-take: if ever it came to close-quarter combat, you'd be far better off shooting your adversary in the head with a pistol.

Every other vehicle had a winch fitted to the front, just above the sump guard. It was a vital bit of kit for hauling out bogged-in vehicles, but it was heavy, hence fitting it to alternate Pinkies. That way, every two-vehicle patrol had a winch should it need one, and it kept the weight down.

Two jerry cans of fresh water were loaded aboard each wagon, plus a dozen ration packs, claymore mines and grenades. When we were done packing our Pinkie was jammed so tight you couldn't fit anything else in. Well, all apart from the Marlboro Lights. Tricky

Right Early days in the Parachute Regiment, before I became a Pathfinder. Those around me are all PARAs, some of whom would go on to become Pathfinders.

Below Myself, left of photo, during High Altitude Low Opening (HALO) parachute training in Nevada, USA. Only a handful of Special Forces units do this highly specialist training, which enables us to drop from very high altitude and plummet to earth undetected.

Above Myself, far left, with fellow Pathfinders preparing for an epic HALO descent in Nevada. We're jumping with our M16 rifles strapped to our sides, which was then the Special Forces weapon of choice. The guys in shorts are RAF Parachute Dispatchers and they're checking that our oxygen breathing equipment is working properly before we jump.

Above Same Nevada drop zone. Myself to right of photo, with jump suits, parachute harness and helmets. We specialise in using HALO and HAHO techniques to penetrate enemy terrain covertly, to seize drop zones and bring in conventional forces.

Right Dressed in full oxygen equipment, state-of-the-art BT80 parachute with full Bergen, prior to a HALO descent and feeling like James Bond in *Tomorrow Never Dies*! With our parachute kit, M16 assault rifle, Bergen full of food, water, weapons, ammo and survival gear, we'd be carrying 100 kilogrammes of kit.

Above Pathfinders about to jump out of a C130 Hercules at extreme high altitude. At three minutes to P-hour – parachute hour; the moment to jump – the pilot would crank out AC/DC's 'Thunderstruck' at top volume over the aircraft's tannoy system. If the adrenaline wasn't already pumping in bucket-loads, that really got it punching through the roof.

Below P-Hour plus . . . We've walked the plank to the edge of the Hercules tail ramp and the wind is tearing like a hurricane around our ears. The lead Parachute Dispatcher stands strapped to the side so he doesn't get torn out by the wind. He's giving 'GO! GO! GO!' and we're diving headfirst into the howling void.

Above Nothing beats skydiving at sunset with the distant horizon a flash of burning fire. We're on a jump over the North Sea to practise flying under our parachutes so as to carry out a covert border crossing. A stick of six Pathfinders drifting silently under their chutes is all but invulnerable to detection by the enemy. We trained relentlessly for using this highly secretive method of penetrating enemy airspace in preparation for operations in Iraq.

Below Patrol in freefall. Terminal velocity is about 150mph. You need goggles to shield your eyes, otherwise it would be like riding a motorbike at that speed with no visor. It's vital to keep visual contact with the blokes in your stick so as not to gain too much separation in the air and lose each other during the descent.

When doing a HALO jump, we dive out of the aircraft on the roof of the world, but we only pull our chutes at very low altitude. This enables us to plummet into enemy territory with minimum time from jump to hitting the target – so giving the enemy the least chance to see and kill us. The most experienced parachutist always leads the stick into the Impact Point (IP).

Top right Yours truly in freefall over the desert, feeling like a giant shuttlecock plummeting to earth. To increase your speed you go into a delta shape, with arms by your side. Conversely, to stabilise speed and maintain your position in the stick, you get your arms and legs out beside you, in the starfish shape.

Centre and below right Still images taken from a video we filmed of one of our sunset HALO jumps. The camera was strapped to your helmet and reviewing the footage after the jump was a great way to learn and perfect the jump technique.

Below Pathfinders, with trusty M16 assault rifles slung over their left side, barrel pointed downwards. You'd always jump with your main weapon strapped to your body, just in case you lost your Bergen during the fall. 13-round Browning pistols are packed in the rucksacks, plus grenades, Claymores and most of the spare mags of ammo, so as to prevent weapons snagging in the parachute when it releases, which could prove fatal.

We're put through highly-realistic conduct after capture and resistance to interrogation training. Here Pathfinders are dragged out of the rear of a truck after being 'captured' by an 'enemy force'. The aim is to get us accustomed to how an enemy will likely treat us when captured on a mission behind enemy lines, and on the physical and psychological pressure we will be put through.

Bound and degraded; after hours of such treatment you either crack or you learn to find your inner peace and to zone out your captors. We were given talks by famous captives, one of whom, General Anthony Farrar-Hockley, had been captured and escaped several times during the Korean War. I will never forget his words: strength of mind was the key to surviving capture, and those who kept faith with their fellow POWs would make it through.

wasn't going anywhere without his forty smokes a day. When out on ops I'd share a ciggie with Tricky. It was a bonding thing. Joe and Steve too. Ciggies were a valuable currency, especially when the shit went down, so we loaded our Pinkie with a few extra crate loads.

The Pinkie is basically a cut-down Land Rover with a strengthened chassis. With three men to each wagon, plus all the water, fuel, weapons, ammo, comms kit and food, we were at the very limit of what it was designed to carry. We couldn't afford the extra weight of ballistic matting, which would provide protection against small arms fire and explosions. On the upside, we had an awesome amount of all-round firepower. On the downside, we had zero protection from incoming.

Needless to say, there was little room for personal kit, either. I had one problem with this: my girlfriend, Isabelle. Or rather, her generosity. She was a sultry French beauty; tall, leggy and with these large breasts that for some reason I was drawn to. Plus she'd got this gorgeous long, curly, dark hair. As a mate of mine remarked, she was a walking wet dream. She also had fantastic taste in French lingerie. She was a lawyer working for a top city firm, so I guess she could afford the best.

I'd seen her just before we'd deployed to Kuwait, and we'd had drinks and dinner in la-di-dah Hampstead. I'd only met her a few times, but I was still hopeful of cracking it that evening. It was what we in the Pathfinders called a 'trap or die' date. I had nowhere else to stay in London but her place, but unless I scored big time I'd be walking the streets until the morning.

I'd worked out the attraction on her part: I was Isabelle the high-flying lawyer's bit of rough. She had all these super-wealthy guys chasing her, but not so many rough as fuck soldiers. I knew that the more I talked that evening, the more chance I had of blowing my chances. So I played the still-waters-run-deep card and kept quiet, leaving Isabelle's imagination to fill in the blanks. It was amazing what a woman would dream up to explain a man's silence.

We ate and drank and she took me back to her swanky Hampstead apartment. It sure beat my one bed basher at Pathfinder camp with the mattress thrown on the floor. She put some slinky jazz music on the stereo, dowsed the lights and lit some candles. No Smudge crooning Kenny Rogers or Elvis here then. I forgave her when she started to dance for me, although I didn't join her for obvious reasons.

Then she asked me if I wanted some cheese. I thought: *For fuck sake, don't start eating garlic cheese whatever you bloody do!* She moved towards me, put down her glass of red wine and kissed me. Then she reached over and turned down the dimmer switch to zero. I guessed the cheese had been postponed until afters, then.

The lovely Isabelle had just sent me this care package out to Camp Tristar. Along with the melted chocolate and the wet wipes, there was a thick tome of a book. The wet wipes were much appreciated. With limited water, there would be days go by when we couldn't wash. They were perfect for getting rid of bacteria and grime around the mouth, so you could eat without getting sick.

But the book wasn't useful. Not at all. It was an appallingly bad novel about some future alien world laid waste by space-age warfare. In her letter she told me the book was especially precious, for her father had given it her on her twenty-first birthday. She asked me to carry it with me wherever I went, and to bring it and me back safely. Isabelle may not have had the greatest taste in literature, but hell, English wasn't her first language, and she did boast the finest French lingerie.

I figured I had to take the book with me into and out of Iraq. It got stuffed into my grab bag, along with the basics for escape and evasion. I hung the grab bag on the exterior of the vehicle, within easy reach of the passenger door. That way if I had to abandon the Pinkie and go on the run, I'd just grab it and go. And if we did have to do a runner, I could always use Isabelle's crappy novel as bog paper.

In the Pathfinders, you treated your vehicle as something extremely special. It was like you were a guy who'd worked all his life and finally managed to buy that dream vintage Ferrari. When not on ops we would barely use the wagons at all. We'd keep the mileage down, and carefully maintain and cherish our steeds. The vehicles were kept in a special hangar, and only once they'd been cared for would a bloke look to his own comforts. *You look after your vehicle – it looks after you.* Even more so when out on operations.

In many ways it was like the experience I'd had with horses as a kid. My mum taught me that you should always put your steed before yourself, for you were dependent upon it. Get the horse groomed, fed and watered first. So I'd give them their mixture of oats, molasses and corn mash, before ever I'd settle down to my own meal.

In an effort to prevent blue-on-blue (friendly fire) incidents, the Pinkies were fitted with BFT (Blue Force Tracker) panels, which were designed to send a signal making us instantly identifiable from the air. All NATO aircraft were supposed to be able to see Blue Force Tracker on their radar screens. At Brigade level they had this computer system that supposedly allowed them to see where all their callsigns were, via BFT. The Pinkies were also fitted with these visual recognition flashes, which were your back-up in case the blue force tracker system failed.

With the Pathfinders operating deep behind enemy lines we were most likely to be at risk from friendly fire, for we would be where the enemy were. We'd be sneaking about on minor roads, tracks or the open desert. We were also painfully aware of how different our Pinkies looked from the American HUMVEEs. From the air, an American pilot would most likely see them as enemy vehicles.

It was the first time that we'd had blue force tracker when on combat operations, and we thought it a fine idea – *that's if it worked*. We knew how easily computers crashed and electronic gizmos malfunctioned in the heat and dust of Iraq. BFT was also a new system that was untested in combat, so it was bound to have its teething problems. There was a lot of scope for it to go wrong.

We packed our NBC kits, as the threat of nuclear, biological or chemical attack was seen as being high. Our NBC detection devices looked a bit like metal detectors. You had to attach this special indicator paper, which would turn a certain colour depending on which NBC agent was present in the air. As far as we were concerned, the NBC kit was just more shit to cram into the wagons, which were already horribly overloaded. If we were to carry more weight we'd rather have had extra ammo, but we'd been ordered to carry the NBC kit.

Over the last week most of the lads had been doing an 'Op Massive' – that is, pumping themselves up in the makeshift gym. They'd piled on extra muscle, largely to put on weight that they could afford to burn when out on operations. When deployed into the field we were unlikely to get enough food. We'd be burning a lot of calories due to stress, pressure, the climate and sheer physical exertion. We'd burn muscle as well as fat, and we'd lose weight rapidly, hence the need for the Op Massive.

A few hours short of H-Hour, John asked the brigade commander to come and have a few words with us. Brigadier 'Jacko' Page had commanded several elite regiments, and his reputation went before him. He spoke to us in the mess tent, tucked away in one corner of the camp. He wasn't the biggest bloke in the world, but he had this ultimate confidence that shone out of him. The atmosphere was electric with anticipation, but Jacko remained measured and calm as he started speaking, as if he was having a fatherly chat with his lads.

'So, Pathfinders, finally we're going across the border. I'm sure all of you are more than ready. As we know this is a US-led war, and I know some of you wish you were deploying ahead of the US Marine Corps and their main force. All I'm going to say to you is that this is very early days. There's going to be a lot of surprises to come and you will get used, so be patient.'

Jacko wasn't bigging it up, like a lot of senior British officers tended to do. His talk was absolutely pitch-perfect for what we were about to do.

'You've done a cracking job during exercises,' he continued. 'Once we're in Iraq I want you to push the boundaries of what's possible. But just because we'll be war-fighting deep inside enemy terrain, that doesn't mean you'll get air cover all the time. You'll need to survive on your wits. I'm expecting the extraordinary from the Pathfinders, and I have every confidence that you will deliver.'

He gave us this steady look. 'Any questions?'

Jacko was a man of few words, and he'd said exactly what we needed to hear. If it had been some pompous speech, someone – most likely Steve – would likely have piped up with: 'Why didn't Chew Bacca get a medal at the end of Star Wars?' But Jacko commanded ultimate respect. John asked the first question, after which I figured it was time to raise the issue that was on the mind of every man in the room.

'Sir, if there is a need for us to insert by parachute, and that is the most tactical way to deploy, will we be jumping in?'

I'd just posed the million dollar question. I hoped I'd put it as diplomatically as I could, but what I was asking was did the will exist within the British military and their political taskmasters to allow us into Iraq by a para-insertion? I could see the blokes eyeing me, their expressions saying it all: *Balls of fucking steel to ask that one, Dave.*

It was more than sixty years ago now, but the British Army remained scarred by the loss of thousands of parachutists at Arnhem. Ever since then detractors had used that example to argue against airborne operations. I'd studied Arnhem at Sandhurst, where it was used to demonstrate the dangers of such a mission. They'd dropped the main force after relying on the intelligence given, and with disastrous consequences – but it was the intel that was at fault, not the method of insertion. Even so, Arnhem was still cited as an example of how many men could be lost when parachute operations went wrong.

The last time the British military had done a para-insertion into combat was almost fifty years ago, during the 1956 Suez Crisis. On 5 November a Pathfinder element of the 3rd Battalion the Parachute Regiment had dropped into El Gamil airfield, in Egypt, which made them the first British soldiers on the ground. The 'Red Devils', as they were called, were unable to return fire whilst parachuting, but as soon as they were down they'd used their Sten guns, their 3-inch mortars and their anti-tank weapons to deadly effect. Having taken the airfield with a dozen casualties, the remainder of the battalion was able to fly in by helicopter.

This was the first in a series of airborne landings. In spite of facing strong Egyptian resistance, and fierce street-to-street fighting, they largely achieved their objective. Working closely with French and Israeli elite units, the British seized the Suez Canal, which was the key military objective. But by then the international political battle was all but lost, and public opinion at home had turned against the war. Facing intense domestic and international pressure, the British and allied forces were forced to withdraw, and the entire Suez campaign was branded a failure.

In fact, Suez had demonstrated the effectiveness of parachute-borne operations in post-Second World War conflict. It embodied the very reasons that the Pathfinders were formed – to enable a small, elite unit to go in first and establish ground truth, so as to allow the main force to follow in some safety. It showed how you only needed to risk a small body of men to prove how things were on the ground. But the perceived failure of Suez had enabled the detractors of parachute-borne operations to brand them overly risky and prone to disaster.

It was that which we were up against now, as we prepared to deploy into Iraq. Jacko eyed me for a second. He was clearly thinking carefully about my question – whether the British military had the guts to send us in by parachute drop.

'You've raised a fair point,' he remarked. 'All I'm going to say is that we do have C130s in theatre. Your parachutes are here. If that is the best or the only way of inserting, and it's possible to do so, then you will be doing it that way.'

Each of us was aware that Jacko had commanded elite units at the time that the Bravo Two Zero patrol went on the run in Iraq, during the First Gulf War. As that patrol had discovered, going in by air and then on foot meant you had far less firepower than inserting by vehicle. But air insertions have a much longer reach, and are far more covert and rapid. Jacko's was an honest answer. It wasn't a firm commitment, but he wasn't shying away from the issue either. His message was that we stood as good a chance as anyone of doing a para-insertion.

After Jacko's talk was done we were issued with our silk escape maps. They covered the whole of Iraq and the neighbouring countries in great detail. But as a result they were absolutely fucking enormous. Spread out, each was the size of a large blanket. Rolled up, each was like a thick cloth belt. The upside was that the scale was superb, and they would be fantastic for navigating hostile terrain. The downside was that we had no idea where to hide them.

Tricky held one open above his head. 'At least now we've been issued with bloody parachutes.'

Steve pawed at his map and started doing a pompous officer impression: 'Now, men, we are here,' he jabbed the map with a stubby finger. 'I want you to go around here, up here, then over here and to take this entire area.'

Whilst he was doing so his finger was covering half a grid, and the map was blowing about in the wind. In the PF you never point with a finger when giving directions – it's far too inexact. You use the tip of a pencil, or something equally fine.

Eventually, we decided to roll the escape maps tight and thread them twice around the waistband of our combats, like a belt. There were no gold sovereigns issued to us, as there had been to the SAS in the First Gulf War. Then, they were for paying off local Iraqis to help the men of the Regiment escape from Iraq, if needed. Steve joked that due to the defence cuts the Army couldn't afford them any more.

In the final hours prior to crossing the border the lads were tinkering with the vehicles. They were checking the tyres for pressure and wear, and for thorns and sharp rocks; they were cleaning, greasing and oiling anything that might creak or squeak over rough terrain; and they were strapping down ammo tins and making sure the stowage cabinets were firmly latched shut. As he went about his work, Dez was mad enough and mince enough to talk to the vehicles.

'Right, so there we are – that's there, where it should be, in its place. Okay, nice and tight and looking good.'

Steve and Tricky took the piss relentlessly. But Dez was the equivalent of a horse whisperer with the wagons – *he could talk to his vehicles*. It was a real comfort to have him with us.

Even at this stage, when we were poised to head into Iraq, Steve was still playing the fool like a good one. He took an NBC early warning device and started tracking back and forth across the sand making this weird bleeping noise. He brought it close to Dez, and the beeping increased in pitch and tempo ten-fold.

'Emergency! Emergency!' Steve announced, in this metallic robot voice. 'Contaminated! Contaminated! This man needs another shower!'

Having alerted Dez to how he was 'contaminated', Steve took the NBC detector unit and attached it to the front of our Pinkie, with some gaffer tape. He stood back proudly once he was done.

'There you go lads,' he announced. 'All we have to do is get the beast up to 88 miles an hour and we can travel back in time.'

I was trying not to laugh. I couldn't be seen to be leading the messing, but I wouldn't ever want to stop it. As far as I was concerned, such larking about was a vital part of unwinding the tension of the coming mission.

With H-Hour fast approaching we grabbed a few minutes of our favourite movie – *Things to Do in Denver When You're Dead*. Steve had scored one from the American PX store, and it was playing on a laptop in the accommodation tent. The old sweats were back together for a final job, and each man had a compelling reason to be there. It wasn't just for the final pay cheque, so they could retire in the sun: each man had a personal reason to do the one last mission.

Andy Garcia plays the lead in the movie, a gangster with his heart in the right place and a whole host of problems. When one of his team is in prison Garcia goes to visit him. The two men touch hands on the dividing glass, and then mouth the phrase 'boats drinks'. It refers to how one day they'll have made their millions, and be on the

French Riviera sipping cocktails on the yacht of their dreams.

Having got a good hit of the movie, we wrapped up with our she-maghs. It was partly practical: they'd keep the dust out of our hair and faces. It was partly for disguise: at a distance we could pass for an Iraqi commando unit. And in part it was psychological: we were easing ourselves into a new skin. We'd have to think and act like the enemy now, if we were to outwit and defeat them.

We slipped on our goggles, because of the dust thrown up by the vehicles in front, and in case we hit a sandstorm. We weren't wearing gloves for the drive in. It was a night move, so it was going to be cold, but if it was any warmer than freezing it was best not to wear them. You needed skin on metal when you were in the fierce heat of a contact and operating all sorts of weapons systems.

By the time we were ready for the off, we were like a convoy of Mad Max lookalikes. As the first of the Pathfinder vehicles moved out into the pitch darkness, I turned to Steve and Tricky: 'Boat drinks.'

They gave me the thumbs up: 'Yeah, boat drinks it is, mate'.

CHAPTER EIGHT

We crossed the night-dark border, heading for the FOB (Forward Operating Base) from which 16 Air Assault Brigade would push further into Iraq. We'd barely got our wheels spinning when the sky before us dissolved into a sheet of flame. There was a massive firestorm on the horizon ahead, like a vast nuclear cloud. We'd been warned that the Iraqi forces might fire the oil wells in an effort to prevent us advancing through the desert. This was the result.

Away from the inferno, the terrain was pitch black and still. It was a vast, featureless sea of nothingness. But right ahead of us was this series of fierce glowing fountains. As we drew closer it became obvious how huge the angry orange eruptions actually were: each was a mountain of fire gushing up from below the earth, some several hundred metres high, and each was slightly mushroom-ish in shape, as if a cluster of atomic bombs was going off in slow motion.

As we got to within a few hundred metres of the first fiery geyser we were no longer cold. Instead, the burning heat was roasting the exposed parts of our faces. Five minutes of driving followed in the scorching heat, a deafening roar in our ears as the fire spurted high into the air, and then we were past that first torched well.

We pushed onwards, further wells gushing fiery volcanoes of oil all around us. For twenty minutes or so the heat was burning our faces and our backs, and then we finally found ourselves heading into the cold blankness of the night. It crossed my mind that each fiery eruption represented millions of dollars' worth of oil going up in smoke. But this was exactly what the Iraqis had done during the First Gulf War, back in 1991. When they were driven out of Kuwait they made sure to leave nothing of value behind them. They left only scorched earth and burning oil, the oil well fires being declared an environmental catastrophe.

I found myself wondering how long it was since the Iraqis had torched these wells. And where had the perpetrators gone? There wasn't the slightest sign of any locals anywhere, let alone the Iraqi military. In 1991 the Iraqi soldiers had largely run away, leaving only abandoned positions and burned-out wreckage behind them. It looked as if they might be planning to do the same this time.

We surged ahead on one of the main tarmac roads that penetrated into southern Iraq. At some stage we veered on to a minor track, and then we were heading into the open desert. We pulled into the location of the FOB, which was isolated from the main highway. It consisted of rocky terrain interspersed with the odd tuft of grass.

First light was at 0500 hours, and by that time we were stationary in our desert leaguer. We'd been on the road for a good few hours, it was freezing cold and the first priority was to get a brew on. As the day dawned it didn't seem to get a great deal warmer. The sky was strangely grey and overcast, and it looked as if the weather might be changing.

We'd been up all night driving, but we were still very much awake, for we've just crossed into a hostile war zone. The 1991 Gulf War had been a race to drive the retreating Iraqi forces out of Kuwait, then home for tea and medals. So far, it looked as if this war was going to go the same way. But even so we were now in a platoon leaguer in potentially hostile terrain, with the vehicles in all-around defence.

A half-hearted sunrise revealed an expanse of featureless rock and sand stretching as far as the eye could see in all directions. It was a flat-as-a-pancake stretch of bare nothingness. In the centre of the leaguer a couple of tents were being thrown up for the Brigade's forward HQ, and above and behind us in the distance we could still see the fiery black clouds of burning oil.

As the dawn light painted the desert a weird, sandy grey, we were doubly alert, and crouched over our weapons. For all we knew there could be Iraqi forces dug in a few hundred metres away, watching and waiting. With the sun well up and no sign of the enemy, we got sentries positioned on a rolling watch, and so began the preparations for whatever operations might be pending.

There were reports coming into the HQ thick and fast. Overnight the Royal Marines had staged a daring helicopter assault to take the Al Faw peninsula – a neck of vitally strategic land that gives Iraq its only access to the sea. The Marines had faced minimal resistance, but the sad news was that they had lost eight men when a helicopter had gone down in a sandstorm. We were also receiving reports that the US Marine Expeditionary Force was steaming north to take the town of Nasiriyah, 200 kilometres inside Iraq. Nasiriyah sits astride the Tigris River, so it was a vital crossing point for forces advancing upon Baghdad.

We now knew that the Royal Marines had seized territory with little resistance, and that the US Marine Corps were moving ahead seemingly unopposed. We also knew that there were SAS and SBS units on the ground in Iraq, doing covert operations. They'd gone in from the northwest of Iraq across the Jordanian border, and they would be recceing Iraqi lines of communications and cueing up air strikes. Plus they'd be hitting suspected SCUD missile sites, to prevent them being used on allied forces or being fired into Israel, as the Iraqis had done during the First Gulf War.

We were starting to wonder when our hour of action – the Pathfinders' moment – was going to come. I thought back over Jacko's words: *I'm expecting the extraordinary from the Pathfinders … There's going to be a lot of surprises … and you will get used, so be patient.* Jacko was right. We needed to be patient, and await the right kind of missions for PF. We had US forces ahead of us, but it wasn't our role to advance up roads to clear and hold ground. Our key role was to be air-dropped ahead of the enemy forces, and to recce and seize terrain deep inside their territory.

We didn't establish a tented camp at the FOB, for we didn't intend to be there for long. Instead, we bivvied up beside the vehicles and tried to catch some rest. We were hoping to get bounced out on ops when the brigade commander got recce taskings that he needed doing. Sure enough, John started calling in the patrols to get their orders. Need-to-know is the foundation of OPSEC (Operational Security) in the PF, and individual patrols often have no idea what the others are up to. You can't tell what you don't know if you're captured.

As 2IC Pathfinders, I sat somewhere in the middle of that need-to-know pyramid. If I was to take over command of patrols on the ground I needed to know the basics of what each of them was up to, without knowing too much to endanger lives. Over the space of the morning all patrols apart from ours got taskings. Three were being projected into the dead ground between the US Marine Corps and us. Their orders were to observe NAIs (Named Areas of Interest) – a series of major road junctions to the north – and cue fast air strikes if they spotted enemy forces.

We watched, enviously, as those patrols left the FOB. Two headed off due north driving into the open desert terrain, whilst a third loaded their Pinkies into a Chinook heavy-lift helicopter. They were to be dropped deeper in the desert somewhere to the northeast of us. We sat around drinking brews and trying to remain positive. We could see for miles in the flat grey light, and there wasn't a thing moving in any direction apart from British soldiers and vehicles. Yet our patrol didn't seem to be going anywhere.

Apart from the British forces on the move, it was eerily empty and quiet. There were no sheep, no goats, no Bedouins and no civvie vehicles. It was like we'd landed in a ghost land, or on a dead planet. Clearly, the Iraqis knew we were coming for they had torched the oil wells, but where on earth had they got to now?

*

Around midday I was called in to the HQ tent, to get briefed on the mission being given to two of the three remaining patrols. Hundreds of kilometres to the north of us lay an Iraqi airfield called Qalat Sikar. It was around halfway between where we were now and Baghdad. The two patrols were being warned-off to recce and mark an HLS (Helicopter Landing Site) at Qalat Sikar airfield, so 1 PARA could insert by Chinook and secure it.

Qalat Sikar had to be a good 150 kilometres inside the Iraqi front lines. Once seized, it would become the stepping stone that would enable 16 Air Assault Brigade to punch far ahead of the Iraqi forces. The British forces, plus the US Marine Corps, would use Qalat Sikar to launch airborne assaults deep into Iraq. In short, seizing Qalat Sikar was the key to the allied advance and to seizing Baghdad, and it could literally win us the war. It was the mission to die for.

One of the two patrols slated for the mission was led by corporal Kurt 'Geordie' Martin, a veteran PF operator who was viewed with massive respect. The other was led by Lance Green, Tricky's sparring partner. We watched enviously as those twelve men rushed around preparing for the mother of all missions. As Pathfinders we all wanted to face the ultimate test, like a pro footballer who was itching to play in a cup final. But right now it looked as if we were going to miss out on the Pathfinder mission of a lifetime.

It struck me that Qalat Sikar was the kind of operation in which all six PF patrols could easily get used. My lot would be the HQ patrol, co-ordinating the others on the ground. One patrol would recce the airfield and then mark an HLS, into which the PARAs could be landed by Chinook. Another would find a suitable DZ (Drop Zone), in case the PARAs inserted by parachute from a C130 Hercules. Other patrols would be positioned to the east, north and west of the airfield, covering NAIs like major road junctions. That way, when the PARAs were inbound we could keep a look out for Iraqi reinforcements, and hit them as required.

During the months of training back in the UK it was always HQ patrol – my boys – that went in to co-ordinate the marking of any crucial DZ and HLS. Other patrols would be out finding the enemy and calling in air strikes to smash them. I felt like we'd earned the Qalat Sikar mission, like we deserved it. I went to have a quiet word with the OC. John and I knew each other well from 1 PARA days, and in a way my relationship to him was like Tricky's to me.

During John's PF selection I had been his DS (Directing Staff) – akin to being his instructor-cum-examiner. At some stage during his selection I was tasked with giving John a 'gypsies warning' – the nod that he was close to failing selection due to what many saw as his over-confidence. As a result, I felt as if John and I had something of a special relationship – just as Tricky and I did – and I wanted to support him in making the right decisions in command.

John was busy on the radio-telephone, so I went to join Jason and Geordie at the ops planning table. Jason and I were hoping that somehow we were going to get a slice of the action on this one. If it turned into anything bigger than a two-patrol mission, John would have to send us, for we were the only other patrol at the FOB.

Jason and I scrutinised the maps and the satellite photos. Qalat Sikar was hardly Heathrow's Terminal Five. It was a minor airfield even by Iraqi standards. But the assessment by our intel boys was that it wasn't heavily occupied, and the airstrip was still usable.

'Can't be driving up to the airfield,' Jason remarked. 'Have a look at the ground – it's wet as fuck up around there. There's no way to get access cross-country in the Pinkies.'

'Too right, mate,' I agreed. 'Para-insertion is the only sound way to go in. We need to warn-off John to get Brigade cueing up the C130s, and to make sure our chutes are ready. Or what about Chinooks, flying in to drop the vehicles?'

Jason studied the map some more. 'Yeah, but they'd have to drop offset from the airfield, from where you'd still have the same problem driving across country. Plus there are outbuildings and there'll be shepherds and goats and shit. They'll hear the helos landing and that'll give the game away before it's even started.'

I turned to Geordie: 'What's your thinking, mate?'

'It's gonna have to be para-insertion,' said Geordie. 'Question is, have they got the balls to let us do it?'

'I'll go speak to John,' I told him. 'Any other way and you're fucked.'

I caught John as he came off the radio. I asked him if the Qalat Sikar mission was a definite. He told me that it was looking pretty damn likely. I asked him if those going in were going to jump. John said it all depended whether the Army high command had the guts to let them do so. The risks of a HALO insertion so deep inside Iraq were real, but we all knew it was the only viable way to make the Qalat Sikar mission happen.

'John, we've got to para for this one,' I told him. 'Can we at least get the Hercs allocated, and make sure they're getting the chutes ready?'

John gave me a grin. 'What's with the "we", Dave?' He paused for an instant to let the point sink in: '*Your patrol's not going*. At the moment, it's Geordie and Lance's mission. I need to keep you in reserve, as you're the only spare team I've got.'

I shrugged. 'We live in hope, mate. Either way it still has to be a para-insertion, and the Hercs are back in Kuwait, as are the parachutes. It's one hell of a lot to organise.'

'Maybe you're right,' John conceded. 'But either way I'll have to go speak to Jacko Page first.'

'If they try sending us in by vehicle we're constrained to use the roads,' I told him, ''cause the terrain up around Qalat Sikar is boggy and impassable. That means we'll be vulnerable to ambush the whole way. And that means we might not even get there. If we want the patrols to get to the airfield without getting compromised and recce and mark it, they need to go in by air.'

John eyed me for a second. I could sense his reluctance. 'Yeah, maybe. But remember Arnhem. Everyone's going to be flapping about the first British para-insertion in sixty years.'

'Yeah, but this isn't Arnhem. It's not dropping thousands of soldiers into an unknown area with bad intel. We're talking a dozen guys. We've trained and practised for this a thousand times, and you know we'll hit the IP.'

The IP is the impact point – the exact spot on which a force doing a para-insertion is supposed to land.

John shrugged. 'I know, but people will still be flapping that once the lads are there they'll be on foot with no vehicles if it all goes Pete Tong.'

Jason appeared at my side. 'Dave's right, boss: there's only one workable route in, and that's by air. It's the only way to do it.'

It was great to have Jason's support. 'We're at war, John,' I added, 'and people can't expect us to do missions like this without any risk. Right now if we don't go in by air, we're …'

'But this war is far from being popular,' John cut in. 'You guys know that. And the last thing the politicians and the generals want is to have another Bravo Two Zero on their hands.'

'Yeah, obviously,' I countered, 'but this is a game of chess, and we have to make the right move. If they want us to recce and secure the airfield they've got to get us there in the most tactically sound way possible. Once we're on the ground the risk is minimised, 'cause 1 PARA comes in on the back of us. We have to do a para-insert. There's no other way.'

There was silence for a second, before John announced that he'd go speak to Jacko about the options for an airborne insertion. As I watched him go, a part of me felt sorry for him. He'd been OC Pathfinders for less than four months and now he had to call this one. No doubt about it, the poor bastard was in at the fucking deep end.

Jase and I went to get a brew. By now Dez, Joe, Steve and Tricky knew there was something big going down, and they pitched in to the debate on how best to do the mission. We were all of the same mind: a para-insertion was the only way to do it. Qalat Sikar was over 300 kilometres to the north of where we were now, and far beyond the Iraqi front line. No one was going to make it in there overland and stay undetected.

If we parachuted in and found the enemy in significant numbers, then we'd radio in their positions and use our air power to smash them. But we would need the PARAs to come in rapidly on the back of us, for a dozen-odd Pathfinders couldn't hold that airfield indefinitely. The runway might be damaged, but we had Special Forces pilots who could fly the first wave of Chinooks in and land the PARAs just about anywhere.

The Special Forces Flight of 7 Squadron RAF had been formed in 1982, in the direct aftermath of the Falklands conflict, and in response to the need for specialist helicopter support to the UK Special Forces. Its pilots operated the Chinook HC2, which had improved avionics, electronic countermeasures, crew protection, fuel tanks and range, plus in-flight refuelling capabilities. If anyone could get the PARAs into Qalat Sikar safely, then the 7 Squadron aircrew could.

Depending on the state of the runway we could even call the PARAs in by C130 Hercules, in a TALO (Tactical Air Landing Operation). I'd orchestrated a TALO before, when the PARAs flew into Lungi Low airfield, in Sierra Leone, at the height of the civil war. The C130s put down with their ramps already lowered, and the PARAs drove off as the Hercs taxied along the runway, and took off again. We could para-insert under cover of darkness, recce and secure the airstrip using night vision kit, then clear the PARAs in for a Chinook insertion or a TALO. And that'd be it – job done.

We'd have leapfrogged the Iraqi front line by hundreds of kilometres. The enemy could then be hit from all sides, which would mess up their command and control, not to mention their supply lines. This was also about force projection: from Qalat Sikar we'd be within striking distance of the prize – Baghdad. This kind of mission was exactly what we'd trained for: the airfield was away from major settlements, it wasn't heavily guarded and it was relatively easy to defend. It was a peachy mission, and we all of us desperately wanted in on this one.

There was another big advantage to seizing Qalat Sikar. An army at war has a very heavy logistics chain – ammo, food, fuel, water. The only way to resupply forces here in Iraq was to drive up by road from Kuwait. Our resupply convoys were massively vulnerable to ambush, and if the enemy blocked the route the logistics chain would be buggered. That in turn would mean the war would take longer, and we'd take more casualties. But if we seized Qalat Sikar, that would open up an air bridge for resupply. Any way you looked at it, the Qalat Sikar mission had to be a winner.

Whichever PF patrols were sent in, they'd most likely go in by HALO as it is the quickest way to penetrate enemy territory, and land a body of men as a patrol, or a group of patrols. The IP would likely be offset a few kilometres from Qalat Sikar airfield, in case enemy forces were present in numbers. From there the patrols would infiltrate on foot and begin their recces.

However, if there was an air-to-air or ground-to-air threat – hostile enemy aircraft or missile batteries – then HAHO (High Altitude High Opening) would be the preferred means of insertion. Likewise, if there was a chance of the enemy detecting the Hercules by radar, which might alert them to parachutists being dropped into their territory, you'd again opt for a HAHO insertion. Saddam's forces were known to have good surface-to-air missile batteries and radar.

In HAHO your canopy would open automatically as you jumped off the aircraft, as each man was attached to a static line. You could be released many, many kilometres from the target and glide in. Each jumper would be wearing a specially insulated suit and mask, as protection against the freezing temperatures at high altitude. That would keep them warm as they drifted into target, the patrol floating to earth together with all its combat and survival gear.

On the front of your HAHO suit was a metal plate with a compass and an SP-GPRS, or 'spugger' as the lads call it. You plotted a course on the GPS to a waypoint – your IP – and the GPS would also tell you what altitude you were at. If there was reasonable ambient light, you'd use your naked eyes to scan for landmarks that you'd memorised from the maps, and to make sure you didn't collide with other parachutists.

HALO and HAHO are very specialist skills, ones reserved exclusively to military parachutists. The greatest height a civilian will normally jump from is 14,000 feet, and even then he won't be carrying anything like the amount of gear that we do. He won't be doing so at night, in difficult weather, and having been on missions already, and so feeling fatigued, and he won't be facing hostile forces.

I'd been on training exercises, and stood on an IP at night, and not heard or seen the parachutists until they had started landing right next to me. The canopy had opened so far away and at such altitude that there wasn't the slightest chance of me detecting it, and the glide in had been steady, stealthy and silent. It was like the parachutists had appeared from out of nowhere, and it reminded me of James Bond's para-descent in *Tomorrow Never Dies*.

You can do both HALO and HAHO in daylight, but doing so at night gives you greater protection from view. Most armies don't have decent NVG kit, and they don't like to operate in the dark. As Pathfinders, we're the opposite: we feel most comfortable deploying and fighting in the darkness.

The main drawback of para-insertions is the limited firepower you can carry. We HALO and HAHO with our personal weapons only, so assault rifle and pistol. We also have a sniper rifle and a Minimi light machine gun within each patrol. That is the kind of firepower that would enable us to find and fix the enemy at Qalat Sikar, and take out their command and control elements, but we'd be lacking any heavy weaponry if we came up against armour.

In PF, the decision to go in via either HAHO or HALO is the choice of the patrols. As a parachutist, you are horribly vulnerable: to bad intel; to equipment failure; to gusting wind; to your aircraft being shot down; to injury or death upon impact; to compromise or capture upon landing. But it's also the quickest, most direct and covert way to reach your target.

HAHO and HALO training is extremely expensive, and we'd recently brought a new parachute rig into PF – the BT80 – plus a new high-altitude breathing system called HAPLSS (High Altitude Parachute Life Support System). HAPLSS consists of an oxygen mask and a protective suit that enables you to survive in extremely low temperatures and at very low oxygen levels. If you were doing a HAHO jump you might be in the air under such conditions for up to forty minutes, whereupon HAPLSS is a lifesaver.

Qalat Sikar was the perfect opportunity to prove that all the investment ploughed into the BT80 parachute system and HAPLSS was worthwhile. But a part of me was worried whether John would win the argument with high command for us to do a para-insertion.

John hailed from a Scottish family, and he'd been to Robert Gordon's College, in Aberdeen. He was tall and distinguished-looking, and whilst he seemed proud of his Scottish heritage he spoke with a pukka southern English accent, which went down well with the generals at cocktail parties. Like all small, elite units the PF needed someone like him to fight our corner, and to keep getting us the resources and training we needed to stay at the top of our game.

John had charisma and a big physical presence, and if he believed in something he could charm and cajole it for the Pathfinders. But he was in a very tough position right now. He'd only been with the PF a short while, and now he was caught in the conundrum that if we para-inserted and it all went to ratshit, he'd be the guy in charge of the next Arnhem/Bravo Two Zero.

But if they tried sending us in by vehicle and we all got captured or killed, that would be equally disastrous.

CHAPTER NINE

J ohn was showing all the signs of being under strain, and in a way it was hardly surprising. But for the men of the Pathfinders, Qalat Sikar was a dream mission. It represented the zenith of what we train for. Even the Hereford boys had never done an insertion as daring as this one, and it was the kind of tasking that the British military would talk about for years to come.

As soon as we had been warned-off to deploy to Kuwait, we'd started doing masses of HAHO and HALO continuity training. Time after time we'd jumped over the North Sea at night, and infiltrated into the UK on NVG (Night Vision Goggles) and using our GPS to navigate. We'd never be better prepared for a mission such as this one.

We were still waiting for the word from John, when I saw H, one of the true legends of the PF, approaching. H was this massive, moustachioed tandem master. Prior to coming to the PF he'd been a farmer in the northeast of England, and by anyone's reckoning he was hard as nails. He and Jason were the best parachutists we had, and amongst the most experienced in the world.

H started chatting to Jase. There was a whole lot of gesticulating, and they were clearly cooking up some kind of plan between them. They came over to me to have words. H could be very abrupt and abrasive when he wanted to get a point across. He said exactly what he thought, and as a bloke he did exactly what it said on the tin. I liked and respected him for it.

He waded right in. 'Dave if there's people bloody flapping about us parachuting, if they haven't got the balls for a couple of patrols to para in, then me and Jase can go in tandem with two others. That way we only risk four blokes and there's no way anyone can say we won't hit the IP.'

'They can drop the two of us and they know we'll hit the target,' Jason added.

'Jase's done shed loads of JTAC-ing,' said H. 'He can call in all the bloody air strikes we need. Job sorted.'

'H, Jase – I know,' I told them. 'I know you blokes could do it. Let's go speak to John and make the offer. But I reckon they'll flap even more about just four blokes going in.'

'Remember Ron Reid-Daly,' said Jason. 'The Selous Scouts. They did scores of two-man HALO insertions into Mozambique, and time and again they proved they worked.'

'Yeah, lads, I know. I hear you.'

The Selous Scouts were the Rhodesian Special Forces at the time of that country's civil war. They were some of the most experienced and battle-hardened elite soldiers in the world. They'd pioneered the technique of using small, two-man HALO teams to penetrate far behind enemy lines and call in air missions, which is exactly what H and Jase were now suggesting they do.

Recently, we'd started doing HALO and HAHO training in South Africa. It was more cost-effective than training in America, our normal venue. We'd done scores of jumps over the deserts and mountains, honing the kind of techniques used by the Selous Scouts to perfection (and similar to the mission described in the prologue to this book).

And right now I had to admire Jason's can-do attitude in suggesting they use such skills to get around the naysayers, and get into Qalat Sikar. I didn't doubt for one moment that he and H had the balls to do it, either.

The three of us went and found John outside the HQ tent. Jase and H hovered whilst I had words. I told John that if Brigade Command was worried about a load of blokes getting scattered all over the Iraqi desert, H and Jase were willing to jump in tandem and guarantee 100 per cent to hit the target.

We left John to mull it over as another of his options. With the approach of last light Geordie and Lance's patrols remained on standby for Qalat Sikar, although their method of insertion was undecided. But that evening we had some highly disturbing news radioed into PF headquarters. In the far north of Iraq a full squadron of SBS – the sister regiment to the SAS – had got compromised. Their entire mission was rapidly going to ratshit, leaving some sixty elite soldiers on the run up near the border with Syria.

The SBS squadron had flown in by Chinook, and had been dropped with their vehicles deep in the Iraqi desert. But over several days hundreds of Fedayeen (Iraqi irregular forces) had hunted down the British force, converging on their positions. The Iraqis had jeeps sporting DShKs (Dushkas) – a Soviet-era heavy anti-aircraft weapon, which is devastating when used against ground forces – plus they had Iraqi army regular units with heavy armour in support. The SBS were driving Pinkies, so they were totally outgunned.

The elite British force had made a fighting withdrawal, but during many hours of intense combat the patrol was split into smaller and smaller groups. Vehicles had got bogged down, and the SBS lads had been forced to blow up their Pinkies to prevent the enemy from seizing them. Yet several charges had failed to detonate. Under cover from allied air power, the main body of the squadron had been airlifted out. But by first light we still had at least two groups on the run, and the word was that the Iraqis would shortly be parading the captured Pinkies before the world's media.

Having those SBS blokes on the run in the north of Iraq was deeply troubling. A force of brother warriors was out there being hunted, and at the enemy's mercy. What had befallen that SBS squadron was the kind of fuck-up that could happen to any small group of elite warriors, when going far into hostile territory. It was a powerful reminder of the dangers we faced here, and of what we wanted to avoid happening to any of our patrols.

But most of all it was God-awful timing for the Qalat Sikar mission. Just as soon as the Iraqis started parading the captured Pinkies on the media, the world's press would be on to the story, so making our superiors doubly sensitive to the risks of small, elite units getting sent far behind enemy lines.

That morning we got the word that everyone had been dreading: John announced that the Qalat Sikar mission had been stood down. No reasons were given, but we figured it was due to the SBS squadron getting smashed and scattered across the deserts of northern Iraq. The two patrols slated for Qalat Sikar were immediately re-tasked. It made sense to get them out on ops, to dampen their sense of disappointment. But still, we were chomping at the bit to get used.

Finally, we were called in for our own mission briefing. It was late afternoon by the time the six of us gathered in the HQ tent. We were hoping for a tasking similar in scope and daring to Qalat Sikar. Instead, we got ordered to go recce two road bridges some 40 kilometres north of where we were now positioned. The bridges spanned a large man-made canal, and our tasking was to confirm or deny if the bridges were intact and crossable by military vehicles. The concept behind our mission was unstated, yet easy to guess at: we were recceing a potential route of advance for 16 Air Assault Brigade. With Qalat Sikar having been called off, command had to be searching for alternative ways of pushing forwards.

The Iraqis had blown the oil fields pretty comprehensively, so there was every chance they'd have blown vital infrastructure too. Our satellite imagery wasn't real time, so you couldn't take it as a given that what was shown on those images was actually there. And less still with the maps, which were even older. So it was our job to go in and prove it on the ground – a classic PF tasking. If the bridges were intact we were to hold them for forty-eight hours, to allow 16 Air Assault Brigade to move through.

This mission was hardly a Qalat Sikar – penetrating deep behind enemy lines – but it was still a potentially important tasking, one that could enable the British war effort to advance significantly. And at least we'd got a mission. We could finally get started.

We set out at last light, heading northeast and driving without lights on NVG. The weather conditions struck me as looking highly abnormal: it was overcast and chilly, and there was little ambient light, for the moon and stars were obscured by scudding cloud. It was totally different to how it had been over the few weeks in Kuwait, and it wasn't good for driving on night vision.

We were using cross-country tactical driving skills to navigate to the mission objective. We stuck to open desert terrain wherever possible, driving as fast as we could in such poor visibility. But there were large areas where rocky outcrops and wadis channelled us on to desert tracks, where we struggled to find a way through.

As we pushed onwards I thought back over our drills for getting a bogged-in vehicle moving again. Back in Kuwait we'd deliberately got one of the Pinkies stuck in soft sand, spinning the wheels until it was down to its axles. Standard operating procedure was for the team from the mobile vehicle to provide a security screen, whilst the team from the bogged vehicle worked to get it free. Folding spades just didn't provide enough digging power, so each Pinkie carried a full-length shovel strapped to one side. It was wrapped in hessian sacking to stop it glinting in the sunlight, or rattling. The slightest reflection or noise could give your position away.

Strapped to each of the vehicles were four lengths of steel sheeting with holes punched in them. Once the wheels had been freed from the worst of the sand by hard digging, the steel sheets were jammed under each of the wheels, to act as 'sand ladders'. The free vehicle was then manoeuvred into position, just ahead and on some firm ground. A reinforced baggage strap – the kind of thing used to lash cargo containers to an aircraft's hold – would be strung between the two wagons. The lead Pinkie would then drag the rear vehicle over the sand ladders and on to solid terrain.

There was never a good time to get the wagons bogged down on a mission such as this one, but at least we had it down to a fine art when it came to getting moving again. I glanced forward to the shadowy form of Jason's wagon. Jase was picking the route, whilst we kept the command wagon 100 metres or so behind. If we stuck closer together and the enemy ambushed us, both wagons were likely to get malleted in the one attack.

The lead vehicle was arguably the one that would get hit first. That was the reason the patrol commander's wagon went at the rear. We had all the comms gear with which to communicate with headquarters, plus the JTAC and his kit to call in air support. If the lead wagon came under attack, we'd use the 50-cal to give Jason covering fire while his wagon moved back beyond us, whereupon it would give covering fire to us. In essence, we'd do something similar to foot soldiers performing fire and manoeuvre drills, but by vehicle.

The further we pushed away from the FOB the worse the terrain was proving in terms of cover. It was a mixture of sparse tufts of grass, rock, some sand, and the occasional small mound. Other than that it was billiard-table flat. It was a nightmare for concealment, but fortunately we hadn't seen a single Iraqi vehicle anywhere. The entire area seemed utterly devoid of life. It was weird. Eerie. Spooky.

We approached the first bridge, whilst all the time trying to make sure we'd got a clear field of view and could fire all around us. In the thick, ominous gloom of the overcast desert night our visibility was down to a few tens of metres. We went firm and closed up the vehicles, so we could talk to each other. We ran through our options, and decided to skirt around to the south and recce a couple of kilometres beyond the bridges. That way we'd scan the terrain for any Iraqi forces, before revealing our actual objective.

We drove this wide, sweeping recce through the open desert, but the entire area seemed utterly deserted. We moved in closer and did a quick recce of the first and then the second bridge, each of which appeared to be undamaged. They were both of an iron girder-type construction, and they were clearly strong enough to take military vehicles. In fact, the canals they spanned were some 50 metres across, and each bridge was as wide as a two-lane highway.

I radioed in a sitrep (situation report) to John: 'Bridges intact. No other crossing points in immediate area. Intention to recce further afield.'

That done, we started driving north to scan for enemy presence, and prove the entire area clear of enemy forces. We did as much as we could do when the terrain all around us was obscured by a thick wall of darkness. The weather showed no sign of lifting, and we'd need to repeat our recces at first light, just to make sure we didn't bring the Brigade into a massive enemy ambush.

As we headed north there was a brooding stillness to the terrain, like the calm before the storm. We'd made about a kilometre when we were hit by the powerful blast of a chill, biting wind, gusting out of the east. It felt icy cold, and it carried with it the distinctive dirty-wet-dog smell of rain falling on baked earth. It had been burning hot for a month now, and we couldn't believe it when the wind was followed by a blast of rain. In no time the rain had turned to sleet, and then to a whiteout of snow.

Suddenly, we were in the midst of a howling winter's gale.

The Pinkies were open to the elements, but it wasn't necessarily a major drama. Recently, we'd been issued with HALO Gore-Tex jackets, which were designed specifically for high-altitude freefalling. They were manufactured from an ultra-thick Gore-Tex layer that was windproof and waterproof, and which provided a good degree of warmth. With that on over my North Face down jacket – designer labels snipped out, of course – I'd be fairly toasty despite the weather.

We'd got similar HALO Gore-Tex over-trousers. We'd only ever wear them when freefalling from altitude, or when the weather turned abysmal, because they were noisy to walk in and could give your position away. We'd also been issued with several pairs of gloves, including leather ones for driving in the cold (they dry out quickly when placed on a warm engine), plus Gore-Tex gloves for para-insertions, or for adverse-weather. Now was most definitely the time to use all our adverse-weather gear.

Jason pulled over and we pulled up alongside him, so we could break out our bad-weather kit. We were halfway through getting suited and booted, when Steve noticed that Tricky wasn't bothering with any of his cold-weather gear.

'So what's with you not bothering with your Gore-Tex?' he asked. 'You waterproof or something?'

Tricky shrugged. 'Nah, but I'm all right without it, mate.'

I glanced behind me to his position on the rear: 'What d'you mean, *you're all right without it*? It's been pissing down and now it's blowing a blizzard.'

Tricky was looking distinctly uncomfortable. He was trying to ignore it, but he was soaked to the skin and getting wetter and colder by the minute, and his position on the rear of the wagon was by far the most exposed.

Finally, he admitted his problem: 'The thing is, lads, I left all my Gore-Tex gear back in the FOB.'

'*You did what?*' Steve and I demanded.

By now Tricky was practically cringing with embarrassment. I'd rarely if ever seen him in such a state, and I was amazed that he could have got himself into such a predicament. Still, he was only human, and if I was honest with myself it had crossed my mind to leave my wet weather gear behind as well. I'd opted to squeeze it into my bergen just to be on the safe side, but I'd been that close to doing otherwise.

It was impossible not to see the funny side of his predicament, and Steve and I started laughing. Jason glanced across at us and smiled. It was rare to get a laugh out of Jase when on ops, but there was real warmth to his smile. He jerked his head in Dez's direction, as if to say – *Get some of this!* Dez was hunched over the steering wheel without a scrap of wet-weather gear, looking soggy and frozen.

'Dez, mate, where's your Gore-Tex?' Jason demanded.

'I left it in Kuwait,' Dez muttered. He looked like a child who knew he'd been naughty and was just getting found out.

'Why d'you do that?' Jase needled him.

Dez shrugged. 'Well, 'cause Tricky left his, so I thought it'd be okay.'

Both wagons were rocking with laughter now, Jason's Popeye cackle kicking in alongside ours. Even Joe was chuckling, though he was trying not to be too obvious about it, in deference to Tricky. That had Steve and me in tears.

Every patrol member could choose what kit to take on operations. After a month sunning ourselves in Kuwait, Tricky had clearly decided to stuff in a few more mags of ammo and throw out his cold weather gear. Dez must have seen him do it and followed suit. It was a bone decision if ever there was one.

Tricky tried a smile and a laugh, but it had a sheepish ring to it. As for Dez, it was like he was sulking. It was coming down in stair rods now. A howling gale of sleet mixed with freezing rain was battering all around us. There was no more recceing to be done with the weather like this, plus the two of them in such a shit state. Beneath the humour, we were all of us aware of how quickly this could turn nasty.

Jase voiced the obvious: 'We've got to go find some cover and get those two into some shelter.'

After twenty minutes' driving we came across a small road bridge crossing a wadi. It was a solid concrete construction that offered us more shelter from the elements than the iron girder canal bridges. We took cover by driving the wagons into the wadi, which got them and us out of sight and below ground level. It also got us out of the worst of the wind. It wasn't a moment too soon. It was around midnight by now, and Tricky and Dez were shivering like fuck. They were clearly into the early stages of hypothermia, and whilst we were sheltered from the worst of the storm it was only marginally warmer down here.

We got the vehicles parked up so we could make a rapid exit if need be. Jase put Steve out on the first sentry duty with his Minimi light machine gun, whilst I sent a sitrep to PF HQ. We'd seen no sign of any Iraqis, and we reckoned the weather was now our greatest enemy. Tricky and Dez didn't seem particularly aware of it, but they were starting to slur their words, as the hypothermia kicked in.

Soaked through to the skin, they rapidly lost body heat. Dez looked to be the worst. His face had an icy tinge to it, his teeth were chattering with the cold and his hands were shaking uncontrollably. Even though we were in some shelter he didn't appear to be getting any warmer. The only option was to break standard operating procedure by brewing up, to get some hot liquid into him.

'Nothing for it,' Jason grunted, jerking a thumb in Dez's direction. 'Let's get a brew on. Joe?'

Joe grabbed a hexy stove – a simple fold-up metal cooking stove about the size of your average book – and dug a scoop in the rocky earth to make a fire pit. He folded the stove into its cooking position, and pulled out a couple of opaque, whitish fuel blocks much like household firelighters. He held a lighter to the first one, dropped it into the stove, and soon had a brew going. He laced the tea with spoonfuls of sugar, then poured it into the patrol mug, an aluminium monster with fold-out steel handles and a pint capacity.

We always shared the one brew mug when out on operations, in case we had to move out quickly. We might get spotted at any moment by the enemy, so we kept it simple and passed the brew around from man to man in the one mug. This time we made sure that Dez and Tricky each got a good half pint of the steaming liquid down them. Joe brewed up a second time, and as we shared that around the chat got going.

I gestured at the storm raging all around us. 'Fucking unbelievable. Just when we get a mission, this shit has to come down.'

'Murphy's Law,' said Steve. 'If it can go wrong it will.'

Jase gave an affirmative grunt. 'Expect the unexpected.'

In the back of each of our minds was the Bravo Two Zero mission, from the First Gulf War. In 1991 eight SAS blokes were airlifted into Iraq and forced to go on the run, whereupon the weather did exactly as it had done now. Those without adequate cold weather gear quickly went down with hypothermia. The weather proved to be the one enemy that they couldn't defeat. Three men died, four were captured and only one escaped. The long shadow of Bravo Two Zero has hung over Special Forces soldiering ever since then. But no one seemed to want to give voice to this, not whilst Dez and Tricky were still in such a bad way.

Steve turned the chat to food. 'You know what, I bet those Yank Spec-Ops guys are loving their treacle pudding, now the weather's turned to shit.'

'Yeah, well they probably need it more than us,' I remarked. 'They're the only ones who seem to be heading for where the enemy are right now.'

It felt to me that once Qalat Sikar had been stood down, we'd been pretty much sidelined in this war. Steve started banging on about some girl he'd been seeing in the UK, while the rest of us tried to get some kip. I burrowed into my sleeping bag fully clothed and with my boots on, my roll mat spread below me. I curled into a ball but I was still cold.

There was a gale howling beneath the bridge, and I couldn't imagine how Tricky and Dez had to be feeling.

CHAPTER TEN

By first light it was still blowing a blizzard, and it was murderously cold. Tricky and Dez were slurring their words, and they were growing noticeably listless. We broke SOPs for a second time and brewed tea, plus we heated up some food. Joe whacked a job lot of Lancashire hotpot into an old ammo tin, chucked in a load of the Tabasco sauce that we'd got off the Spec-Ops boys, and bunged it on to the hexy stove. None of us had ever dreamed of eating Lancashire hotpot in Iraq. It is a thick meat stew with balls of dough swimming in it, and it was the perfect scoff for these kind of conditions.

With the weather continuing to batter us there was no way we could do any more recces. With Tricky and Dez in such a bad way *and worsening*, I put the call through to PF HQ. I explained our predicament to John, and he made the decision to call us back in. There was little more we could achieve here, especially not with two guys fast going down with hypothermia.

Crawling along at 45 kph in a raging storm the wind-chill factor was deadly, and the drive back was freezing and bitter. It felt neverending, even for those of us with every part of our bodies shielded by Gore-Tex. Tricky had refused to swop his position on the 50-cal for somewhere more sheltered. We stuck to the main roads to speed things up, and get him and Dez back to the FOB as quickly as possible. By the time we reached it their faces had turned horribly puffy and blue.

We stuffed them into dry, warm clothing, then into sleeping bags and bivvie bags and into one of the tents. We forced them to eat some more hot food, and to drink endless brews. In the shelter and the warmth they slowly started to thaw out and come to life, and it was clear that the worst was over. It was now that we felt able to give the pair of them the slagging they deserved.

'Didn't you blokes ever read B2Z?' I ventured. B2Z was the slang we used for Bravo Two Zero.

'Yeah, that lot hit the worst snow storms in decades,' Steve chipped in. 'Remember? Just like we've done!'

All we got from Tricky and Dez were some sheepish looks. Still, I guessed they'd learned their lesson. I was amazed that Tricky could have gone out on operations without his cold-weather kit. He was an old hand. The ultimate PF soldier. It was almost unthinkable for him to have made such a basic error.

I'd first run into Tricky back in 1999, in Sierra Leone. I'd been there with 1 PARA, and Tricky had been there with the Pathfinders. I'd witnessed him and the other PF lads in combat in the jungle, smashing the murderous Sierra Leonean RUF rebels, and it was that experience that had made me decide to go for PF selection.

It was an SAS veteran – Aidey Warren – who first devised PF selection. It works on the SAS model, but it is shorter – six weeks, as opposed to six months. Basically, the salient tests of physical and mental fitness were pulled out of SAS selection, with the same times required to pass. Some claim that PF selection covers the same ground as SAS in less time, which makes it more intense and challenging. Others argue that is bollocks: it is quicker, which lowers the attrition rate. Most of us in the Pathfinders don't particularly care either way. It's PF selection. It's unique. It does what it says on the tin.

I'd pitched up for selection in the Brecon Beacons in the midst of a bitter winter. There were thirty-five of us, and we knew only a handful would make it. We were straight into the 8-miler forced march, which had to be done in one hour sixteen over the hills. We started losing guys in the first ten minutes, with knees or ankles gone, or simply from exhaustion. But it gave me a massive confidence boost when I recognised that my DS for that 8-miler was Tricky.

From the start Tricky made it clear that we had to really, really burn for it if we wanted to get into the Pathfinders. If you didn't truly burn for it, you were welcome to start VWing (Voluntary Withdrawing) yourself at any time. Tricky was taking the fitness and communications modules of selection, plus he was one of the six guys demoing how to go down the ranges. It was awesome watching him work his weapons. It was like the final scene from the movie *Heat*, when the bank robbers have to fight their way out of this trap set by US law enforcement agents.

Tricky also got up on the hills with us. He led the most extreme tabs in the worst possible weather, showing by example how to deal with the atrocious conditions on the mountains. In the Pathfinders you had to be able to operate in all kinds of climates, so on group exercises you'd pretty much go out in any kind of weather. You were more likely to get hypothermia or be injured on the individual test marches, but even then the DS would only pull you off the hills in absolute extremis.

We'd come off the Brecon Beacons into the showers, then we'd be straight on to tests in navigation, mountain safety, cold-weather kit and survival. Too many guys had died on SAS selection, so you had to prove you knew how to survive before they threw you alone and unaided on to those unforgiving peaks. All of which made it doubly surprising that Tricky had been caught out so badly by the weather in Iraq.

PF selection is run from the same camp over the same routes as the SAS. I can remember the times I dragged myself out of bed at an exhausting 0300, to shovel down a massive breakfast, and then clamber into a four-tonner truck for the long drive to the Elan Valley. You'd huddle together to share body warmth, because the thin canvas let the cold air come streaming in. I'd find my mind playing tricks on me. *Do I really need this?* I'd be thinking. *I could opt for an easy life with the lads back in my unit.*

– 117 –

By the time we'd reached the Elan Valley one guy or more would have decided to VW. They'd be left sitting on the truck as the rest of us set off into the hills. And occasionally someone would VW right after the tab was over: 'Staff – I'm not doing that again.' Ever more extreme forced marches followed, interspersed with weapons drills, and medical, comms and demolition skills lessons. And every day your pack was filled with more and more gear.

The starting weight of your bergen was 35 pounds, not including water and food. It was increased in 10-pound increments, all of which weight was necessary for military or mountain survival. No one carried any dead weight just to make up the load. Your kit included a GPS beacon that enabled the DS to track you over the hills. It was a bulletproof way of stopping people from cheating. If they noticed your tracker beacon was suddenly moving at 80 kph, they'd know you'd hitched a lift and you'd get binned immediately.

There were random checkpoints along the routes, where the DS would weigh your bergen, to make sure you hadn't filled it with water at the start and then emptied it out. You had to carry a deactivated SLR assault rifle, which you had to keep gripped in your hands at all times as you marched. On PF selection you're forbidden to use any roads or tracks that a vehicle can navigate, plus you're forbidden to use your weapon as a walking stick, which at times of sheer exhaustion was hugely tempting. If you got caught doing any of those things you were made to run up and down the nearest peak, and then told to carry on.

We were all dressed in combat fatigues with no markings, but a DS was set apart by wearing the distinctive maroon top of the Pathfinders. It sports the PF cap badge – a directional arrow, superimposed over wings, with a parachute in the middle. Even though you're totally fucked after the first week, and your feet are sore and blistered, and you're permanently dizzy from dehydration, you have to try to be reasonably together when you reach the DS manning the checkpoints. You were free to leave selection and return to the unit you came from at any time. All you needed to say was: 'Staff, I want to VW.'

There was one guy on my selection who was an Army ultra-marathon runner. He was extremely fit, and he had a 'No Fear' tattoo on his right shoulder. I'd spotted it early on when we were in the showers. We came to the final, 64-kilometre endurance march, the ultimate test in PF selection. We hit the 2-kilometre mark, where the route starts to climb this massive, all but sheer mountain. I was one of the last to set off, and I was part way up that horrendous cliff face when I spotted that bloke doubling back and coming down past me. I never did see him again. Incredibly, he'd fallen at the final hurdle and VWd.

I passed PF selection, although an injury on that final endurance march came very close to killing me. And once I was into the Pathfinders proper the real challenges began. It was then that I had to learn the craft. Invariably in a PF recce unit the maximum force you'll ever reach is a six- or twelve-man patrol. You needed to be happy operating as a small group of very determined individuals. In the regular infantry it was all about going forwards and attacking as a company or a battalion – so 100 or 700-plus strength, and with the might of the Army and the Air Force behind you. In PF you'd be a tiny, isolated unit far into hostile terrain.

If you came across an enemy position it was likely to be a company at least, and you'd expect to be heavily outnumbered and outgunned. Your skills were all about how to break contact, extract from the kill zone and disappear. That had to be slick and instinctive if you were to have any chance of survival. You practised to death how to respond to contact from front, side or rear. The IA (Immediate Action) drill was that whoever was contacted put down rounds, and shouted 'Contact front left!' or whatever. As a unit you'd concentrate fire on that target.

Whoever spotted a piece of cover to retreat to would shout 'Peel left!' or 'Peel right!' Any individual could then nominate a rally point: 'Rally on me!' You practised with full bergens and day sacks, and you rehearsed your 'man down' procedures for getting an injured bloke on to your shoulders and out of there. In the Mobility Cadre of PF training you repeated that process, only this time with your vehicles. You also did your specialist comms and recce training.

You learned how to find, assess and report the info that the brigade commander needed – the recce mission objective. You learned to report via long-distance HF radio, bouncing signals off the ionosphere, and by data-secure cryptographic means. You learned how to make rapid sketch maps of enemy positions, whilst wearing surgical gloves so that your reports remained clear and legible, despite the fact that you were filthy dirty.

But as much as Pathfinders were challenged physically, we were also challenged mentally. We were taught to operate in a different reality, to embrace what others feared. We were taught to possess the night, to inhabit the darkness. We were taught to be totally at home under moonlight, in starlight and in sheer black. Darkness was the cloak with which to hide our operations. We learned to love the darkness and make the night our own.

We were taught to seek out bad terrain, margins, arid desert and remote bush – anywhere abandoned by humans. And we were taught to seek out the worst, shittiest weather imaginable – conditions within which covert operators like Pathfinders could thrive. Or at least, where we were *supposed to thrive*.

After our first Iraq mission, I didn't hold Tricky's failure to bring his cold-weather kit against him. After all, we were all human. Whilst Tricky and Dez recovered from their ordeal, the rest of us wrote up the patrol report on the bridges mission. I read it back to the lads before submitting it, just in case I'd missed anything. We had no idea if the Brigade would use the route across the bridges to advance further into Iraq. It wasn't our need to know.

In spite of the appalling weather conditions we'd accomplished our mission, and we were expecting to get rapidly re-tasked. But we hadn't slept properly for several nights now, and were badly in need of some kip. It had stopped raining and snowing, but it was still bitterly cold. There were no tents available, so we wrapped up well and crashed out beside the vehicles, which did provide a little shelter from the wind.

The other patrols were all out on missions, so we could only pre-sume that they'd got far sexier taskings than our bridges recce. The one consolation was this: if any mission did come in to PF HQ it would have to be given to us, for we were the only patrol left in camp.

At first light – 0500 – I was woken by the PF sergeant major, Ray Oldman, AKA the 'White Rabbit'. Ray looked almost albino in appearance, with his snowy hair and blue eyes tinged with red. He had a wild intensity about him, which made it all the more appropri-ate that he'd earned the White Rabbit nickname. Like many soldiers who'd seen a massive amount of combat, he had a wired look about his eyes that's also known as the 'thousand yard stare'.

Ray warned me off to prepare for our next mission. He had this weird gleam in his eyes as he did so. He gave me the nod. This was the big one.

'Better get your arse into the ops tent,' he told me. 'Qalat Sikar is back on …'

From being in the midst of the deepest sleep, I was instantly wide awake. This was the equivalent of being pulled off the reserve benches, and being told you were on for the world cup final. I was fucking buzzing. I told myself: *Fuck having a brew!* I needed to see John soonest and find out what exactly he'd got in store for us.

I'd taught myself to be good at coming instantly awake. I needed to be able to snap out of a deep sleep and make immediate decisions. One of the tricks of doing so was to eat well and to drink bucket loads of water before going to sleep. You might need to piss in the night, but you'd wake up with good energy levels and feeling well hydrated.

I woke the lads: 'Boys, orders in fifteen minutes.'

Jason grunted: 'What for?'

I said the magic words: 'Qalat Sikar.'

As soon as Tricky heard that he was up instantly and into action. Jason wasn't an early morning person, and he always took a good few minutes to get fully active. But even so the words 'Qalat Sikar' had got him crawling out of his doss bag and rubbing the sleep out of his eyes. As for Steve, he lay there for a second grinning like an idiot.

'Just give me a mo' while I deal with me semi,' he remarked, dreamily. There was this horrible, rhythmic rustling from within his sleeping bag. I hoped to hell he was bluffing, the dirty bastard.

I glanced at Joe. 'Joe?'

Joe shook the sleep from his young head. 'Qalat Sikar – wicked.'

I turned my gaze on Dez. 'Best you pack your Gore-Tex,' I joked.

Dez gave a sheepish grin. 'Just got to hope the sun keeps shining on us lot, eh?'

Inside the HQ tent it was buzzing. John had the PF signallers rushing around gathering documents, comms equipment and sat photos.

He nodded at us as we entered: 'All right guys? All good? Slept well?'

As the six of us took out seats John gathered his shit together, laying out the mission folders on the briefing table. He took a stand out front, the White Rabbit on his shoulder.

He gave us this warm smile: 'Right, lads, you got it: Qalat Sikar is back on.' He paused, letting the words hang in the air. 'But we need to wait one before I can do the briefing proper, 'cause you've got a three-man Engineer Recce Team coming with you.'

John could read the reaction on our faces. We were about to go far behind enemy lines and we'd got this dumped on us: we were getting a unit of Engineers tacked on to our patrol. The Engineer Recce Teams were exactly what they sound like: Royal Engineers trained-up for recce taskings. They were a newly-formed unit, and the reasoning behind having them was so that they could come in on the back of a mission like Qalat Sikar and repair the airstrip.

There was no selection process prior to joining an Engineer Recce Team. Needless to say, they weren't supposed to do the actual recce insertion and be the spearhead, which was the *raison d'être* of the Pathfinders. We'd never worked with the Engineer Recce blokes, but we knew they weren't para-trained and that they didn't know our SOPs. On a mission such as this one it was the very last thing that we needed.

John held up his hand to silence any objections. 'Guys, *I know*. It's far from being ideal, but mostly this is politics. You'll need to trust me on this one and go with it, okay, 'cause those are the orders.'

The CO of the Engineer Recce Teams was an ex-SAS bloke that I knew well. We Pathfinders had long been nurtured by the SAS, and he was clearly calling a favour back off us, by inserting his Recce Team on to our mission. We had to presume that he'd selected three of his best, in which case it was a fair one. Either way this was an order from on high, so we had no choice but to crack on. John told us to ready the patrol so we could deploy in three hours' time. He'd brief us fully on the mission once the Engineer Recce blokes had arrived.

We got busy refilling water bottles, and double-checking the wagons. Dez had never once stopped tinkering with the vehicles, and they were pretty much shipshape and ready to go. But I figured we wouldn't be needing the Pinkies on this one. We were going in to take Qalat Sikar and that had to mean parachuting in, and maybe with the Engineer Recce Guys tandemmed to us.

With Qalat Sikar being a good 300 kilometres away we clearly couldn't go in on foot. If we tried to drive in, we'd be risking the same fate that had befallen that SBS squadron that had got so badly compromised in northern Iraq. The fate of those sixty elite operators had to play to our advantage, and make the chances of getting cleared to go in via parachute that much higher.

At 0545 we gathered in the HQ tent for John's briefing. The atmosphere was electric. The three Engineer Recce guys joined us and took their seats at the back. Typically for Engineers, they were big, beefy blokes.

'Right, guys, as you know, Qalat Sikar is back on,' John announced. He was clearly excited, but he was trying not to show it. 'The situation is that 16 Air Assault Brigade, along with the US Marine Corps, wishes to seize the airfield and use it as a base from which to mount attacks into the rest of Iraq.'

Because we were the only patrol left at the FOB, the mission had fallen to the six of us, John explained. As Qalat Sikar had been originally tasked to two PF patrols – a dozen men – it made sense to have extra blokes with us, and so the Engineer Recce team had been asked to make up the numbers. John went on to outline the one major downside to the Qalat Sikar mission as it was now constituted: when push had come to shove, high command had baulked at an airborne insertion.

Instead, we were being ordered to go in using the vehicles, which meant that we had a massive drive ahead of us into the heart of hostile territory. If we were to attempt this mission overland, I figured that having one extra vehicle mounted with two GPMGs – the Engineer Recce Team wagon – might well prove useful. But either way, switching from a para-insertion to a vehicle insertion was about as close to madness as ever you could get in the British military.

It was a golden rule of soldiering that you never interrupted the OC's orders. At the end of his brief was the time to get vocal, if you needed to. And for sure I had several issues I needed to raise with John on this one.

'The mission is being led by your patrol, David,' John continued, 'with the three guys from the Engineers in support. What's your names, guys?'

'Ian Andrews.'

'Simon James.'

'Stephen Altry.'

'Okay, Ian, Simon, Stephen – welcome to the party,' said John. 'This is your collective mission: move by vehicle to Qalat Sikar airfield. Recce and mark the airfield in order to facilitate a 1 PARA battle group SH insertion.'

SH stood for support helicopters – Army-speak for Chinooks. Once we reached Qalat Sikar we'd need to mark an HLS (Helicopter Landing Site) for the Chinooks to put the PARAs on to.

'Timing,' John continued. '1 PARA battle group L-Hour 24-0400 Zulu.'

This meant that the Landing Hour for the PARAs was 24 March, at 0400 Zulu – local – time. I was immediately thinking: *Fuck me, that's less than twenty-four hours from now!* In the meantime we had to work out a mission plan and the possible routes in, decide actions-on, plus get ourselves to the airfield.

Once we reached the airfield we'd got to do a 360-degree recce, and clear and mark an HLS. Plus we'd got to get the Engineer lads checking for any obstacles and making good the runway, so the airfield could be made usable as quickly as possible. In short, it had all the appearance of a race against time on mission bloody impossible.

John moved on to the intel brief. 'The intel picture is as follows: the US Marines are advancing towards Nasiriyah, 150 kilometres to the north of us. They're expecting to encounter limited Iraqi resistance, so there will be contacts, but nothing overly significant. There is assumed to be "no significant enemy threat" in Nasiriyah.'

'Between Nasiriyah and Qalat Sikar there are no known Iraqi positions,' John continued. 'The intel assessment is that the area is "relatively benign". There's an intel pack in the Ops Box with satellite imagery, humint [human intelligence] reports and other bits and pieces, plus Geordie and Lance's patrol planning file.'

John finished with this: 'Brigade absolutely needs you to make 1 PARA's L-Hour, and so you need to reach and secure that airfield urgently. That's the deal, guys. Any questions? And keep 'em short ...'

'The obvious one: why by vehicle?' I queried. 'Why can't we para-insert?'

'I forgot to say,' John replied. 'There are no air assets available for this mission.'

'What, no air support at all?' asked Tricky.

'Nope. Nothing,' John replied. 'There is nothing available for this mission.'

'Isn't there even any SH?' Jason asked.

I knew what he was thinking. If we couldn't para-insert, at least we could go in by Chinook and get dropped with the vehicles, so we weren't channelled on to roads the whole way there.

'There's nothing available,' John repeated. 'The first time any air is coming online is at 0300 tomorrow, to get 1 PARA inserted for their L-Hour. That's it.'

Fuck. Hugely frustrating didn't cover it. The cash-strapped British military didn't have the airframes available to drop us over target, even if the will existed to do so. But in a way it was hardly surprising. We'd seen for ourselves how short was the supply of air assets to support the Brigade. In any case, we'd always known that Qalat Sikar was going to be dangerous whichever way we went in.

In the Pathfinders we have an unofficial collect – a poem that defines the ethos of our unit: 'Happiness shall always be found by those who dare and persevere; wanderer – do not turn around, march on and have no fear.' If they'd ordered us to insert by swimming up the Tigris we'd probably have done so, we wanted the Qalat Sikar mission so bad.

We weren't going in by air. We were going in overland. So be it.

CHAPTER ELEVEN

'I need you to get moving as soon as possible,' John prompted. 'Are your vehicles ready?'

'They're good to go,' I confirmed.

'David, I need you to back-brief me as soon as you're ready to depart. Can you do that by 0730 at the latest?'

I looked at the guys. They gave me the nod. *Sure we can.*

I said. 'Yeah. Can do.'

'And David,' John added, 'you'll need to use your charm and charisma with the US Marines to make sure they let you break through their lines and get to Qalat Sikar well ahead of them.'

I told John no problem. I sensed what he was driving at here. The US Marines had an H-Hour of 0800 this morning to start their push into Nasiriyah, 150 kilometres or so to the north of us. Up until their front line we could assume that the terrain was pretty much clear of Iraqi forces, and so secure. But once we reached Nasiriyah we were going to have to push ahead of the Marine Corps' front line, and break through into enemy territory. We were in one hell of a rush to make Qalat Sikar, and it was likely going to take some careful persuasion to convince the US Marine Corps commanders to let us through.

The mission was moving so quickly that we had little time to liaise with the US military on this one. We had a US liaison officer co-located within Brigade Headquarters, but even if we did get to brief him on our mission, the message might never make it out to the US front line. We were going to have to rely on our wits to convince the Yanks to let us push on through.

The briefing broke up. Jason grabbed the maps and started to scrutinise the ground between us and Qalat Sikar. I grabbed Geordie and Lance's patrol planning file, and started ploughing through the intel reports. Tricky headed off to Brigade signals to sort out the comms. He needed to grab the frequencies for the various TACSAT nets, which were changed regularly, and especially those for the air cover and the CSAR (Combat Search and Rescue) teams, if we ended up in the shit.

Tricky left Joe to sort comms with the Engineer Recce wagon, so he could patch them into our net. Steve scrutinised the sat images to find the best route in, whilst Dez started triple-checking the vehicles, plus I gave Jason actions-on.

The only way we'd be able to communicate directly with the US Marines was by routing a radio call via our HQ to theirs. Even then they'd have a different kind of crypto fill to ours – the software that scrambles signals to make them immune to intercepts – so we'd only be able make contact using insecure (unencrypted) means.

The US Marines would be running 300-odd radio nets out on their front lines, so each platoon could speak to its own men. They'd be changing their frequencies every twenty-four hours or so, as a precaution against enemy intercepts. Getting comms with the US Marines on their front line was going to be very, very challenging, and probably next to impossible.

From the sat photos the Qalat Sikar airfield looked like a small, military-use airstrip. The resolution was good enough to reveal a small control tower, plus a couple of hangars, but there were no aircraft or military vehicles present as far as we could tell. Normally, known enemy positions would be marked on the sat photos, and there were none shown. The date and time of the sat photos was to within a few weeks, so no more recent than that. The intel brief was hugely long-winded and full of waffle, but it boiled down to the fact that there were no known Iraqi forces present.

The first blindingly obvious thing from the maps and sat photos was that the area north of Nasiriyah was a lot wetter and more vegetated than where we were now. The sat images revealed canals and thick patches of undergrowth. At first it looked as if there was no way through off-road. But the more we studied the images, the more we were drawn to a couple of dirt tracks that looped northeast from Nasiriyah. They seemed to skirt the marshland all the way to the airfield.

We settled on a two-stage plan. If the intel picture held up when we reached Nasiriyah we'd take the main road – Route 7 – direct to Qalat Sikar. It would be the quickest route in, plus the intel picture said that it should be doable. We'd prefer to go off-road. That was always our first choice when on a vehicle-mounted mission. But the dirt tracks criss-crossed scores of canals, so all it would take was for one bridge to be down and we'd be buggered. However, if the intel picture proved badly wrong once we were past Nasiriyah, our fall-back option would be to take our chances and use those tracks.

From the maps, Jason figured it was a drive of some 290 kilometres to Qalat Sikar. We could average 50 kilometres an hour if we did it all on the main highways, so it was a six-hour drive minimum. That meant that we should be able to make it with ample time to recce, secure and mark the airfield, but it all depended on how well the intel picture held up once we hit enemy territory. If we ran into serious resistance, all of that would change.

From being an ultra-covert insertion, jumping from a C130 Hercules at high altitude, this had now become a mad dash up the main highway with a serious Charge of the Light Brigade feel about it. But there was no other way of getting in. In any case, ever since my time in 1 PARA we'd always been asked to do crazy operations with minimal kit and support. We'd done as much in Kosovo, Sierra Leone and Afghanistan. It's what the British Army is renowned for.

It was the intel that worried me most. We hadn't seen a single Iraqi soldier in the entire time that we'd been here. We knew that the

Yanks were moving towards Nasiriyah full steam ahead, and meeting little or no resistance. So maybe the intel picture – 'relatively benign' – was accurate. But somehow I doubted it. Relatively benign meant that no hostile forces were known to be present in the area. However, there was always a time lapse between intel being secured and the here and now. Plus we knew that the Iraqi Fedayeen – militias fiercely loyal to Saddam Hussein – weren't stationed in permanent bases as such. The Fedayeen were mobile, irregular forces and they were hard to pin down.

But we were where we were. We were being sent in with the best information available, and we were being asked to discover the ground truth. If the intel was wrong, it was only the six of us – or nine with the Engineer Recce blokes – that were at risk. And that was exactly the role for which the Pathfinders had been created.

The Engineer Recce Team consisted of a sergeant and two lance-corporals. We'd made it clear that they were free to chip in if they wanted to, but they'd seemed happy to defer to our expertise. With the mission plan pretty much done, Jase explained to Ian, their vehicle commander, the order in which we would proceed.

'Ian, this is the orbat [order of battle]: my vehicle in front, Dave's vehicle to the rear, yours in the middle. D'you want to send your blokes away so you can be ready for the off as soon as? Dez: go with them and help them get their wagon sorted.'

We began checking and rechecking our gear, especially our personal belt and webbing kit. A lot of care and attention went into it, for that was the one set of equipment we'd always have on us, even if we were on the run and had lost everything else. First priority was ammo. Each man had six thirty-round mags for his assault rifle in his webbing, the first facing forwards and the right way up, so it would slot directly into the weapon. Every few days we'd de-bombed our mags, getting rid of any dust and grit, then check and oil the spring and reload it. Some guys only loaded up twenty-nine rounds per mag, so as not to overstress the spring.

Second priority was grenades. Each bloke packed four HE (High

Explosive) grenades into two pouches. The side you carried them on depended on whether you were left- or right-handed. The primers were kept separate from the grenades, and screwed into them prior to going into combat. Third priority was food. Each man packed enough scoff for a normal twenty-four hours of operations, but not a full twenty-four-hour ration pack. Generally, we'd carry two boil-in-the-bag meals, which would likely be eaten cold. Food was stuffed into a rear pouch, for it was the last thing we'd need to reach for in a hurry.

If we did go on the run we might allow ourselves one boil-in-the-bag meal every three days – so just enough to keep us alive. With the food went a key piece of kit, the spoon, generally attached to our webbing by a length of para cord. If we lost our spoon we'd be forced to eat with dirty hands, which was asking to get sick. Fourth priority was water. We each packed two plastic one-litre bottles, one of which sat in our plastic mug to save space. Some of the blokes also carried a fold-up mountaineering water bag, which could be used for gathering extra drinking water.

Fifth priority was survival kit. This included steritabs for making dirty water potable; a personal first aid kit; a penknife; matches; plus a lighter (usually the cheap disposable kind). One emergency field dressing would be taped to the front of our webbing with green Army tape, where we could easily rip it off and slap it on to a gunshot wound. Sixth priority was a PRC-112 radio. This was an emergency UHF ground-to-air comms system. It was a Walkman-sized piece of kit, with an antenna that folded out so as to talk to the air. It provided line of sight comms only, and like a lot of our kit it was archaic and frequently broke down.

Seventh priority was our position-marking gear. We had classified and secret tactics, techniques and procedures, plus specialist equipment, which we used to covertly mark our position and to call in a search and rescue team via helicopter.

We each also carried a DZ marking kit in our webbing, consisting of a pop-up cone of fluorescent material that would be used for marking a DZ (Drop Zone) – a safe and cleared area for parachutists to drop into. Lastly, each man might opt to carry a hexy stove and some fuel tabs. It was relatively heavy kit, and we could survive on cold rations, but a hot brew was great for morale and it could be a lifesaver. Again it was personal choice.

At 0715 we back-briefed John on the mission plan. What we were attempting to do was complicated and a lot could go wrong. It was an isolated, unknown area deep behind enemy lines. The back brief complemented the patrol file, leaving headquarters with a clear picture as to our intentions, plus actions-on in the event of trouble. It also gave a clear sense of our route, in case John had to send in a CSAR team to find us.

I briefed John that our intention was to be at the airfield by 2200 hours latest, leaving us five hours to recce, secure and mark the HLS. We'd stop short with the vehicles, and do an initial recce on foot. We'd then use one vehicle to cover the others, as we did a 360-degree check of the runway. We'd do the first 360-scan using our SOPHIE thermal optics, which were outstanding pieces of kit.

SOPHIE has a 2000-metre effective range as we would be using it, and you can zoom it in to get up close and personal with whatever you are viewing. We used it primarily as an optical aid for CTRs (Close Target Recces), but it could also be used as a targeting aid to take out whatever enemy forces had been identified. If there was heavy activity at the airfield we might not be able to do a 360-degree sweep on foot. In that case we'd make clear to PF HQ exactly where we'd found Iraqi forces, and recommend that they put the PARAs down offset from the airstrip.

We'd mark the HLS using torches with IR filters (only visible by night vision), and our purpose-made IR markers. We'd radio through GPS co-ordinates of the exact spot for the helos to put down. There were only enough Chinooks available to do a company-level insertion, so 1 PARA would arrive in three waves, each consisting of three helos and some ninety men at arms. The rest of the battle group would follow on later. I finished back-briefing John on our plan, and Jason started to outline the actions-on.

'Enemy pre-seen: we go firm, report enemy location, and ID alternative route to avoid them. Contact: we return fire, break contact, send contact report, then carry on with the mission. Ambush: we return fire, drive through ambush and carry on with the mission. If the patrol gets separated, we go firm, wait thirty minutes, then return to the last ERV, of which we have three north of Al Nasiriyah.'

As we couldn't mark-up ERV (Emergency Rendezvous) points on the maps, each of our ERVs had to be an easily recognisable and memorable feature. I'd picked an electrical relay station as our last ERV point, en route to Qalat Sikar. It consisted of a forest of pylons lying just off the main highway a short distance down a dirt track. It was unmissable.

There were two more ERVs between there and Nasiriyah, each of which was a prominent road junction. Each ERV was calculated with a set stand-off distance and bearing, to reduce the risk of a blue-on-blue (friendly fire) incident. The ERV point was set 200 metres to the east of the landmark, and we were to approach it from the east.

On approach you'd go firm outside the ERV, which you scanned with your NVG kit and SOPHIE sight. You'd only actually go into the ERV point when you were certain that it was clear of the enemy, civvies and stray dogs. And you made sure that any friendlies present were aware that you were coming in. If the ERV was unusable for any reason, you'd move on to the next one.

If we had to call in CSAR, we'd mark a HLS for the CSAR aircrew to come in on, with a pre-arranged lay-out using either stones or IR markers. We'd adopt a non-aggressive posture as the CSAR helicopter came in – weapons on the ground, hands on our heads and kneeling. We'd be treated like the enemy posing as British soldiers until proved otherwise, for obvious reasons.

Jason rounded off the actions-on. 'Presence of enemy forces at airfield: conduct CTR, report enemy strength back to PF HQ, and neutralise if necessary. Blue-on-blue: do not return fire, take cover, and ID patrol as friendly forces.'

Tricky did a comms brief, which was short and sweet. We had two Scheds daily, one at 0800 and one at 1600. If we missed one or more Scheds John would presume we may have been compromised and were on the run. If we got into a 'lost comms' situation, where we couldn't contact friendly forces, we'd move back to the US Marine Corps and beg, borrow or steal some comms kit. There was no point in securing a HLS at the airfield if we couldn't communicate that it was all clear for 1 PARA to come in and land.

Finally, Tricky reminded everyone of our call-signs: 'Patrol call-sign is *Mayhem Three Zero*. Dave's call-sign is *Maverick One*. And the mission code name is *Operation Death or Glory*.'

His last comment lightened the mood. Everyone laughed. The mission didn't have an official code name as such, but as unofficial ones went Tricky had hit the nail on the head with that one. At the end of the mission briefing we synchronised our watches. When out on operations we needed to ensure that every member of the unit was working to the exact same minute and second. This is crucial for many reasons, and particularly for the air picture.

The Pathfinders' communications specialist, Pete, stepped forward. He held out his left arm, and gazed intently at his watch.

'In approximately two minutes it'll be seven-fifty-seven Zulu,' he announced.

We each of us moved the hands of our own watches to one second away from 0757. We now had two minutes to kill before the synchronisation second, and we spent it checking over the maps and sat photos of Qalat Sikar.

'Sixty seconds,' Pete warned. 'Thirty seconds. Seven-fifty-seven Zulu in fifteen seconds. Five, four, three, two, one. Mark!'

On Pete's call we each set our watches running, and were synchronised. Pete would have done the same thing himself earlier that morning, getting his time-synch from the RAF HQ in Camp Tristar. What was going on here was much bigger than simply a ground war in Iraq. The British and US forces had air missions flying in from all points of the compass: from carriers steaming off the coast, to fast jets flying out of Jordan, Saudi Arabia and Cyprus, and even B52s launched from bases in the UK.

You'd never run an entire air campaign from one location, for that would make it highly vulnerable to having its airbase attacked. But co-ordinating the air campaign across so many different countries and time zones was a complex and challenging task, hence our time-synch coming down from RAF headquarters. One air vice-marshal – British or American – would be in charge of the entire air campaign, and his timing would be co-ordinated directly with the Pentagon and PJHQ (Permanent Joint Headquarters). The air vice-marshal would delegate time synchronisation to his chief of staff, who would filter it down the chain to every ground unit, including ours.

Pilots would be flying in from a myriad of time zones, while having to co-ordinate their actions with ground troops down to the second. If you were on the ground you might get close air support allocated to you for a very tight time window – a few minutes or seconds even – and you needed to be one hundred per cent certain you were working to exactly the same local – Zulu – time. The same would go for a HALO jump over target, or for a CSAR extraction. Military precision was the key here, as was wearing a reliable timepiece!

I wore a Bvlgari watch, and had done for several years. Few people realise this, but cheap watches tend to lose a few seconds every day. Over time that mounts up. My Bvlgari had cost me £2000, money that I had had to scrimp and save for. Each Bvlgari is individually numbered, and I took pride in its fine, simple lines and its precision Swiss engineering. It had no flashy features – just a ruggedised black strap and an elegant, clean face that told the time precisely and accurately, which was exactly what I needed it to do.

It also had a sapphire crystal glass face, which was pretty much indestructible. Sapphire crystal is the hardest oxide crystal known to man, so up there with diamonds on the hardness scale. (Diamonds are at ten on the Mohs hardness scale, sapphire crystal at nine.) Sapphire crystal has the qualities of extreme strength, hardness, heat resistance and corrosion resistance, which meant my watch face wasn't likely to fall apart mid-mission.

A lot of soldiers tended to wear so-called 'military' type watches, ones that sported a button for every eventuality. The trouble with those was that as a Pathfinder, you'd often find yourself crawling through the undergrowth on your belt buckle. And whilst you might have turned off all the bleeper and light functions, it was all too easy to lean your weight on your watch or catch it on some undergrowth and reactivate them. Imagine being within yards of a hostile position, when suddenly your watch started to flash or to bleep.

The Bvlgari had no light function whatsoever, just a gently luminous dull silver dial. It had no bleeping functions either. During my officer cadet days I used to box for Sandhurst. I'd been forced to wear that Bvlgari on my right arm, because my left arm had been left swollen and bruised after I'd knocked out an opponent. I figured wearing the watch on the right had brought me good luck, for whilst I was doing so I was one of the few officers selected to join the Parachute Regiment.

I'd decided to wear the Bvlgari on my right wrist ever since. It didn't run on batteries, so there was no room for Murphy's Law coming into play: *If it can go wrong it will.* There was no danger of the battery giving out just as we were approaching Qalat Sikar airfield.

'It's 0758 and we move out in twelve minutes,' I announced to the lads on my patrol. 'Right, let's go.'

As we exited the HQ tent I spared a fleeting thought for John. Shortly, he'd have all six PF patrols out on operations. Over the past forty-eight hours he'd given orders and received back-briefs from all of us, and he'd been on the radio net 24/7 liaising with his patrols. He was also supposed to be present during the Brigade orders groups, and to have a view on what the Pathfinders could contribute. He was on information overload and had to be close to burnout. It struck me again that as PF 2IC I had the best of both worlds.

Before we set off I did a final verbal check with the other wagons. 'Jase, good to go?'

He nodded: 'Yep.'

'Ian, good to go?'

The big Engineer bloke gave me a thumbs-up: 'Yeah.'

At precisely 0810 we got our wheels rolling.

CHAPTER TWELVE

Barely had we pulled away from the FOB when Steve turned to me. 'Dave, are we there yet?'

He repeated it a few times, like Donkey does in the movie *Shrek*, until eventually I cracked: 'Steve, fuck off will you, mate?' But I was pissing myself laughing.

The weather had done an about-face. It was calm and sunny and without a hint of rain. We had smocks on with shirts underneath. That was all. In the dawn light the terrain looked cinematographic: it was a sea of flat, open plateaus, dotted with patches of yellow rock and rolling, golden sand.

The Pinkies picked up speed across the hard ground and I began to feel euphoric. *Finally, we'd got Qalat Sikar.* It may not have been a para-insertion any more, but it still promised to be epic. *We were underway on the mission of a lifetime.* I glanced around at the other lads and I could tell that they, like me, were lit up.

With the dawn light sparking off the glittering desert, I grabbed my sunglasses. They were Persol Havana 714s – hand-made glasses with arms and lenses that collapse in on themselves. When folded they were basically the size of a small compass, and they fitted perfectly in the top left-hand pocket of my smock, which made them great for operations.

As we drove across the empty desert a thought struck me from out of nowhere. Maybe Tricky had forgotten his cold weather gear on our first mission *for a reason*. If he hadn't done so and we hadn't been called back to base early, we'd still be out there minding those bridges, and we'd likely never have got Qalat Sikar. Maybe that was why Tricky had decided not to take his Gore-Tex kit. Maybe he'd had a premonition. I'm a big believer in fate: maybe Tricky had dumped his Gore-Tex so we could get Qalat Sikar, this peach of a mission.

After twenty minutes, driving through the open desert we hit Route 8, the tarmac road that stretches all the way to Nasiriyah. Route 8 is a four-lane highway with a metal barrier running down the centre, a lot like a British dual carriageway. We began to speed along it in line astern at 65 kph. The sun was beating down, there wasn't an enemy in sight and it felt like a road movie, like driving to Vegas. When Jason pulled over in the desert sands for a map check, we pulled up in line abreast, each vehicle covering its arcs of fire. But still there wasn't an Iraqi to be seen.

Jason had got his hands on some munchies, and was having a good scoff as he pawed his map. Food: that was Jason's vice. Dez was hovering near and trying not to ask too many questions. In the wagon's rear Joe was trying to have a quiet ciggie without blowing smoke on the others. Jason was the vehicle commander and he'd got to lead the crack, which was pretty much non-existent in their wagon. I could see Joe glancing over enviously at us. Steve and Tricky were taking the piss out of everything – especially the US Marine Corps grunts that had started to thunder past us in this long line of wagons.

A massive convoy of American military vehicles was doing the road move north. There were HUMVEEs, 4-tonne trucks and hulking great M1A1 Abrams main battle tanks. We felt tiny and puny beside them. Part of the American convoy went static nearby, young buzz-cut marines jumping down and deploying in all-around defence, flat on their belt buckles and assault rifles levelled into the distant glare. One glance at us lot and they could tell that we weren't US forces, but thankfully we did have the recognition flashes on our vehicles.

We shot past the static US convoy and were making good progress – nine Brits in three Land Rovers overhauling the thousands of troops and hardware of the mighty Marine Expeditionary Force. We were moving through the US armoured fist that was punching into the soft underbelly of the enemy, or at least that was our understanding. And we knew that our tiny team constituted the vanguard of the British advance into southern Iraq, which was a fantastic feeling.

There wasn't a lot of chat possible as we drove, for the wind rushing past the open-topped Pinkies was deafening. But I could see by the expression on the other blokes' faces, and the look in their eyes, that they were loving being on the move at last. We had VHF radios to communicate between the vehicles, with a handset that sat on the side of the Pinkies. We also had Cougar personal radios for secure comms between individual members of the patrol. Each of us had an earpiece stuffed in one earhole, and a handset the size of a massive 1980s mobile phone hooked into our webbing. But even with those radios, the noise of the wind rushing past made comms next to impossible.

Over time the Pathfinders had developed a series of hand signals to get the basic, vital information across when on a vehicle move: *speed up, slow down, enemy seen, stop*. A lot of the US vehicles we were passing were loggies – supply trucks and the like – and it was clear how enormous and ponderous the US resupply chain was. It was also clear how vulnerable it was to ambush or disruption, as there was only the one road – Route 8 – heading north into Iraq. It was a reminder of the urgent need to make Qalat Sikar happen.

We had this supreme sense of mission now. The minutes were ticking down towards H-Hour, and we had less than nineteen hours in which to get to Qalat Sikar and clear the PARAs in to seize it. Every now and then we were forced to a halt by a broken-down US Marine Corps vehicle choking up the traffic. We couldn't just go screaming past through the open desert to one side, for then some trigger-happy marine might decide to unload on us. It was very likely their first operational tour and they'd be jumpy as hell. Instead we had to wave and smile and thread our way through carefully – *Her Majesty's finest coming through.*

We slowed to a halt at one of those choke points, and this figure emerged from between a couple of HUMVEEs. He was dressed in the distinctive blue flak jacket of the press. He'd got a battered blue base-ball cap jammed on to his head above mad professor-style hair, and these bizarre glasses propped on the end of his pointy nose. There was only one thing that this guy could possibly be: an American jour-nalist embedded with the Marine Corps.

After making a beeline for our stationary vehicle he stopped right by my door. He had a tape recorder clutched in one hand and I'd seen him press 'record', although he'd done his best to hide it. He looked me in the eye, and fired off a first question in this self-important manner that just demanded to be answered.

'Hi, Matthew Johnson, CBS News. So where are you guys going?'

I pointed north: 'Thatta way.'

I figured it was pretty obvious really, as everyone was heading north. At that moment Jason pulled away, the RE vehicle followed, and Steve gunned our engine.

'Hey, wait up …' the reporter shouted after us. Then, when he real-ised we weren't stopping: 'Okay, see you guys next time in Hereford!'

I felt like yelling back: *We're not SAS, we're Pathfinders. Can't you tell the difference? That's like confusing a BMW with a Ferrari!* But if I did I figured he'd have an even bigger story.

We pushed onwards up the main drag. On open stretches we were making a good 80 kph now, but we were forced to a crawl whenever we hit the US convoys. I figured our average speed had to be around 30 kph, at which rate we should still hit Qalat Sikar within ten hours. That left us plenty of time to do the necessary.

Visibility was great, and we could see for several kilometres in any direction. We'd yet to see a single Iraqi, civilian or military. It felt really weird, for here we were driving up this massive fuck-off highway into the heart of Iraq. If it wasn't for the US Marine Corps it would have felt as if we were moving across the Planet of the Apes post the Apocalypse, it was that devoid of any human presence.

At 1100 we'd been on the road for a good three hours, and we stopped for another map check. We figured we were just a few kilometres short of the southern outskirts of Nasiriyah. It was now that we detected the distant signs of battle. Stationary in the desert as we were, we caught the first crump of explosions. I glanced northwards, and on the far horizon I could see thick, oily plumes of smoke drifting with the wind. Cobra helicopter gunships were circling and whirling in the air, pounding targets below, and there was tracer arcing skywards in return.

We moved forward a few hundred metres, and there was a shattered HUMVEE plus an LAV-25 APC (Armoured Personnel Carrier) lying by the roadside. It seemed as if the Iraqis were putting up some kind of resistance after all. The LAV-25 was a big hulking beast of a machine. It was still burning fiercely, a thick cloud of acrid smoke billowing across the highway. We slowed to a crawl, and there were the distinctive puncture marks of what looked like RPGs (Rocket Propelled Grenades) torn into the side of its thick armour plating.

There was no sign of any American casualties, so we figured that whoever had been in the APC and the HUMVEE must have got out pretty much unscathed. And there was still not the slightest sign of any Iraqis. We presumed that a small, mobile force had mounted a snap ambush here, before melting away into the desert.

Weirdly, we were almost relieved to see some sign of an enemy presence, concrete evidence that we were at war. We were almost a third of the way into Iraq, and we had yet to see a single Iraqi fighter. But equally, we'd yet to see a single Iraqi soldier surrendering, and they were certainly not laying down their weapons in their droves.

Nasiriyah is a Shiite town, as opposed to being Sunni. We'd learned as much from the intel briefs. The Sunnis were the traditional allies of Saddam Hussein, and the local Shiite inhabitants here were expected to be friendly. That contributed to the 'relatively benign' intel assessment that we'd been given. For the moment at least the intel seemed to fit with what we were seeing on the ground.

We pushed onwards for a further 5 kilometres, alert to the slightest movement around us. But apart from the Cobra gunships wheeling above the horizon, which had to be somewhere over the centre of Nasiriyah, there was nothing. Finally, we spotted what looked like a US Marine Corps command post some 200 metres ahead of us. To one side of the road was a cluster of tents and vehicles, plus scores of radio antennae fingering into the air.

The command post was surrounded by a line of US marines, lying on their belt buckles in all-around defence. None of them had dug in yet, so we figured they'd been here for only a matter of hours, and that there was no immediate threat. We could see for several hundred metres in all directions, and there was no sign of enemy forces. We figured the US Marine Corps commander would have units stationed 360 degrees around his command post, which meant we could be fairly relaxed around here, although we knew we had to be approaching their front line.

Under the watchful eyes of the Marine Corps grunts we pulled up on the roadside and dismounted. Tricky set up the TACSAT to send a LOCSTAT back to HQ – a report on where we were and what we were up to. Jason and I moved forwards on foot, heading for the command post. We were looking to secure some concrete intel on what might lie ahead of us, what kind of resistance the US Marines had met in Nasiriyah, and our best route through.

I'd grabbed my SA80 from where it was lodged between the driver's seat and mine, alongside Steve's Minimi light machine gun. Jason had also grabbed his, plus we'd got our pistols in our thigh holsters. There was the solid bulk of an Amtrak (Amphibious Armoured Tracked Vehicle) protecting the command post from the road. We skirted around it and approached the first tent. It had a curtain-like flap that shielded the entranceway. It was there so that light didn't leak out at night, revealing the tent's position to the enemy.

I reached forwards and lifted the flap. A big, square-shouldered Marine Corps orderly sergeant glanced up. He was clearly surprised as hell to see us. He stepped forwards and held out his hand, palm towards us, blocking the way. He had these massive, thick-rimmed sunglasses shielding his eyes, so there was no way of reading his expression. He didn't say a word, but he clearly wanted some kind of explanation as to what planet we'd just jetted in from.

'Hi, I'm David, a British Pathfinder,' I told him. 'This is Jason, my 2IC. Is your Ops Officer around? We have a mission to go north and I need to speak to him.'

He gestured for us to step forwards into something like a tented reception area. He seemed slightly less daunted after I had spoken – *and in English* – but I figured that about the last thing he had been expecting was two Lawrence of Arabia-type figures turning up out of the blue and stepping into his domain.

He gestured to a side table. 'Sirs, please put your weapons and your webbing down and leave them here.'

He got us to dump our longs and our pistols, plus our webbing. It was less that he was disarming us, and more that there wasn't the room in the ops tent for war-fighting gear. We followed him inside, and immediately we could sense the tension in the air. You could cut the atmosphere with a knife in there. Things were clearly in deadly earnest, and we sensed that the US Marines had taken casualties.

This was the Marine Corps' Regimental Combat Team 2 (RCT-2) HQ. They were part of the 1st Battalion, 2nd Marines, which made up Task Force Tarawa (TFT) – the force spearheading the assault into Nasiriyah. The guys here looked shocked and exhausted, and we realised it had to be proving pretty heavy out there. Our escort gestured towards this big, beefy Marine Corps major. He was positioned to one side in a vehicle that opened into the ops tent, and he was busy mouthing into a radio telephone.

'Ops Officer is on the net, sirs,' the Marine Corps sergeant told us. 'Figure he may be busy for some time.'

The Ops Officer was chewing tobacco and spitting in between issuing orders, and he looked as if he'd been on the go since well before dawn. He had his chair pushed back and his feet on a desk, and he was clearly having a tough time trying to control whatever was going down with his front line units. He was totally focused upon what was going on up ahead of him, and only marginally aware of us.

There was a moment when he nodded in our direction, and he looked as if he was about to break off from what he was doing to have words. But then some urgent message must have come in over the net, and he was yelling into his hand piece again. The delay was frustrating, but the longer we were here the clearer it became that things weren't going to plan in Nasiriyah.

With the major still yelling into his radio, one of his deputies pulled us to one side. He confided in us that they'd got three Marine Corps companies pinned down in the centre of the city. They'd lost a lot of blokes already that morning, and Nasiriyah was proving far from being the pushover that everyone had predicted.

Finally, the major dropped his handset and turned our way. As rapidly as I could I explained our mission. In response he just stared at us in exhausted silence. He had this expression on his face as if Jason and I each had our tackle hanging out, or something.

'Listen, guys, all I can say is there's no fuckin' way you want to be going north any time soon.' He eyed us in silence for a few seconds. 'You go pushin' north into all of that,' he jerked a thumb over his shoulder in the direction of Nasiriyah, 'then you gotta be on some kind of a freakin' death wish or something.'

Before I could respond there was a burst of static on the net, and he grabbed his radio to take another call. Jason and I had no option but to return to the Pinkies, and await developments. Back at the wagons I briefed the guys on where we were at.

'Right, the US front line is 1000 metres to our north. The Yanks are in heavy contacts, and they've taken casualties. They've got war-fighting to do and casevacs [casualty evacuations] ongoing, and that's what's holding us here. They're saying it's not secure enough for us to move forward. I'll keep checking in with their HQ, so be ready to move in half an hour, an hour, whenever. Okay?'

The lads seemed pretty relaxed about the hold-up, which was good. We broke down into groups and started studying the maps, trying to figure out if there were any better routes through. But with the time available to us rapidly shrinking, straight up Route 7 looked like the only way we were going to make it.

This was the problem with going in overland: it made the patrol highly vulnerable to hold ups. With time fast running out, I tried to figure out if there was any way we might beat the clock. It might well be that we would reach Qalat Sikar with only enough time to do a rushed recce, and that we'd have to clear 1 PARA in with minimal security. It was far from being ideal, but it could be the only way to get this thing done.

There was a part of my brain that couldn't help thinking: *Fuck me, if only we were stood on the tail ramp of a C130 right now, with AC/DC's 'Thunderstruck' playing at top volume and a HALO jump ahead of us. 'Sounds of the drums. Beatin' in my heart. The thunder of the guns. Tore me apart. You've been thunderstruck ...' We'd be on the ground in a matter of minutes and getting the job sorted.*

Jason was obviously thinking the same. 'You know, if me and H had tandemmed in from a C130, we'd have recced that bloody airfield by now.'

I nodded my agreement. 'I know. But we are where we are, mate.'

The more we got into serious operations mode, the more I saw that Jason was rising to the challenge. I reckoned we were going to work fine together now that we were at war, despite the previous tension between us. Faced with the relentless, overriding pace of this mission all those petty rivalries had been left behind us, or so I hoped.

Tricky had managed to raise PF headquarters on the radio. It can be frustratingly hard to raise HQ, so I was relieved he'd got through. There was no watchkeeper on the HQ radio, so it relied on one of the signallers picking up our call. And with six patrols out on the ground, everyone at HQ would be running to stand still. Half of the time John and the White Rabbit would be in Brigade briefings, so even when we did get through there was often no one there who could make any decisions.

Thankfully John was present, and I proceeded to brief him on where we were at. I told him we were liaising with the US forces, and I gave him our grid, beyond which we were unable to move. I warned

John that it might take us some time to get through Nasiriyah. I asked if it was possible to roll back 1 PARA's H-Hour, as we'd got held up. I told him again we were static, and could be held here for some time.

But John reiterated the urgency of getting to Qalat Sikar for 1 PARA's 0300 insertion.

CHAPTER THIRTEEN

We waited an hour, during which we could see and hear more of the battle raging over Nasiriyah. It was fierce. The tension and shock on the faces of those in the ops tent had said as much to us – that right here and right now something was fucking with their shit. Now we were starting to get a real eyeful of it. In Nasiriyah at least, the Iraqis certainly weren't rolling over and giving up for dead.

While Joe got a brew on, Jason and I decided to pay a second visit to the US command post. If anything it was more tense and chaotic than ever. I didn't even try to bother the major. Instead, I got a heads-up from one of the Marine Corps lieutenants as to what kind of trouble they'd stumbled into. He spoke to Jase and me over a map of the city that they'd got pinned up in the centre of the ops tent.

The vital strategic importance of Nasiriyah was that it straddled the Euphrates River plus the Saddam Canal, he explained. These were the two major waterways that would block any further advance northwards into Iraq. In downtown Nasiriyah a pair of bridges carried the main highway – Route 8 – over those watercourses, opening up the road northwards to Baghdad.

The Marine Corps' present mission, codenamed *Timberwolf*, had been meticulously planned and timed to seize both bridges intact. The short length of highway linking the two bridges had been nicknamed 'Ambush Alley', for it was such an obvious place to hit the advancing US forces. So instead of heading directly up Ambush Alley, the Marines had planned to loop eastwards through open ground, moving fast from one bridge to the other and taking any enemy by surprise.

However, *Timberwolf* had gone to ratshit before it could even get properly started. The previous night a convoy of supply trucks from the US Army's 507th logistics battalion had somehow managed to pass through the US Marine Corps' front line positions unchallenged. The convoy threaded through the final screen of M1A1 Abrams main battle tanks, and carried on driving. It then headed into the centre of Nasiriyah, without anyone from the 507th realising they'd crossed the US front line.

At 0600 hours they'd crossed the Euphrates River bridge and entered Ambush Alley. It was then that they realised their mistake, and tried to make an about turn, so they could retrace their route. But by then it was too late. The Iraqi forces had been alerted to their presence, and they proceeded to unleash all hell upon the lightly armed convoy. Truck after truck got hit, and the 507th took horrendous casualties. Scores of drivers, including Private First Class Jessica Lynch, a female soldier – were variously killed in action, posted missing in action or presumed captured.

The dark, oily columns of smoke that we'd seen hanging over the centre of Nasiriyah marked the burning remains of the trucks of the 507th. In the process of blundering into the city, the 507th had blown any element of surprise that the Marine Corps might have had. Instead, the Marines were forced to advance into a raging firefight. Worse still, they'd had to race into the city at breakneck speed, in an effort to try to rescue the trapped soldiers of the 507th. They'd headed directly down the throat of Ambush Alley and had got torn to pieces in the process.

Dozens of US soldiers had been lost that morning, either wounded or killed in action. They'd faced regular Iraqi forces armed with T55 main battle tanks, self-propelled anti-tank guns, mortars, RPGs and smaller weapons. Plus they'd been hit by irregular Fedayeen-type

gunmen, who had been hiding amongst the city's civilian population. It sounded like sheer hell out there, and I could well understand
the major's reluctance to let us proceed.

We left it another hour, then visited the command post for a third
time. The atmosphere seemed calmer. It was now more like brute
shock and exhaustion. The Marines had secured their objectives –
the bridges over the Euphrates River and the Saddam Canal – so
opening up a road route through Nasiriyah. But in the process they'd
been hammered, those two bridges costing them dear.

Whilst we waited to speak with the major, the captain briefed us
again. Their forces were split, one company around the northern
bridge, and one around the southernmost crossing, with a third
sandwiched somewhere in the middle. They kept trying to send
troops forward to relieve the northernmost positions, but they were
getting shot-up all along Ambush Alley. It was anyone's guess as to
how the fighting would shake out in there.

Finally, we got to speak with the major. 'My radio net's overloaded
big time,' he told us. 'I don't have proper comms with all my units. It's
very, very confused out there right now, there's a shit load of fighting going on, and we're still evacuating our casualties. You go north,
that's what you're heading into, and I'd very strongly advise against
it.'

'I hear what you're saying,' I told him, 'but we've been waiting here
for three hours, and we've got our mission's L-Hour fast approaching. We can move ahead, speak with your forward company commanders, and scope it out from there.'

He eyed me for a second, weighing what he was going to say next.
He knew he couldn't order us to stay put, for we were British soldiers
not under his command. But it was obvious that he could make life
very, very difficult for us if he chose to.

He gave this resigned kind of shrug. 'Okay, guys, it's your call. You
wanna move forwards, you've been warned. I've strongly advised
against it, but it's your call, guys.'

I nodded. 'Thank you, sir, I appreciate your support. We'll move forwards to your first company, and liaise with them. We'll then move on to the others, and do the same. I'd appreciate it enormously if you could radio a warning that we're coming through.'

'I'll do my best – that's if I can get comms with my guys on the ground.' He paused, running a hand exhaustedly across his features. He brought his fatigued, bloodshot eyes up to meet mine. 'You know, guys, we got this one APC blown on to its side, and we've not managed to get anyone to it yet. We presume they're all dead, but we just don't know. When you move ahead could you guys push through to that APC, and check for survivors?'

I considered this for a moment. He was a Marine Corps commander with the armoured might of the US Marine Corps behind him. I was a Pathfinder captain with nine blokes and three soft-skinned Land Rovers. We'd got a mission ahead of us that could turn the course of this war, and time was running out. You could say it was taking the piss, what he was asking of us. But I could tell that he was in shock, and that his men had taken a real mauling.

'I'll speak to my blokes and see what we can do when we get there,' I told him. 'What we can do, we will do, of that you have my word.'

We returned to the vehicles. Before moving out we had a quick 'Chinese parliament' – a group discussion amongst all on the patrol. We figured that if we could just get through Nasiriyah, we could do the drive to Qalat Sikar under cover of darkness on NVG, and that would be our best chance.

It got dark around 1600, which left us a good eight hours to get to the airfield, do the recce and get 1 PARA in for their H-Hour. But we all knew there was only one possible route through the city. We had to cross the first bridge that was being held by the US Marines and run Ambush Alley.

At 1300 we mounted up the Pinkies and moved out. We took Route 8 north into Nasiriyah, heading first for the Euphrates River bridge. We were moving away from the Marine Corps command post, when Steve turned to have words with me. I figured maybe he'd seen something of significance.

He leaned over and yelled into my ear: 'Dave, I need a wee.'

'Steve, will you just shut up for one minute!' I yelled back at him, in Shrek's broad Scottish ogre voice. 'Just for one bloody minute!'

But in spite of myself I was laughing. You had to love him for the sheer bloody torment he could deliver, anytime, anyplace, anywhere.

We'd each forced several litres of fluid into our bodies before setting out again, for maximum rehydration. We'd only sip sparingly now. On a mission such as this one the last thing you needed to be doing was stopping all the time in order to rehydrate, or so Steve could take a piss!

We'd spent hours studying our maps minutely, and memorising the roads that we needed to follow into Qalat Sikar. The entire route was clear in my head, as it would be with each of the other PF blokes on my patrol. That way, if we somehow got split up or separated from our mapping, we'd still be able to navigate our way to the mission objective. With one eye on the milometer, it should be easy enough to steer a way through the various road junctions.

Word was that the blokes from the US 507th logistics convoy had no maps with them when they blundered into Nasiriyah. That in part explained how they had ended up getting so hopelessly lost, and stumbling into the mother of all ambushes.

We pushed ahead at a dead slow, scanning our arcs of fire and alert to anything suspicious. Wherever any one of us PF gunners looked, our weapon would be pointing, for we moved the barrels of our machine guns in synchronisation with our heads and eyes. That way, as soon as we spotted a threat or a target we could open fire and mallet it.

The terrain changed quickly, and soon we were passing through a network of irrigation canals plus dense palm groves. This was the biblical area of Babylon and the Garden of Eden, and suddenly it had turned very green, closed in and claustrophobic.

Before we were into the city proper we stumbled upon the first signs of battle. Four khaki-coloured wagons were skewed across our side of the road, their gutted shells spitting orange fire and spewing out great gouts of oily black smoke. These had to be the remains of some of the 507th trucks that never made it out of the cauldron of Nasiriyah. Flaming tyres were pouring out thick clouds of acrid black smoke, which was barrelling into the air.

The way ahead was all but obscured by the drifting, oily darkness. Our forward visibility was down to near-zero, which made this the perfect place to ambush us. As we pushed ahead we were hyper-alert to any enemy presence. We crawled past the first wagon and we could see that the paint was blackened and blistered from the scorching heat, the truck body riddled with bullet holes.

Here and there great rents had been torn in the soft-skinned vehicle, as RPG and other large calibre high explosive rounds had torn into it. The heat was scorching on our faces, and the sickly-sweet smell of burning flesh made me gag as we passed by. We heaved up our shemaghs to shield our exposed skin, and I said a quick prayer for the poor bastards who were caught in all of that.

A couple of kilometres further on we hit the deserted streets of the city. There was an eerie, brooding silence in the place that did not bode well. Now and then we caught a dog's distant howling, or a half-glimpsed figure flitting down a side alleyway. Otherwise, there was bugger all moving out there.

Two kilometres into the city proper the first bridge reared up ahead of us like a giant, humpback whale. All around the massive concrete and iron structure there was this scene of absolute carnage. There were wrecked Hummers and the armoured hulks of Bradley Fighting Vehicles strewn along the roadside, spitting angry smoke and flame.

We reached the first group of marines. They were positioned at the bridge, and they'd gone firm in all-around defence. But they seemed glazed and shaken, as if they'd just seen a terrifying ghost. These were the men of Alpha Company, the first into Nasiriyah that morning, and they'd lost a dozen men as they had taken the bridge, maybe more.

Bravo Company had moved through them to storm Ambush Alley – the stretch of road leading from the first bridge to the next – and to relieve the trapped soldiers of the 507th. There they were likewise smashed, their Abrams tanks and APCs getting bogged down in the mud of a swampy, sewer area to the east of the highway.

Bravo Company had regrouped in an open patch of waste ground, before going in to assault Ambush Alley for a second time. Charlie Company then came through in an effort to relieve Bravo, and seize the second bridge. They had taken a real hammering before they had managed to force a way ahead and take the bridge over the Saddam Canal.

The scene at that first bridge was surreal. A US Marine Corps battle group had been fought to a standstill here. Its vanguard had been hammered to such an extent that blokes were wandering about pretty much lost and confused. I wondered how these guys, the cream of the US military, could be so shocked and so frozen. It was as if they had come in here not expecting a shitfight, and had then suddenly realised – *Oh my God, we're being ambushed and attacked!*

I guessed the answer had to be pretty simple, really. Their intel was likely appallingly bad; way wide of the mark. They'd probably sat through highly inaccurate briefings, telling them that Nasiriyah was going to be a pushover, and that the Iraqis would throw down their weapons and run. Instead, they'd stumbled into a veritable shitfight.

I sensed that the fighting was largely over now. There were still Cobra helicopter gunships circling overhead, and loosing off bursts of cannon fire. But it wasn't as if my sixth sense was screaming at me that it was all about to kick off. This felt like the exhausted, brutalised stillness after a big, ugly, bloody battle had gone down. Still, when the guys of Alpha Company heard that we were pushing on across the bridge, they warned us to take it real careful. It was bad up ahead. *Real bad.*

We spotted the massive form of an Abrams main battle tank creeping forwards, and we pulled the Pinkies in behind it. Using the cover provided by its massive armoured bulk, we crawled towards the apex of the bridge. We went firm just as we reached the downward slope, from where we had a panoramic view over the battle-torn city and directly forwards into Ambush Alley.

Smoke was pouring out of buildings to either side of us, and the nearest palm grove had been stripped bare by whirlwinds of shrapnel. There was the rhythmic '*thwoop-thwoop-thwoop*' of a helicopter gunship above us, and a Cobra came barrelling through the distant smoke, unleashing a long, deafening burst of cannon rounds as it went. Then it circled high above us.

A group of figures emerged from the shot-up palm grove. They were males dressed in local dish-dash robes and turbans. They moved towards us – lean, tanned and sure of foot in their light leather sandals. These were the first Iraqis of any sort that we'd seen since our arrival in their country several days earlier.

They pointed over their shoulders and started gesticulating. Then they yelled out in guttural, broken English: 'Soldier Americani! Soldier Americani!'

Is this where the major back at RCT-2 headquarters had lost his APC? Is this where he wanted us to check for any survivors? Or were these Iraqis trying to lure us into some kind of a trap? We looked where they had indicated. I could see a Bradley Fighting Vehicle lying on its side, half-sunken in the river mud. The back door was hanging open, and I reckoned I could see a dead or injured figure in there. But to confirm it either way we'd have to cross over the bridge and turn east on to the riverbed.

My instinct told me to stick with our mission. But still I wanted to do something at least to help. I opted for a halfway house. Whilst Tricky tried to raise Pathfinder HQ on the TACSAT, so we could file our 1600 Sched, Jason and I headed off on foot to find the Alpha Company commander. We asked a couple of marines where to locate him, but they were like zombies. All we got were a series of indistinct grunts and gestures. I guessed it was a fair one. It was like a champion boxer had taken on the underdog and got knocked to the floor. They'd been left reeling.

By luck rather than their directions we stumbled on to the Alpha

Company HQ. It was situated at an Amtrak, forwards right of the northern end of the bridge. The company commander was a Marine Corps major. He was out on foot a few paces away from the vehicle, gazing north into the cursed city and mouthing into a radio. We identified ourselves, and alerted him to the whereabouts of the Bradley and its grim cargo. It was adjacent to Alpha Company's right flank, so easy for them to investigate. Or at least it should be. I couldn't quite tell if he'd registered what I was saying. He seemed frozen; shell-shocked; all over the place.

There seemed little chance of getting any usable information out of him about what lay ahead. I tried asking, but he'd got dead, injured and missing marines scattered across the battleground, and he had his own shit to deal with. A focused briefing for the nine of us just wasn't happening.

We returned to our position on the bridge and I gazed up Ambush Alley. It was there that we needed to go. There was movement down there now. I pulled out my Nikon binoculars, a civvie purchase that I'd made just prior to deploying. They were compact and semi-waterproof, and they boasted low-light intensifier lenses. Via the binos I pulled Ambush Alley into sharp focus. I could see young women wearing dull black and beige headscarves scurrying this way and that, plus a couple of old biddies bent double with bags. Kids too. It looked as if the civvie population had broken cover to make some last-minute moves before nightfall.

There was no way the locals would be out and about if it was still Murder Central down there. It was a sure combat indicator when civvies disappeared from a city's streets. Conversely, when they reappeared you could pretty much conclude that it had all gone quiet. It was almost dusk now, and I figured it was time we pushed on.

For some frustrating reason Tricky couldn't raise PF HQ, but we couldn't afford to delay any more. It was 1530, and we'd likely miss our 1600 Sched, for we couldn't make the call on the move. But we could try again just as soon as we got into a static position with some security. In any case, I'd spoken to John just about every hour whilst we were halted at the Marine Corps command post, so he knew in detail what we were doing.

I asked Jason what he reckoned. He figured it was okay to move ahead. We'd press onwards and make the final call on the mission at the northern bridge. With the light fading fast we needed to move. Out of everything we do, operating at night is our absolute area of expertise.

We owned the night, and right now we had to get moving.

CHAPTER FOURTEEN

I'd been forward, speaking with Jason, and it was only when I went to return to my vehicle that I noticed what was happening with the Engineer Recce guys. They were flapping like they were about to take off. It turned out that their Land Rover had suffered a puncture. They'd been twenty minutes trying to change the tyre, and they couldn't seem to work out how to use the jack properly.

The Pinkies use a high-lift jack system, one that resembles a big chunk of steel pipe and levers. It consists of half a dozen parts, which you click together like a Meccano kit. With the arm under a jacking point, the high-lift can ratchet up the wagon to some considerable height. It's far lighter than a trolley jack, and it allows you to get right beneath the wagon if you need to, for repairs.

In the PF we kept our high-lifts strapped to the left-hand side of the wagon, right next to the spare wheel. Unbelievably, the Engineer Recce guys didn't seem to know where the various pieces of their jack were, or how to assemble it properly. As I watched the cluster fuck they were making of trying to change a tyre, I was boiling up with frustration.

We spend several months of every year training for vehicle-mounted mobility operations. The very basic first rung of such training is learning to deal with a puncture. We'd been refused the option of a para-insertion for the Qalat Sikar mission, and instead we'd been lumbered with an overland insertion, plus three guys who couldn't change a tyre. Right now they were putting the lives of my blokes in danger by their ineptitude. It would have been bloody laughable if it weren't such a fuck-up, and that was the root cause of my anger.

Perched on a bridge over the Euphrates in the midst of war-torn Nasiriyah was hardly the time nor the place to teach those guys how to change a tyre. We had little cover, and I wanted to get us moving pronto. Not a hundred yards away was a blown-up Amtrak, so the Iraqis had clearly been unleashing some big pieces of weaponry on the Yanks. Those Engineer Recce blokes had been bolted on to us to up the numbers, but right now it felt as if a massive ball and chain had been tied around our ankles.

By now Jason had also clocked the tyre-changing charade. The Engineer Recce blokes had yet to get the jack fitted together properly, and he was staring at them in utter disbelief. I saw him jab Dez in the ribs, and then Dez was staring at them in utter bemusement.

I caught Jason's eye and gave a nod in Dez's direction. 'Jase, get Dez on to it will you?'

In a flash Dez was off his wagon and over by the Engineer Recce vehicle. He was like a Tasmanian Devil: bam, bam, bam and it was done. Puncture sorted. From the sheepish looks on the Engineer Recce guys' faces, I guessed they knew how badly they'd messed up here. Had their vehicle got bogged down in the sand, and they'd not known how to free it properly, we might have cut them some slack. But this was so basic it was outrageous. *A recce team who couldn't change a tyre – in my book it was beyond fucking useless. It was amateur hour.*

That tyre-changing crap had wasted us a good twenty minutes, and it was 1600 dead when finally we moved off. We'd wrapped our faces in our shemaghs and dirtied ourselves up as much as possible. In the semi-darkness, and from a distance, I hoped very much that we could pass as locals. Bravo and Charlie Companies were 3 kilometres ahead of us, so that was how far we had to go.

We were driving on NVG, and up ahead Ambush Alley was bathed in a sea of fluorescent green brightness. There was good ambient light from a clear sky and we could see well to drive. We left the bridge and moved on to the flat, empty expanse of the darkened highway. We were alert and manning the weapons, whilst at the same time trying to make like we were some kind of local Iraqi militia. We were so used to patrolling in vehicles that we could have the weapons in a relaxed pose, but very quickly bring them to bear and put down murderous fire.

Ambush Alley seemed totally deserted now that it was dark, and we were the only thing that appeared to be moving out there. There was the odd, bullet-riddled, shitty white estate car abandoned by the roadside, and here and there light leaked from a cracked door or a window, but no one seemed to notice our passing. It was a tense, ten-minute drive before we reached the rear unit of the American forces. We'd asked the Alpha Company commander to radio Bravo and Charlie that we were moving forwards: *Beware, British Path-finders coming through*.

I spotted a group of Amtraks to the left of the road, in an expanse of flat, open ground. The road was elevated, and we could see further armoured vehicles to the right of us, in all-around defence. We stopped beside the first vehicle that had radio antennae. I went to introduce myself and to ask if this was the Company HQ. The guys here appeared more than a little surprised to see me, and I figured no radio message had got through. They also looked shell-shocked, and were clearly on the alert for further attacks.

One of the marines made a vague and exhausted gesture into the gathering darkness, pointing me in the direction of the Company HQ. We moved on and reached the second bridge, the one that crossed the Saddam Canal. It was smaller than the Euphrates River bridge, consisting of a flat concrete structure about 200 metres long. We crawled across it and at the northern end we located the Charlie Company HQ. Looking west I could just make out the lowrise silhouette of the city, about a kilometre away. To the east there were no buildings of any significance except for a few scattered huts.

We were on the northern outskirts of the city now, and as far as our intel briefings had told us there was only empty rural terrain ahead. It was 1700 and almost completely dark. All seemed quiet. Jason stayed with the blokes in the vehicles, as I moved forward on foot to speak to the Charlie Company commander. We were right on the front line, and it was best that Jase stayed with the wagons in case anything kicked off.

I moved through the men and vehicles of Charlie Company, the most forward unit of the US Marine Corps in Iraq. The grunts seemed hugely battle-fatigued, but they weren't as totally finished as their comrades from the Alpha and Bravo Companies. I found one of the Charlie Company commanders in his vehicle, and I made my introductions.

'Hi, I'm David, a British Pathfinder. We've got a recce mission 120 kilometres north of your front line. Have you seen any sign of the enemy north of your positions?'

'Yeah, I just got a radio message you Pathfinder guys were coming through,' he confirmed. 'But no,' he shook his head. 'No contact ahead of here for the last couple of hours.'

'And is your intel the same as ours – that there's nothing significant north of here in terms of the enemy?'

The guy eyed me for a second. 'We don't *believe* there's anything much out there.' He was choosing his words carefully. 'We don't *believe* there is. But, you know, we don't know for sure.'

'So as far as you know it's relatively benign?'

He nodded. 'That's the intel picture all right. But then again, there weren't supposed to be any significant hostile forces in Nasiriyah, and look what Alpha and Bravo got hit by, plus my boys. Lord only knows what might lie ahead of us.'

'Okay, but your best guess is that it's relatively benign?' I persisted.

'Yeah, right now we got nothing better to go on. So, I figure it's still relatively benign.'

'Okay, then we're going to press ahead and proceed with our mission. Where is your last vehicle?'

For a moment he stared at me. He seemed lost for words. It was like the idea of the nine of us pressing onwards into the unknown just didn't compute.

I repeated the question: 'Where is your last vehicle?'

He glanced at his map. 'It's around 300 metres to the north at the next road junction, a T-intersection where the main highway makes a sharp turn eastwards.'

I knew the road junction well from the maps: it was burned into my memory. 'Okay, and thanks,' I told him. 'We'll be seeing you.'

'Good luck with your mission,' he called after me. 'And one more thing, buddy: you'd best keep a watch out for any US warplanes, as much as you do the enemy. Two of our AAVs were hit by A10 tank-busters, and I lost a lot of good guys. So you'd best keep one eye on the skies.'

He asked me if we had Blue Force Tracker. I told him we did. He told me it had done little to safeguard his guys, so we'd best keep checking the skies. At the height of today's battle, two A10 Warthog tankbuster aircraft had pounced upon Charlie Company's AAVs (Amphibious Armoured Vehicles), as they tried to push through Ambush Alley and take the northern bridge. In the fog of war, the A10s had made several strafing runs with their 30mm cannons, before they'd realised what a horrific mistake they'd made.

By that time one marine from Charlie Company was dead and seventeen were wounded. The warning of the threat of friendly fire was ominous, but there was little I could do about it now. I thanked the Charlie Company commander for it, and returned to my patrol.

'Okay, guys, this is the sketch,' I told them. 'They haven't seen anything, or been in contact for the last couple of hours. Their intel picture echoes ours: north of here, relatively benign. Let's move forward to their last vehicles, which are at the T-intersection, and ask them what's what. If there's no change, I say we crack on.'

There were murmurs of agreement all around. We took a momentary pause, whilst each of us heaved on our Kevlar body armour, which until now had been sat in the rear of the vehicles. If we felt the situation warranted it we'd opt to wear the stuff, and now was as good a time as any to put on the Kevlar.

We checked that all the vehicle-mounted weapons had a round in the chamber, and we did likewise with our personal weapons. We'd been locked and loaded from the very moment of setting out from the FOB, but it never hurt to double-check.

Safety catches would be left on until the moment we were engaged or had to open fire. They needed to be, in case the vehicle hit a rut and you had a negligent discharge – the shock of the impact making the gun go off of its own accord. Your finger remained resting on the safety at all times, so it could be flicked off and you could open fire in one fluid movement.

But right now I was feeling fairly confident that we could push ahead without being compromised. I figured the drive along Ambush Alley had proved one crucial thing: a tiny force like ours could pretty much slip through undetected, if making like locals and driving at night on no lights and NVG.

I leaned forwards and flicked a switch on the dashboard, which cut all the circuits to the wagon's lights. Having done so, none of the Pinkie's lights would come on, not even the brake lamps. We pulled our shemaghs – our chequered Arab headscarves – up over our faces, until only our eyes were showing. We then roughened up our combats, our assorted rag-tag of uniforms.

We checked our weapons one last time: our personal assault rifles and pistols; magazines; ammo; grenades; grenade launchers; rocket launchers; plus the four GPMGs (General Purpose Machine Guns) and the two 50-calibre heavy machine guns mounted in the wagons. Finally, we flipped down our NVG, and waited for our eyesight to adjust to the smudgy, fluorescent-green alien-world glare.

We moved off and skirted around the US command wagon, pushing ahead until we were 2 kilometres north of the Saddam Canal bridge. As we approached the road's T-junction we slowed, searching for the last US Marine Corps vehicles. But there was nothing that we could detect in any direction.

We scanned the surrounding terrain first with our NVG, and then with our SOPHIE thermal imaging sights, but there was not a single Amtrak, Bradley or Abrams tank that we could make out. We figured that either the Charlie Company commander was mistaken about the location of his last vehicles, or the platoon had moved.

We paused for a few minutes to have a collective heads-up. We'd seen no sign of the last American positions, but equally we'd seen no sign of the enemy. Nothing had changed about the intel picture or the state of play, as far as we could tell.

If we'd got any concrete warnings from the Americans that there were Iraqi positions up ahead of us, then we'd have had to re-visit the mission plan. Maybe we'd have opted to try the tracks that looped eastwards, keeping off the major roads. But as it was, Charlie Company had been here for several hours and seen nothing. We figured we must have entered some kind of no man's land – that we'd pushed past the American front line and were into uncharted territory – but still I felt reasonably confident about moving ahead.

The American forces were driving HUMVEEs, Amtraks, Bradleys or Abrams tanks, all of which were hulking great armoured monsters, and unmissable. They dwarfed the Pinkies. We were in open-backed wagons wearing shemaghs over our faces, and dressed in a motley collection of uniforms. We reckoned we could flit past any Iraqi positions that might be out there, and those that did see us would take us for an elite unit of the Iraqi Republican Guard, or something similar. The vote was to crack on.

It was 1730 when we made the turn at the T-intersection heading eastwards, the start of a short dogleg that would take us from Route 8 to Route 7 – the freeway leading all the way to Qalat Sikar. The airfield was 120 kilometres north of here, and we had nine hours in which to make it, and get the PARAs in for their H-Hour. It was all doable.

In the confusion of trying to locate the last friendly positions, and get some usable intel off the Americans, Tricky and I had forgotten to send our 1600 Sched. Not sending it would trigger a process which would force PF HQ to consider us compromised and on the run, and to cue up the CSAR teams. But we didn't realise that we'd missed our Sched.

We moved out, heading north into the darkness and the unknown.

CHAPTER FIFTEEN

Almost unconsciously, our senses had become hugely heightened as we moved forwards. We'd left the protective screen of the US Marine Corps, and we were out here on our own. But we were not here to recce this area. We had the draw of Qalat Sikar airfield pulling us forwards, and that was our focus.

We headed eastwards, the road passing through open, rural terrain. All around us there were thick palm groves, and the dense undergrowth was interspersed with the shadowy forms of low, mud-walled huts and farm-like structures.

We were hyper-alert to the presence of any US vehicles, in case they'd pushed ahead of the T-junction. The last thing we needed was a Bradley Infantry Fighting Vehicle opening up on us. The Bradley boasts an array of fearsome weaponry that could chew our Pinkies into shreds in seconds. But there was no sign of anything. No American armour. No Iraqi military positions. No civilians. Nothing.

My brain felt unusually calm, quiet and clear. There weren't a hundred different thoughts crashing through my mind, as there often are when out on exercises. It was like a form of meditation, this tuning in to the night environment and our surroundings. I opened up my mind and my senses to any changes in the atmosphere and the setting, and I was hyper-alert to any sense of threat. But there was nothing that I could detect.

We approached the second T-junction, where Route 8 ran into

Route 7. It was here that we'd take the turning heading north, and that would complete the short dogleg around the outskirts of the city. We'd then leave Nasiriyah behind us. We slowed to a crawl as we swung around the junction, and as we did so I caught sight of the first substantial building that we'd seen since leaving the US front-line positions.

Just to the east of Route 7 there was this large, mud-walled compound. It was dark as the grave, and it seemed to be utterly deserted. But still there was something ominous about the place, and I sensed that it represented real danger and ... evil almost. It was weird, but the sense of blackness that emanated from the place was more than just visible. I could feel it.

A chill went up my spine as we began to sneak past at a dead slow. We were puttering along at 30 kph, our 2.5-litre diesel engines purring softly in the still night air, our tyres making just the faintest hum on the tarmac. We'd drilled and drilled and drilled for this kind of noiseless driving. The secret was making no sudden movements with the Pinkies – no noisy acceleration, or engines growling, or gears grinding, or the scrunching of tyres on the road. All was smooth and silent, and we were as soundless as the wind. A soft gust would cover our passing.

And then I heard it. *Voices.* It was just the faintest snatch of Arabic hanging in the cool desert air. I tuned in, my ears hoovering up the sound. The voices seemed louder than they really were in the night-dark quiet. I could tell that these weren't raised voices, that this wasn't someone shouting in alarm. This wasn't someone yelling: *What the fuck are those vehicles?*

I swivelled my head and my weapon about, trying to catch the chatter, so I could pinpoint what direction the voices were coming from. And then, in the periphery of my vision, I caught sight of the figures. I swung my eyes directly on to them, and as I did so I was sighting down the barrel of my gun. At one end of the dark compound a group of seated men were chatting away, and each was cradling a weapon in his hands.

They were 50 metres or so away from us, but I could tell by the cut of their forage caps that they were Iraqi soldiers. I figured it had to be a platoon-strength position, so maybe thirty men in all. I didn't know if Jason had seen them, for his wagon was 250 metres in front of us. All the Iraqi soldiers needed to do was glance towards the road, and they'd see me sighting them down the barrel of my GPMG.

The Gimpy as we call it – pronounced 'jimpee' – has a very simple set of metal sights, and the stark iron 'V' was outlined in the glow of my NVG. I was poised to flick off the safety, and open up on those figures, at the faintest sign of any trouble. I knew that the moment I did so the GPMG would spit out a funnel of fire, annihilating the figures before my eyes.

I didn't need to check that Tricky had clocked where I was aiming, and that he'd got the 50-cal ready to drop thunder if they spotted us. Even though there might be thirty enemy soldiers, we could easily outgun a platoon of Iraqi troops, especially when we had surprise on our side. We had the 50-cal and the GPMG mounted on a very stable fire platform. They had thirty hand-held AK47s.

As we crept forwards my heart thudded in my ears, but no one seemed to notice our passing. Within seconds we were leaving that sinister building and its occupants behind, apparently without anyone spotting us. Breathing a long sigh of relief, I swung my weapon and myself back to face the way ahead. The road looked flat and straight for several miles. It was dark and deserted as far as I could see, and devoid of any movement or headlights.

We were running along a raised embankment. To the west, the ground dropped away. To the east it rose to a low ridge, which was dotted with a scatter of outbuildings. There wasn't the slightest glimmer of light, or any sign of life anywhere in all directions. We gathered speed, and all I could hear was the hum of tyres on tarmac, and the rush of the night wind. I presumed that we were through the Iraqi front line positions now, so from here on it was a straight drive to Qalat Sikar. We were free-running all the way towards the mission objective.

Up ahead were the reassuring forms of Jason and the Recce Engineers' Pinkies. I had no doubt that we could still pull off the mission. For a moment I reflected on what we'd learned whilst passing through Nasiriyah. If the intel could have been so hopelessly wrong about that place – which by anyone's reckoning had spawned the mother of all battles – maybe they'd got it equally wrong about the area running north to Qalat Sikar airfield.

It was hardly a pleasant thought, but it was one worth considering. Maybe it wasn't relatively benign out there at all. Maybe the airfield wasn't largely unoccupied. But if so it wouldn't be the first time that the intel picture had been so hopelessly out of kilter. Either way we were at war, and as Jacko Page had told us back in Kuwait, he was expecting the extraordinary out of the Pathfinder Platoon.

The reason why the British Army had formed the Pathfinders was to take the risks required on the intel available, and to go forwards. That way we risked six, and not 600 or 6000 men. We might lose a couple of vehicles, and a few good blokes, but not an entire battalion. What we were doing now defined the PF: it went with the territory.

We were a kilometre north of the T-junction when for an instant I thought I caught the sound of voices again. We'd upped the speed to 40 kph by now, so I had to strain my ears above the roar of the wind to hear. Sure enough I could just make out the faintest gabble of Arabic. The night vision goggles tended to channel your sight into a tunnel of green light wherever you were looking, and your vision went dark and foggy towards the periphery. I glanced left, in the direction of the voices, and suddenly I spotted the source of the chatter.

There was a pair of soldiers strolling towards us on our side of the road. They were sporting smart forage caps, and each had an AK47 slung across his right shoulder. There was a slight hesitation in the step of the guy in front as his eyes met mine, and I could tell that there was a momentary freezing of his mind. I knew for sure that he'd seen us, and it was as if he was thinking – *What in God's name is that?* He was no more than 5 metres away as we rolled silently past him, and I was gazing right into his eyes.

Everything seemed to wind down to ultra-slow motion. I could see the Iraqi soldier's mind scrambling for some kind of comprehension, some sliver of understanding, some clue as to what this dark vision that had emerged silently from the night might be. My face was covered by my shemagh, my eyes shielded by the night vision goggles. All that he could see of me was the faint, other-worldly glow that the NVG threw off, making two pinpricks of fluorescent light, like frog-green alien eyes.

An instant later we'd shot past. I had to force myself to resist the temptation to swing the GPMG and myself around. That wasn't the ruse here. If we were a unit of elite Iraqi troops – say Republican Guard Special Forces – we were hardly going to pay those two Iraqi soldiers much heed. We would thunder on regardless, Saddam's elite treating those two Iraqi conscripts with the scant regard that they deserved.

The psychology here was a lot like kids out vandalising a car, when the cops drive by: *Don't look, or they'll know it's us.* We just had to carry on as if we had every right to be here. We wanted to leave those Iraqi soldiers with the firm impression that Saddam's finest were coming through. We'd got to hope we could bluff our ticket, and slip away silently into the night.

Once we were past them I concentrated on covering my arc of fire – from 8 o'clock to 2 o'clock in front of the vehicle. For all I knew there might be more enemy troops ahead of us on the road, and that was what I was searching for in the darkness. I knew that Tricky would be watching the rear. If it looked as if those two Iraqi soldiers were going to open fire, Tricky would mallet them with the 50-cal.

My thoughts as we sped onwards into the night were these: *Fuck me, that was outrageous!* I'd just passed an Iraqi soldier at arm's length, whose brief it was to kill me, and I'd looked him in the eye man-to-man. He was close enough to reach out and strangle me, or for me to reach out and grab him. I'd never heard of anything like this happening, not in the PF or any other unit. Whenever we got to the airfield and got the PARAs in, the blokes on my patrol would sure have some stories to tell.

The image of the Iraqi soldier that I'd eyeballed was burned into my mind. A lot of the Iraqi conscripts tended to look like a sack of shit, but not that guy. He was neat and professional-looking, his drab olive cap matching his drab olive uniform, and his weapon slung on a smart, polished leather sling. The bloke was lean and clean-shaven, with a neatly-trimmed moustache. He had one hand stuffed in his pocket, and his right hand resting easily on his slung weapon.

His buddy was smoking a ciggie. I'd seen the glow blooming green and smudgy in my night vision. I was struck by how relaxed they both looked as they strolled along Route 7. I compared their appearance to that of the US Marines, just a few kilometres to the south. The Iraqi soldiers appeared calm but ready. Compared to the US Marines that we'd encountered during the day, they had an air of cool about them. They certainly weren't flapping that the US Marine Corps was massed just to the south of them, and on the warpath.

Those two soldiers were so close to Nasiriyah that they had to be part of the unit that had been engaged in battle with the US Marine Corps that day. I figured that they were part of a company that made up a battalion, one that had been ordered by Saddam to repulse the US Marine Corps' advance. Their easy self-confidence had surprised me, and it was strangely unsettling.

It was the right decision not to have opened fire. Our job was to get to the airfield and facilitate 1 PARA's insertion, not to start brassing up the first enemy that we came across. If we passed by unnoticed, or were gone too swiftly for them to challenge us on our identities, then all the better for the mission.

An elite Iraqi Republican Guard unit would most likely be driving GAZ jeeps, a Soviet-era four-by-four used widely by the Iraqi armed forces. The Gorky Automobile Plant (GAZ) started manufacturing their jeep in the 1940s, so it hailed from a similar era to the Land Rover. At first glance the GAZ was not dissimilar in appearance to the Pinkies. The GAZ jeep was an open-backed four-by-four, with distinctly rugged, Second World War lines. You'd have to study our wagons carefully to be certain that they weren't

GAZs, especially when they shot past from out of the darkness.

I'd read confusion in that Iraqi soldier's eyes, plus real surprise, but there was no sudden realisation there that we were the enemy. I had to presume that for now at least the bluff was working. I knew instinctively that Steve and Tricky had also seen them. We'd lain in OPs (Observation Posts) for days on end, shitting into bags and hearing each other's life stories. I'd known instinctively that we were all on to them, and that each of us had clocked exactly what the others had seen.

When we went firm as a patrol we'd compare notes, just to make doubly sure that we'd all seen the same things. Any one of us was free to open fire, if he judged that he had to. But we'd only do so if we were being engaged, or if we were about to be engaged. The rule was to wait, wait, wait, because we might get through unchallenged and get away with it, just as we seemed to be doing right now.

We pushed onwards in a tense silence for another kilometre. A small building appeared on the left-hand side of the road. Clustered around it I could see a dozen Iraqi soldiers lounging around with their weapons. At the minimum this had to be a platoon-sized position, but it was a hundred metres or more away from the road, and I reckoned we could slip past unnoticed.

The nearer we got the more details I could make out. There were five guys sitting outside the building, and I figured there had to be more inside. They were not so much on sentry duty as hanging out and shooting the shit. Maybe it was some kind of checkpoint, but it was too far from the road to be effective. Still, I found myself thinking: *Jesus, more fucking Iraqis!* I had hoped we were through the main concentration of their front line positions by now.

A couple of the enemy soldiers got to their feet, but still they were chatting away unconcernedly. They clearly hadn't seen Jason's vehicle, or the Engineer Recce wagon. I saw a head flicking in our direction, but by the time the soldier thought that maybe he'd heard something we were flitting past, onwards into the night. I told myself that maybe that was it. Surely by now we'd pushed through the Iraqi front line, and more or less without being seen. I sure bloody hoped so.

We pushed onwards for another 5 kilometres. Nothing. The road up ahead was reassuringly dead. Dark. Deserted. It was great for using the night vision, for there were no man-made lights visible anywhere to flare it out. There was little limit to what we could see range-wise in this kind of ambient light. The terrain was totally silent. There wasn't a human voice, nor a dog barking, nor a farm animal bleating, nor an engine grunting anywhere, and all I could hear was the roar of the wind above the quiet purr of our vehicles.

I was starting to hope that the intel picture would hold up now. I was hoping that we'd sneaked through the Iraqi forces, and that we were in the clear. I glanced to the rear of our wagon and there was not the slightest sign of anyone in pursuit. We'd bluffed our way through at least three groups of Iraqi troops, which in itself was amazing going. I allowed myself to relax a little, as I shifted my weight behind my weapon.

We hit the 10-kilometre mark – 110 still to go – and there were some outbuildings to the east of the road. They were set back on a ridge some 500 metres away, and mostly they were dark. From one or two I got the occasional glimpse of light, as if a candle had been left burning behind a partly-shuttered window.

Jason's vehicle started to pick up speed. We followed suit. Soon we were barrelling along at 70 kph. It was a good call. There was no point hanging around in utterly deserted territory for any longer than we had to. Then I spotted a lone pair of headlamps far ahead of us.

I studied them closely with the NVG. The lights were close to the road, so it had to be a car, as opposed to a jeep or a truck. As the vehicle got closer I could make out that it was some kind of white sedan. It looked like an Iraqi taxicab. We'd been told to expect the occasional civvie vehicles on Route 7, for it was the main highway to Baghdad.

If we pulled off the road to avoid this vehicle we might have to do the same all the way to the airfield, especially if there was a lot of civvie traffic about. In any case, that wasn't the deal here. The bluff was that we were an elite Iraqi unit, and if we were spotted skulking about by the roadside we'd have blown our cover. As the vehicle drew closer, Jason made the call to carry on driving north up the highway. It was exactly the right thing to do as far as I was concerned.

I saw the car pass Jason's Pinkie, and it visibly slowed. As the Engineer Recce wagon neared, the driver momentarily flicked his headlamps on to full beam, fully illuminating the wagon. By the time we were approaching the sedan it was barely crawling along, and there was this face pressed close to the windscreen and peering up at us.

Tricky, Steve and I flipped up our NVG, to prevent the car's headlamps whiting out our night vision and blinding us. As the vehicle got nearer, the driver flicked his lights from dip to full and back again. He had our Pinkie fully illuminated in his headlamps, so he could get a real good look at us. We shot past and I could see the driver staring up into my face. He was a fat, moustachioed geezer dressed in a dish-dash. He looked like some Iraqi version of Ron Jeremy, the fat American porn star with a droopy moustache. I guessed he was your typical Iraqi cabbie, one who used his taxi to drive to the local corner shop he was that flabby.

But whilst he was overweight and paunchy, his brain appeared to be pretty sharp. He took this great, long look at us, and I could see this expression of total consternation spreading across his features. There was alarm and disquiet in those pudgy eyes, like he was suddenly on to the fact that we were far from being his fellow Iraqi brothers in arms.

A thought flashed through my mind: *Never take the third light*. It's an old Army saying from the First World War. In the trenches, the guy who struck the match would alert the enemy to your position. The second light would give the enemy something to aim at. And with the third light … he'd pull the trigger. Hence you never accepted the third light.

We were the third vehicle in our well-spaced convoy. I figured with

Jason's wagon the Iraqi cabbie had thought – *What the fuck was that*? With the Engineer Recce truck he'd slowed down and asked himself – *Are those Iraqi vehicles*?

And with us his eyes had started bulging with disbelief – *Who the hell are those guys*?

CHAPTER SIXTEEN

As we pushed onwards into the night I was not sure exactly what the fat cabbie's facial expression had meant. He'd seen these weird alien warriors steaming out of the night, but did that mean that we'd been compromised? And would anyone listen to him if he tried to raise the alarm? If the cabbie knew what was best for him he'd keep quiet, for who was ever going to believe his story?

We carried on driving, and it was Steve who broke the silence. 'Did you see fucking Ron Jeremy giving us the once-over?'

'Yeah, what d'you reckon?'

'I pity the poor Iraqi bird that's married to that one.'

That was Steve's way of saying that we had no choice but to crack on. Of course we could always turn around and shoot up the enemy forces that we'd seen behind us, but that wasn't our mission. We had to presume that we'd had another lucky escape with Ron Jeremy, and continue with the mission.

We'd got 15 kilometres under our belts since Nasiriyah, so 105 left to go. From the sat photos of Qalat Sikar we figured it was pretty much open desert some 30 kilometres this side of the airfield. Once we hit the 30 kilometres to target mark we could leave the road and head overland, which meant all we needed to do was get near enough to that open terrain.

I felt a sudden sharp whack on the shoulder from Tricky. 'Dave! Dave! Lights coming up fast from behind!'

For a moment I went to check my rear-view mirror, before remembering the wagon didn't have one. At night, wing and driver's mirrors can reflect street lamps and car headlights, so giving your position away. During the daytime, if the sun caught a mirror it could flash a blinding reflection across enormous distances, and directly into the eyes of the enemy. In fact, small mirrors are often carried by SF units as a last resort, to signal a position to a rescue party. I had one stashed in my grab bag.

I turned my head and gazed backwards along the length of the Pinkie. I could see this dazzling light beaming out of the darkness, and bleaching out my night vision. It was a lone pair of headlights coming up fast from behind. The nearer the headlamps got, the more I was convinced that it was the same vehicle as before – Ron Jeremy's taxicab.

As we were the last in line it was with our vehicle that the fat Iraqi cabbie first pulled level. He had one hand on the wheel while the other was fiddling in the pocket of his dish-dash, and he was staring up at us in total amazement. He pulled out what looked like a mobile phone, and started gabbling into it. I spotted the distinctive flick of an antenna poking out of the top of it, and realised that it was some kind of radio.

Suddenly, Ron Jeremy was no longer just a run-of-the-mill Iraqi cabbie. They didn't carry those kinds of radios. But if he was Iraqi military, he was well out of shape and far too old to be a junior-ranking soldier. So maybe – just maybe – he was some kind of Iraqi commander heading back to his front line positions. If he was, and if he was radioing through our presence to headquarters, that was seriously bad news.

Still, he needed to know exactly where he was on the road to give our position accurately. It was night, and there had been no noticeable landmarks in the last 10 kilometres or so. It wasn't going to be easy for him to pinpoint our convoy, even if he had pinged us. For a moment, I considered blowing the guy away, but he was driving a civvie vehicle and he was dressed like a civvie, and I couldn't see any weapon.

If I brassed him up I'd have to live with that for the rest of my life, and PF or no PF, I wasn't up for murdering civilians. In any case, we'd been given very specific rules of engagement for Iraq. We knew that we had to be able to positively identify an Iraqi with a weapon, one who was a clear and present threat to us, before we were permitted to open fire.

The car dropped behind us, overtook again, then pulled in behind Jason's Pinkie. I was certain that he was 'dicking' us – a phrase that we had used in Northern Ireland when we had an enemy disguised as a civvie spying on our patrols. I was equally convinced that he was reporting back all that he could see to some form of higher control. But I had no proof that this was so.

I'd seen no weapon, he'd not opened fire on us, and he wasn't causing us any physical harm. Even though we'd seen him dicking us, unless we were under heavy and accurate fire it was best to stay covert for as long as possible when on a mission such as this one. In short, I couldn't find the slightest excuse to blow his brains out, which one part of me was very tempted to do. One other thing was absolutely clear. Whoever the hell the guy was, he had balls of total steel to do what he was doing. He was getting eyes-on with our vehicle, then the next and the next, and all the while he was a sitting target. *Balls of fucking steel!*

I wondered what it was that had fingered us as a non-Iraqi unit. Our wagons had military number plates on them, but they were non-reflective and I doubted that he could see them. With the amount of kit hanging off the Pinkies they could easily be GAZ jeeps, for their shape was all but totally obscured. We were probably physically bigger than most Iraqi soldiers, but we certainly wouldn't look like any US marine did in the video games that Ron Jeremy played.

Finally, his vehicle dropped behind us again, and his lights disappeared. All I could think was – *Thank fuck he's gone*. We were 25 kilometres in now, but I could sense that the net was starting to close. Yet there was still no sign of any Iraqi forces on our tail, and we had to hope that we'd got through the worst.

We were a good quarter of the way to Qalat Sikar, and the worst we'd had was some ballsy Iraqi cabbie-cum-fat-controller fucking with our shit. It was a lot of ground to have covered without a single shot being fired, and I figured that we were getting there. I could see a long, long way in front, and there wasn't a vehicle or a building in sight.

Even if the net was closing, they still had to find and catch us, plus there was no way we could ever go back the way we'd come. I could guess at the size of the Iraqi force that was positioned behind us, which had to be a couple of companies at the very least. I'd got a sense of their calibre too. They were going head-to-head with the US Marine Corps, and they were hardly running away or throwing down their weapons.

We had to presume that Ron Jeremy had alerted the Iraqi force commanders to our presence, so they'd be waiting for us, and that meant the element of surprise was totally gone. There was no option but to keep pushing north. Still, I couldn't shake off this creepy feeling that we were driving into a trap, and that in turn got me thinking about how to survive if the enemy did capture any of us.

We'd recently attended a talk by the British general Sir Anthony Farrar-Hockley, who was then a living legend in elite forces circles. Some generals had one medal earned on peacetime ops, but Farrar-Hockley was the real deal. During the Korean War he'd been taken prisoner by the enemy, and had escaped and been recaptured several times over.

It was amazing that he was still alive after all he had been through, let alone so pin-sharp in his presentation. He had to be well into his eighties, and it was a true privilege for every bloke in the PF to hear his stories from the Korean War, which was still the fiercest conflict fought by British forces since the Second World War. What he had been through – the repeated hell of capture and torture and interrogation – was very much what we dreaded happening to us on our kind of missions.

The general looked robustly healthy, and he was unlike any man that I'd ever seen of that age. He told us that the secret to staying youthful was to keep the mind busy and occupied. He talked about how he'd kept himself mentally strong under duress as a prisoner, and how strength of mind was the key to surviving such horrors. During one escape attempt he'd made it all the way back to his unit, only for it to get attacked again and for him to be recaptured.

He told us how they were fed very little in captivity, getting a few bowls of rice between many prisoners. There were two types of people who emerged at those times: those who shared a bowl of rice with you, and those who did not. He stressed how the more selfish prisoners who didn't share tended not to make it, whilst those who were generous with their fellows somehow had the strength and the will to survive. Against the odds it was the good guys who made it through, reflecting how mental fortitude was the absolute key to survival.

As Farrar-Hockley had talked us through all this, I'd wondered whether Jason was the type to share his bowl of rice with you. Back then, just a few months ago, I'd figured that he most likely was not. But right now on this mission, and heading into the heart of enemy territory, I was changing my mind fast on that one.

At Sandhurst I'd been taught to lead autocratically, by right and by rank. When I joined the Pathfinders I'd realised very quickly that was the wrong approach completely. I had to give the lads on my patrol far more respect than that. I'd done so to the ultimate degree with Jason on this mission, and he'd risen to the challenge. He was leading from the front, making a lot of command-type decisions on the fly, and I'd yet to fault a single move that he'd made. I guessed if I were prone to insecurity I'd see this as threatening my role, and seek to rein him in. Thankfully, I wasn't. As much as ever we could be, we were a team of equals.

The other thing that Jason was showing in bucketloads was sheer bravery and raw courage. There was a simple rationale behind putting your command vehicle in the rear: it meant the patrol leader and your command communications had greater protection. By taking pole position Jason's wagon was going to be first into any ambush. He knew that, and he'd never once baulked at it.

I was torn away from my thoughts by a distant crackle of gunfire. I turned my head and way behind I could see tracer rounds arcing high into the wide, starlit heavens. The fire was coming from some-where back near the US Marine Corps' front line, and I had no idea who was firing at whom or why. But it sounded as if a firefight of sorts had sparked off again.

I had little time to dwell upon it. Up ahead the road was no longer a clear run through. Instead, there were two sets of headlamps bear-ing down upon us, pinpricks of light in a sea of blackness. They were larger and brighter than Ron Jeremy's cab lights, and they showed up like massive, smudged green frog-eyes in my NVG.

I could ID the lead vehicle pretty much right away, for the lights of the rear wagon were shining through and illuminating the one in front. It was a white minibus, and I could see by the silhouettes inside that it was packed full of women wearing burka-type head coverings. The vehicle behind looked to be a similar vehicle carrying a similar load.

It seemed as if some form of civvie transport – the local Nasiriyah bus service? – was bearing down upon us. We'd got to be doing a combined speed of 130 kph, and the distance between us narrowed rapidly. We rushed past the first minibus, and no one seemed to pay us any heed. Within seconds we were past both vehicles, and the road was clear again.

One thing occurred to me when we were passing, something that I hadn't really noticed before. Those minibuses had shot by on our left-hand, passenger side, because here in Iraq we were having to drive on the wrong side of the road for British vehicles. The Iraqis drive on the right, and it suddenly struck me that maybe that had been the giveaway to Ron Jeremy. How could we possibly be Iraqi Special Forces, if we were using right-hand-drive vehicles – *those that are driven by the foreigners*?

Steering wheel on the wrong side: it was glaringly obvious when you thought about it. He'd certainly spent long enough staring up at our wagons in the full illumination of his headlights to clock the fact that we were driving foreign vehicles. Up until now I'd just presumed that we could pass as an elite Iraqi unit. Suddenly, I was convinced otherwise. Ron Jeremy had clocked us: the question is, what would he and his Iraqi brethren do about it?

I flicked my eyes across to the milometer. We were 40 kilometres along Route 7, with 80 more to go. I checked my watch. In addition to the Bvlgari's indestructible black leather strap, it has a faintly luminous dial, which makes it easy to read. It is also waterproof to a depth of 600 metres, which made it all but bulletproof in terms of the kind of soldiering we did in the PF. It was approaching 1800 and it was as quiet as the grave out there. We had to press on.

All the satellite images and intel reports had suggested that there were no major Iraqi settlements along Route 7, the whole way from Nasiriyah to Qalat Sikar. The maps showed a couple of minor villages and a scattering of oil wells, but no major towns, and certainly no Iraqi army bases. Yet we were just 50 kilometres in when we hit our first major obstacle. Up ahead we could see the distinctive orange halo-like glow of street lamps. Street lamps had to mean a significant Iraqi settlement of some sort, for the smaller villages didn't even have them.

A kilometre in front of us and closing fast the road was bathed in a sea of orange light. As we drew closer I could see a dense cluster of buildings to the right, eastern side of the highway. These were the first street lamps that we'd seen since Nasiriyah. They reared above the highway like a long row of dinosaur necks, heads poised to strike downwards at their prey. Our convoy would be illuminated for the entire length of the highway on which they were situated.

We were a good 500 metres out when we were forced to discard our NVG, due to the blinding orange glow. We flipped up the goggles on their brackets, before the street lamps whited out our vision completely. Even so, it took several seconds for our eyes to adjust to the new light levels.

To the east of the road I could make out more of the buildings. There were groups of flat-roofed structures two or three storeys high, running for a good 300 metres along that side of the highway. Most were totally dark, but from the odd window a sliver of light spilled out from behind a curtain. This was a substantial human settlement, and it was clearly occupied.

The land rose up to a ridgeline several hundred metres high, and about a kilometre to the east. The buildings were set on the slope running up to that ridge, so they were higher than we were, with good views of the road. It looked as if this was some kind of a purpose-built settlement, and just about every building covered a huge killing area on the slope below, stretching down to the highway – Route 7 – itself.

It was an ominous proposition having to run this stretch of road in the full glare of those street lamps, and being so visible. I glanced to the left – western – side of the highway, to see if there was a way through off-road. But there was a wall of vegetation looking thick, dark and impenetrable. There was no point heading off-road that way, and going east would only take us directly into the built-up area. There was only one possible way through and that was dead ahead.

I saw Jason's wagon speeding up, and Steve pushed his pedal to the metal to keep up with the lead Pinkies. We hit 90 kph, and I figured Jason's plan had to be to run the street lamps at top speed and hammer on through. It made total sense to do so. There was no point trying to be all sneaky-beaky and creeping along, when we were going to be 100 per cent visible. That would make sitting ducks out of us.

We hit the pool of light beneath the first street lamp, and the instant we did so I felt horribly exposed. It was like being in the pitch black of night, and suddenly having a police helicopter put a massive searchlight over you. I could see the vegetation to the left-hand side very clearly now. It was a thick, tangled mass of bush, with palm trees arching over it. We were right keeping to the road.

Steve was gunning the engine, which was screaming and revving hard. I could feel the Pinkie weaving about as he fought for control over the steering. The wagon was painfully overloaded with all the weight in the rear, and it handled like a complete pig at anything like this speed. All we needed now was for one of the Pinkies to suffer a blowout, and we'd be fucked.

I held my breath as we barrelled through, the street lamps beaming down on us like fizzy orange daylight. I felt horribly naked, deprived of the cloak of darkness. As Pathfinders we shun the light, and running this stretch of road bathed in the glow of the street lamps felt like we were asking to get smashed. There was a shoulder-high wall along the eastern side of the road, one that provided a little cover from view, but still we were sticking out like a pair of dog's bollocks.

The tension was fucking horrible. Surely, someone had to see us. Jason's wagon hit a gap in the wall, and a series of sharp, staccato shots rang out into the air.

'Crack! Crack-crack! Crack!'

When the Engineer Recce wagon reached the gap, exactly the same thing happened: shots punched the night. 'Crack! Crack-crack! Crack!'

As we came upon that same opening we heard a dozen-odd rounds tearing into the air. 'CRACK! CRACK-CRACK-CRACK! CRACK!' The fire was close: it had come from somewhere on the far side of the wall, but no way were the rounds aimed at us. There wasn't a lot of difference in the noise made by our own 5.56 mm (NATO) rounds and a 7.62 mm short – the bullet fired by an AK47. They both made the same, distinctive sharp crack. And in these calm, cool, dry, desert conditions we could tell how close the gunman was.

Often, it was hard to tell where a round had come from exactly, but you always knew if you were the target. You saw tracer zipping past, the sound was amplified by the punch of pressure waves, and you might see bullets hitting the road or your vehicle. The bursts of fire from behind that wall had been squirted high into the dark night sky. But I didn't kid myself for one second that they weren't linked to our presence somehow.

The bursts of rounds had been synchronised with each wagon's passing. Whoever the gunman was, it almost felt like he was signalling that we were on our way. *But who was he signalling and why?* Again, I had that horrible, creepy feeling. Ice running down my spine.

We're driving into a trap.

CHAPTER SEVENTEEN

We sped out of the area lit by the street lamps and onwards into the welcoming blackness up ahead. I locked eyes with Steve. He leaned across to have a word.

He had to yell into my ear to make himself heard: 'See, mate, the thing about women is …'

At least it burst the tension bubble.

I flipped down my NVG, as we pushed onwards for another few minutes. Nothing. Blank darkness and an empty silence. I checked the milometer. We were 75 kilometres in now, so over halfway to Qalat Sikar airfield. Whoever the gunman may have been signalling, there didn't appear to be anyone out here, so maybe it wasn't a signal after all?

I got the answer to my question at the 85-kilometre mark. Up ahead a massive settlement emerged from the gloom. It straddled both sides of Route 7. By rights – and according to our intel and sat photos – it shouldn't even exist. But here it was, squat and dark and menacing, bang in front of us. This settlement was far larger than the first. It was more built up, with dozens of buildings three or four storeys high. But the strange thing was that it was completely dark. There were no street lamps, and barely a window was showing any light.

For a moment I wondered if it was deserted. Maybe it was a not-yet-finished town, or maybe it had been abandoned. I wasn't left in doubt for very long. As soon as the approach of our vehicles could be heard from the settlement, we started taking incoming fire. It was pitch dark all around us, but we could hear these long bursts of fire come rolling in. '*Brrrzzzt! Brrrzzzt! Brrrzzzt!*' Whoever was trying to hit us, they were loosing off on automatic, and from the sound of the gunfire it was coming from a good half a kilometre away.

The hot, green slug-trails of tracer arced through our night vision, going way above us in the sky. Our attackers clearly couldn't see our wagons to aim at. We held our fire. If we opened up on the source of those tracer rounds, all it would serve to do was give our position away. We train and train and train for being under fire. We do so in the wagons, driving under fixed gun positions that squirt rounds over our heads. We do so on our belt buckles, crawling beneath barbed wire over which machine guns are pumping bullets. It gets you used to the terrifying noise and feel of being under attack.

The natural human reaction to being shot at is either fight, freeze or flee. We had taught ourselves to ignore such instinctive responses, so we could assess how best to deal with any combat situation – like now, when Tricky and I held our fire and Steve drove on through. It would be a cardinal sin in the PF to get a flap on. We needed to be able to think calmly and clearly when under intense pressure and danger. Anyone prone to panicking would've been deselected at an early stage, most likely when poised to jump off a C130 Hercules' tail ramp. But all the training in the world doesn't make you any the less shit scared.

There was more fire coming from the eastern side of the road now. There were maybe half a dozen AK47s squeezing off wild bursts, plus a heavier machine gun had opened up. But there was no way that they could see us. They were aiming at a speeding chimera, at ghosts.

As we hit the heart of the settlement the fire started to get more and more concentrated. I heard the unmistakable '*tzzzinnnggg-tzzzinnnggg-tzzzinnnggg!*' of rounds cutting through the air barely yards from our vehicle. Someone had to be spotting our progress, and calling through our position to the gunmen, to better direct their aim.

Whilst few of the Iraqi gunmen would have NVG, it would only take one commander with such kit to be doing the spotting. He would radio through our movements to his forward positions: *Enemy vehicles passing by the green mosque now.* That would give them a specific enough target area to aim for.

A couple of bigger, GPMG-type machine guns had joined in the one-way firefight. I could hear their throaty growl echoing around the darkened hillside, amongst the sharper crackle of the AKs. They were most likely Kalashnikov PKMs, Soviet-era belt-fed 7.62 mm tripod-mounted weapons, accurate up to 1000 metres or more.

As with the GPMG, the PKM is an area weapon, and it doesn't take pin-point accuracy to smash an adversary with one of those. It was a horrible feeling knowing that the PKM would be spitting out some 650 rounds per minute, and that every one of those bullets was trying to find us and smash us. Standard ambush drill is always to keep driving. It was far better simply to speed on through. If you tried to stop, fight or turn your wagons around, you made yourself a sitting target and you'd likely get killed. But still, I couldn't help wondering how the other lads were faring up ahead.

Just as we were almost through the settlement, I saw the fiery trail of an RPG (Rocket Propelled Grenade) streaking out from the ridgeline. Whilst I couldn't make out the warhead in the glow of the NVG, the exhaust trail appeared like a massive green comet roaring across the sky. In the thing came. It was heading right towards us. From the trajectory of the flaring green rocket trail, it looked as if it was aimed right at mine and Steve's heads. Instinctively I ducked, and the warhead thundered across the bonnet of our Pinkie, missing it by a bare couple of feet.

Targeting a vehicle moving fast at night and showing no lights is extremely difficult, even with a machine gun. To do so with an RPG from over 500 metres away was next to impossible. But that rocket had been horribly close – a one in a million shot. We thundered onwards and out of the built-up area, Steve gunning the Pinkie like crazy into the welcoming embrace of the night. Gradually, the fire started to fade away behind us. There was the crackle of gunshots and the odd crump of a powerful explosion in our wake, but they were firing into the space that we'd just vacated.

I was searching in the darkness up ahead with the GPMG, scanning my arcs, half expecting there to be a follow-up attack, or maybe a blocking group placed upon the highway. But all there seemed to be was open, deserted road stretching as far as the eye could see. Steve turned to me. I was readying myself for another wisecrack about women, or a peachy line from *Shrek*.

'That was small arms, HMGs, RPGs,' he yelled above the road noise. 'It's getting closer. Best we pull off the road and assess the situation.'

It was standard operating procedure in the Pathfinders that if any man saw something of crucial importance, he had the authority to call a halt to the patrol. It was the same as when you were in a contact, and you called a spot of ground to retreat to. Steve had made the call that we should stop and get a heads-up, to try to assess the state of play and see what exactly was happening.

Being in the PF was like being in a football team: anyone who saw the break or the opportunity to score could call it, and Steve's was a good call to have made. I sensed Tricky leaning forwards from the rear of the wagon. He was raised up on the 50-cal turret and he would have the best all-round view.

'Dave, they lobbed a load of mortars after us,' he shouted. 'They were creeping nearer, until we managed to outrun the fuckers.'

I nodded an acknowledgement. I hadn't even realised we were getting mortared. Those mortars had to have been called in by an enemy spotter – one who could see us, and was tracking us as we speeded north. I had this horrible feeling that the net was closing on us big time. We needed a plan – something to allow us to escape from whatever trap had been set for us.

My mind groped for some kind of inspiration. I was the leader of this mission, the Pathfinders' 2IC. If anyone was supposed to come up with the brainwaves at times like this, it was me. I glanced all around me, desperately trying to detect the source of the threat. I smelled the faint scent of burning diesel from the engine of the Pinkie up ahead, the reek of oil burning on a hot exhaust. There was the muffled rattle of ammunition in one of the crates beside me, and the ghostly hiss of the wind in the trees. Otherwise, there wasn't the faintest sign of life out there.

We were a long way from home now, and a good distance from Camp Tristar and the relative security of our FOB, just this side of the Kuwaiti border. Wherever the enemy might be, there was no way I was going to flush them out of hiding. But I was convinced they were out there, somewhere in that darkened landscape, watching, waiting and preparing to strike. If I couldn't think of a plan, it was now more than ever that I needed the lads. We needed to get our heads together, and pool our thoughts, and maybe that would lead to something.

I leaned over to Steve. 'Pull up abreast of the Engineer vehicle.'

He accelerated until we were next to their wagon. I gestured at them to prepare to stop. I shouted across to Ian, their sergeant: 'Get ready to pull over, mate.'

He gave me a thumbs-up, and we moved forwards and did a repeat performance with Jason. It was easier to do it physically and verbally than to try to use the radios. That way, you got the clarity of face-to-face communication, plus the earpiece on the Cougar was flimsy, and not well-shielded from the wind noise.

Up ahead Jason slowed and started searching for a place to stop. We dropped back again into our original position. The golden rule was that you never broke the order of march, not unless you came under fire and you were doing a vehicle-based fire-and-manoeuvre drill. It was crucial to know where the other vehicles were at all times.

Jason's wagon was positioned around 200 metres in front of ours, with the Engineer Recce wagon sandwiched in between. We figured that our wagon had been targeted by the worst of the incoming fire, and that Jason might not be aware of how fierce and heavy it had been. A light mortar has an effective range of around 1000 metres. Jason's vehicle would have been 300 metres or more ahead of where those shells were landing, to the rear of us. It was highly unlikely that he even knew that we'd been mortared.

Half a kilometre further on Jason's wagon slowed, then pulled off the road. The Engineer Recce wagon followed suit, and us with them. We nosed into a patch of dense palm groves and undergrowth. Jason pushed ahead some 50 metres, until he reached a position where he figured we were hidden from the highway.

The thick vegetation provided cover from view only. Cover from view stops you being seen, but it doesn't stop a bullet. We'd need a ridge, a thick wall or a deep wadi to provide cover from fire. But we couldn't push any further into the undergrowth, or we'd get stuck. There was a wall of tangled palm groves to the west of us.

Jason's wagon did a U-turn, until it was nose-on to the road. The Engineer recce vehicle did the same. We looped around the back and pulled up alongside Jason's wagon, likewise facing the highway. Joe, the top gunner on Jason's wagon, automatically covered his arcs to the west, away from the road. Every other weapon – that was four GPMGs and one 50-cal – covered the direction east, towards the main threat, Route 7.

We cut the engines.

We were now in a snap ambush.

It was dead quiet. We were close enough to have a Chinese – a group heads-up – without moving from the vehicles. We flipped up our NVG. Whenever we were talking to each other like this we needed to have genuine eye contact. For a few moments everyone was silent and listening for signs of the enemy, but it was ominously quiet and still out there.

Jason and I began checking the map. First priority was to work out exactly where we were. We nailed our position, then compared notes on what we'd seen since leaving Nasiriyah, some two hours earlier. It turned out that Jason had no idea of the weight of fire that had been levelled against us. Being the front vehicle he'd got through well before the worst of the shit had kicked off. He'd missed the RPG and the mortar rounds completely.

'I had no idea it was that heavy,' Jason whispered. In the quiet hush we were alert to making the slightest noise.

After the drive thus far north from Nasiriyah nothing seemed to make much sense to us. The Iraqi front line positions somehow seemed to stretch all the way up Route 7. We'd hit two company-strength positions at least, directly as we left Nasiriyah, and we'd just been fired upon by what had to be another company-strength position. Jason added one crucial bit of info to the overall picture.

'Did you see the fat cabbie in the Datsun trying to take us on?' he asked.

I shook my head. 'No, mate. What happened?'

'He pulled off the road just ahead of us, drew this pistol and started waving it out the window. He loosed off a few wild rounds into the air as we charged towards him, the fucking idiot.'

Jason gave this Popeye gap-toothed smile in the darkness. I couldn't help letting out a chuckle.

'I swung the Gimpy on to him,' Jason continued, 'and he soon stopped waving the shooter about. That fat Iraqi cabbie's been watching too many cowboy movies.'

There was a part of me that was surprised that Jason hadn't mal-leted the guy, but I guessed that would truly have blown our cover. Jason had just finished telling me about the fat cabbie attack, when I caught the faint snarl of an engine breaking the night's stillness. It was far to the south of us, and I was unsure at first if I'd heard it. I strained my ears and I could hear it again, deep, throaty and powerful.

I locked eyes with Jason and I could tell that he too had detected it. We swung our heads away from the Pinkie's dash, where we were gathered over the map, and gazed southwards, towards the direction from which the sound was coming. Our sight was still adjusting to its natural night vision, as opposed to the artificially boosted luminosity of NVG. We strained our eyes in the darkness, trying to work out what it might be that was moving on the road out there.

From out of the flat blankness of the desert there came this vision, like a bloody great mirage. Gradually, the entire length of the road to the south of us came alive with the glare of vehicle headlights. The convoy approached, headlamps glaring like the eyes of a swarm of angry insects.

We had no idea what the hell was coming out of the night.

But of one thing we were certain: they were coming for us.

CHAPTER EIGHTEEN

As the lights drew closer they disappeared from view, for the vehicles were passing through the slight cover of a natural depression. By the time they reappeared, the silent night was being torn apart by this deafening rumble, one that was shaking the very ground at our feet.

I could make out the lead vehicle in the convoy now. It was a smart Toyota-style pick-up truck. The open back of the wagon was crammed full of fighters, plus there was the unmistakable form of a tripod-mounted DShK (Dushka) HMG (Heavy Machine Gun) poking ominously forwards from the rear.

The convoy thundered towards us along the highway. It was moving fast, with the vehicles closely spaced, the drivers making no effort to move tactically. With a strength and firepower such as theirs, I reckoned they didn't feel the need to. In the rear of each truck there were ten to fifteen Iraqi fighters, perched on bench seats. Those who were closest had their backs to us, but those on the opposite side would be staring right at us over their fellow warriors' shoulders.

I counted fifteen sets of lights, and still there were more coming. Each wagon was an identical white Toyota pick-up, crammed full of fighters. The convoy was bristling end-to-end with Dushkas, so I guess Saddam must have purchased a job lot off the Russians. Fucking nice one. The Dushka is the Russian equivalent of our own 50-cal heavy machine gun. It can only fire on automatic, and it unleashes its big, armour-piercing, high-explosive rounds at the rate of 600 a minute.

The Dushka's 12.7 mm bullets can chew their way through walls and trees. Body armour or no body armour, a direct hit from one of those would rip an arm or a leg from your body, and take your head clean off. It was a devastating weapon when used against aircraft, or lightly armoured vehicles, and it'd make mincemeat out of our soft-skinned Pinkies. One round into the diesel tank of our wagon, and that'd be Tricky, Steve and me nicely torched and done for.

The convoy was so close by now that I could lob a cricket ball into it, with a good hefty throw. As the first Toyota drew level I could see that the guys on the back weren't regular Iraqi army. In contrast to the smart soldiers in forage caps that we had stumbled across earlier, these guys were dressed in white dish-dash robes, and they had red and white checked shemaghs on their heads. This, we knew from the intel briefs, was the trademark dress of the Fedayeen.

The Fedayeen were Saddam loyalists recruited into a specialist paramilitary militia. They were able to rove around in fast, highly-manoeuvrable vehicles doing guerrilla-style hit-and-run operations. They were mobile, they had an organic, flexible command structure, and their purpose was to engage us in unconventional warfare. And from the looks of these guys they were well-disciplined, plus they were very well-armed.

We were here in Iraq expecting to face conscripts lacking in morale. That's what the intel briefings had told us to expect. We were expecting to confront soldiers who didn't want to fight and who couldn't think for themselves. Instead, we were up against Fedayeen in brand-new SUVs actively looking for a scrap, and packing some serious firepower. They looked and felt hardcore.

They were passing so close that no one dared breathe a word. We had cut our engines as we went into the snap ambush, so they were unlikely to hear us. But just to the north of our position there was one small area devoid of any vegetation, where we had zero cover from view. All it would take was for one Fedayeen to glance our way as he passed that gap, and he'd see us. We just had to hope that with all the light their convoy was throwing off, none of the enemy had attained any great degree of natural night vision. Hopefully, they'd be blinded by their own headlights, and with our wagons being totally dark the night would shield us.

These Fedayeen had to be a hunter force sent to find us. It was clear that there was no way that we could outrun them. A Toyota four-by-four is faster than a Land Rover, plus with all the weight we were carrying we were bound to be far heavier than their vehicles. We were part-dismounted from the Pinkies with the engines turned off, which was hardly great for making a getaway. And we were boxed in by thick vegetation to the west, so the natural route of escape was closed to us.

If they saw us we'd have to open up with everything we'd got. There was just a chance that with the element of surprise we'd be able to mallet the lot of them. They were too bunched up to avoid being hit by our firepower. But still, I didn't exactly rate our chances.

The first few encounters with the enemy, plus the one sustained contact just south of our position, hadn't really made me feel threatened. We could have been killed, but equally we could have taken on and smashed the enemy, and we had escape options. This felt very, very different, and it made my gut drop like a stone.

They were right on top of us, wagon after wagon pounding past, and we knew in our hearts that they'd been sent out to find, fix and kill our patrol. Playing hide and seek with these guys wasn't going to be fun. I had to fight off this strong sense of nausea that was rising within my throat.

It didn't escape my notice that this was exactly the same kind of hunter force that had gone after the squadron of SBS in northern Iraq – those sixty-odd lads who had been forced to go on the run. That entire squadron of elite soldiers had been torn apart and scattered across the desert by a similar number of Fedayeen. We were nine. The SBS had been sixty. The odds were horribly stacked against us.

After what felt like an age, but could only have been a matter of a couple of minutes, the last Fedayeen vehicle thundered past. I had this anxious, sickly feeling as I waited to see if its occupants had spotted us. I was well in control and my head was still together, but my larynx was tight and dry with all the tension. I breathed a long sigh of relief as that last Fedayeen vehicle proceeded north at full speed, and without faltering. They clearly hadn't seen us.

That was a mobile force of some 200 hunting for us, with scores of vehicle-mounted Dushkas. It was clear now that we must have passed through a couple of major enemy positions to the south, if they'd managed to rustle up a convoy of that size and lethal power. You never made a hunter force more than 25 per cent of your main body of men, so we had to presume there were anything up to 1000 Iraqi troops positioned to the south of us, and possibly far more.

We remained silent and observed the situation. For five minutes we watched the tail-lights growing ever smaller in the distance. Those five minutes felt to me like fifty. And then, some 3 kilometres ahead of us, we saw a row of brake lights blinking on, red and angry in the night. We watched as the Fedayeen vehicles slowed and pulled off the road to the eastern side. There was a bit of shunting backwards and forwards, dust shining golden in the beams of their head-lamps, then all lights were extinguished.

Darkness.

Engines killed.

Silence.

I figured they had to know that we were headed for Qalat Sikar airfield. They must have known that they were moving faster than we were, and that they had passed us somewhere on the road. And now, their ambush was set. Everyone was silent, staring at the spot where the enemy convoy had gone static. I knew what the rest of the lads were thinking: *How the hell were we going to make it through to the airfield, with that little lot sat bang in our way?*

We had to make the airfield for 1 PARA's L-Hour, so that the first airborne forces could come in. By now they'd have the 1 PARA lads positioned somewhere near the Brigade HQ, where they'd marry up with the Chinooks and move out. They wouldn't get airborne unless they got a signal from us giving the green light, and they wouldn't get the Chinooks in unless we'd marked the HLS, that was for certain.

The Chinooks would have been bouncing around from one air mission to another, and they very likely only had a specific time slot available to get the boys into Qalat Sikar. It was vital that we made the H-Hour. The Chinooks cruise at no more than 10,000 feet, as they have no oxygen for the troops they carry. From the FOB to Qalat Sikar it'd be around an hour's flight. So from us giving the green light it'd be an hour minimum prior to the PARAs coming in, with attack helos in support. Getting the timing right was critical.

But I had this growing feeling that time and fate was fast turning against us. If we pressed on up Route 7 we'd doubtless take a lot of the Fedayeen with us. We had the advantage of NVG, which gave us some stealth and surprise, but there was little doubt that we'd get annihilated. Our only chance of achieving the mission was to remain covert, and we couldn't do that any more if we stuck to the highway.

I turned to Jason, and nodded for Ian, the Engineer Recce sergeant to come closer.

'That's it – enemy ambush set,' I whispered. 'There's no way through on the main road north.'

It was stating the obvious, but someone had to say it.

'Enemy ambush bloody set,' Jason hissed, in confirmation.

'Yep,' Ian, the Engineer Recce sergeant, muttered. 'Looks like they've gone well firm up there.'

Ian had a face like death, and he clearly wasn't relishing the thought of those several hundred Fedayeen being so close on our tail. For that matter, I didn't figure any of us were.

Jason grabbed the map and we placed it under the tiny, hooded map light set in the Pinkie's dash – one specially designed to beam a tiny cone of illumination downwards, whilst allowing the minimum of light to escape from the vehicle. We figured the airfield was 45 kilometres away, no more. *It was so fucking close – less than an hour's drive on good roads.*

We couldn't head south to box around the Fedayeen ambush, because south lay the settlement and the main body of the enemy. We couldn't go further west, for the vegetation was impenetrable that way. The airfield was north-northeast of us. It was obvious that we'd got to try to cross over the road and box around the Fedayeen by going east, and then hooking around northeast.

'Only one thing for it,' I ventured. 'Cross the highway and see if we can link up with those dirt tracks.'

'Yeah,' Jason agreed. 'We've cracked most of the distance on the main road. We'll do the remainder cross-country.'

We knew the rest of the lads would have overheard what we were saying. Their silence meant they were in agreement with us. We were deep behind enemy lines, we'd been compromised and now we were being hunted. In situations such as this making the slightest noise could end up getting you killed, so we kept the chat to an absolute minimum.

The ground we were on was slightly lower than the road. Jason's vehicle led off, its engine whining horribly as it hauled the heavy Pinkie up the shallow incline. In the deadly quiet the noise sounded deafening, like a bloody great jet aircraft taking off. We just had to hope there was no way the Fedayeen could hear us from 6 kilometres away.

Jason halted by the roadside, did a careful visual check both ways, and then crossed over. Once he was over he waved the Engineer Recce vehicle forwards, whilst providing cover with the weapons on his Pinkie. As their wagon nosed on to the road, we were covering it with our weapons from the rear. Ian went firm on the far side, from where they provided cover for us, as we moved across the deserted highway.

At a dead crawl we pushed into the humped and jumbled shadows to the east side of the road. We were back on NVG now, and the vegetation was clearly sparser here, but the going seemed rough as fuck. The Pinkies were cannoning into potholes and kangarooing off ruts, as the suspension struggled to cope with the weight and the terrain.

We dropped our speed to 5 kph, and at that kind of a dead crawl it was just about possible to keep pushing ahead. But still it felt like we were three sick camels stumbling through the darkened desert. For a moment I considered what would have happened if we hadn't followed Steve's suggestion, and pulled off Route 7 when we did. Presumably, the Fedayeen would have caught up with us, and we'd have been in the battle of our lives.

We'd been incredibly lucky to have evaded them as we had. I could barely believe that those hundreds of Fedayeen had failed to see us. Even so, the whole game had changed now. I could sense it from the tense, strained atmosphere on our wagon. In an instant we'd gone from being the hunters to being the hunted.

All around us there was the intense '*rubbittt-rubbittt-rubbittt*' of frogs croaking in the bush. Somewhere nearby there had to be water, and the frogs were beating out an eerie rhythm. Somehow, it seemed to reinforce how, with each passing moment, the trap was fast closing. It was a struggle even to think straight, with all the racket they were making.

One thing was clear: far from being the Charge of the Light Brigade, this was all about stealth and concealment now. If we were to have any chance of making Qalat Sikar we had to remain undetected. We were nine men in three overloaded Pinkies, trying to evade 200 Fedayeen in dozens of fast pick-ups. Staying hidden was infinitely preferable to facing all of that in a full-on firefight.

What made it all the worse was that we didn't know how the three Engineer Recce guys would hold up under serious fire, for we'd never been to war with them. They could prove to be rock-steady; or they could lose it and crumble under the pressure. Either way we just didn't know, and it was that lack of shared combat experience which made them such an unknown.

When driving across rough, heavily-vegetated terrain as we were now, we had to bunch the vehicles closer together. It was easy to lose sight of one another in an environment like this, and the last thing we needed to be doing right now was making radio calls, and trying to locate lost wagons. We'd got maybe 25 metres between each Pinkie and were crawling along at a dead slow, when I noticed both Jason and Ian's vehicles come to a juddering halt.

Jason's wagon was most forwards. Ian's had stopped alongside it, but set a little way back. We pulled up on the opposite side of Jason's Pinkie, so together our three vehicles formed a shallow 'V'. I jumped down and went to cross the couple of metres to Jason's wagon. As I did so, I caught the faintest glimmer of moonlight on a stretch of water just to the front of us.

I peered through the undergrowth, and as I did so the noise hit me. Jason's wagon had halted on the very lip of a canal, and the frogs were going nineteen to the dozen down there. The waterway looked about the size of a normal British canal, the type that carries barges full of holidaying families. I glanced across the water, and I could just make out the dark silhouettes of a clutch of low hut-like structures on the far side. They were set back 300 metres or so from the canal, and they looked like some kind of agricultural outbuildings.

I turned to the lads and made a signal like a knife-cut across my throat – PF talk for 'cut the engines'. We needed to take a view on where we were heading, now that we'd hit the first Iraqi waterway. All three wagons powered down. Once the engines were cut, the only noise from the Pinkies was the whir of the fans trying to cool the hot engines, and the weird, rhythmic click-click-click of cooling steel. It sounded as loud as gunshots in the eerie night stillness, and I wished to hell it would quieten down.

Jason pointed towards the glimmer of moonlight on the water, and spoke into the silence.

'Dave, there's no fucking way the wagons are getting through that.'

I rubbed my hands across my face, trying to massage away some of the tension. 'Don't I know it, mate.'

Standard British Army Land Rovers have a breather tube fitted to one side, the end of which pokes above the driver's door. The diesel engines can suck in air through those tubes, which gives the wagons a good couple of metres of wading capability. But the Pinkies don't have them, for the cut-down open-topped design means there's nowhere to bolt the tube on to. In any case, the water in front of us had to be deeper than that, and we had no idea what the canal bed was like. The water looked more or less stagnant, and below it was very likely soft, clinging mud.

'I'll tell you something else,' Jason hissed. 'We fucking well nearly drove the Pinkie over the edge and into the drink. We didn't see the canal bank until the last bloody moment, what with all the undergrowth. And with all the weight we're carrying, the wagon most likely would've flipped over. That would have been the lot of us head down in the water. Fucking nice one ...'

'I know mate,' I cut in. 'The going's fucking horrendous.'

Jason pointed north. 'Plus there's fucking that one too, and God only knows how many more.'

From his vantage point in the vehicle he was a little higher than I was. I had to crane my neck to see where he was indicating. Just to the north of us there was what looked like a side canal coming in from the direction of the road. The canals had to form part of an irrigation network, and we were effectively boxed in. It wasn't looking very good. Those two waterways barred our routes east and north, the very directions in which we needed to go.

Apart from Jason, the lads on the wagons were silent, peering into the dark wall of bush all around us and scanning their arcs. We were clearly going to be here for some time, as there was no obvious way through. It was good that we had the wagons in a snap, silent ambush, especially with that hunter force just to the north of us.

I caught Steve's eye, and nodded eastwards: 'Steve, mate: sentry.'

Without a word he removed his Minimi from the wagon, and moved off stealthily on foot. He stopped some 30 metres away on a slight rise overlooking the canal, and then he went firm, his weapon held at the ready but not in the aim. Once he'd stopped moving his form faded into the background darkness, until he was all but invisible.

'Jase, maps,' I whispered.

We gathered over the dash of my Pinkie, and we got the map

under the hooded light once more. We figured we'd gone no more than 500 metres east and were moving away from the main highway. There were no waterways marked on the map at the point where we now found ourselves. Either the maps were bang out of date, or the canals were too small to be marked. Whichever, it was a complete gang fuck.

From the maps alone we had no way of knowing what other canals might be out there, and no means of mapping a possible route through. Jase and I didn't need to give voice to this. We both knew it. And we were racking our brains as to what to do next.

'What about the sat photos?' I whispered.

The images from Qalat Sikar airfield were burned into my mind, with the level of detail revealing individual control towers and vehicles. They were more than detailed enough to show watercourses the size of the canals that we'd run into. It was standard operating procedure not to carry sat photos with you, for they constituted too sensitive a source of intel to fall into enemy hands. But I was hoping that Jase might have spirited a couple on to his wagon, knowing how crap the maps might prove.

I heard him give a snort under his breath. 'Sat photos – I fucking wish. Back at the FOB.'

I felt a hand on my shoulder. I turned around. It was Tricky. He motioned towards Steve on sentry. I looked over, and I could see that Steve was standing tense and motionless, his Minimi hard in the shoulder and in the aim. He'd clearly seen something. I reached for my SA80, and moved off, ghost-walking, to join him. As I did so, I saw him glance over his shoulder.

The expression on his face said it all: *We've got fucking company.*

CHAPTER NINETEEN

Steve turned back to whatever it was that had spooked him. His stance was fire-mode, eyes down the barrel of his weapon pointing northeast. I picked my way through the undergrowth, silently feeling a route through, my weapon in the aim. I came to a halt just behind and to the left of Steve. It was the position his shoulders had presented to me.

He gave me the signal to keep silent, then gestured towards where his barrel was pointing. I heard them before I saw them. Voices speaking Arabic, drifting across to me on the cool night air. Whoever it was, they were speaking loudly and animatedly, and moving ever closer to our position. I presumed it had to be a search party, a follow-up from the Fedayeen hunter force. Maybe they were checking both sides of Route 7 on foot, back from their ambush position. Combing the ground to flush us out of hiding. If so, we'd have to open fire and break contact without having a clue as to where we were going.

The voices grew louder. There was dense undergrowth all around us, so we couldn't yet see them. Plus there was a thick mist rising off the canal and curling into the vegetation, which added this weird horror-movie feel to things. We were both of us working without NVG, for we'd flipped up our units when we stopped to get the heads-up. If we changed to NVG now, it'd take too long for our vision to adjust properly, especially with the enemy right on top of us.

In the eerie silence and stillness the guttural Arabic of the voices was growing deafening. Figures appeared on the far side of the canal. We could see their feet below the thick bush, their heads above it. I could see the dull glint of gunmetal reflecting off whatever weapons they had slung over their shoulders, and the smell of cigarette smoke reached me clearly across the still water.

They were 15 metres away, and it seemed impossible that they wouldn't spot Jason's Pinkie, the nose of which was poking out into the mist-shrouded canal. Steve and I were frozen, following the Iraqis in slow motion with our gun sights. My finger was achingly tight on the trigger, a hair's breadth away from opening fire. My heart was racing, pounding in my ears. It felt so loud, like it alone was going to give us away.

Steve whispered: 'Dave, I'm gonna slot 'em.'

I motioned for him to hold his fire.

'Dave, I'm gonna slot 'em.' Steve's voice was tight with tension.

Again, I signalled for him to hold his fire. We had to try to remain covert until the last possible moment. I was convinced that the success of our mission – not to mention the chances of our getting out of this alive – depended on it.

Slowly, so slowly it was physically painful almost, the figures drew level with us. Slowly, their voices faded away into the thick mist and the tangled, brooding bush. Unbelievably, they didn't appear to have seen us. For five minutes we remained totally still and silent, just in case there were more of them, or they were doubling back to attack our position.

With the urgency of our mission, and the God-awful situation that we had found ourselves in, those five minutes felt like an absolute lifetime. Finally, Steve lowered his weapon. I gave him a nod, then crept back to the vehicles. In a whisper I explained to the others what we'd just seen. Then I was back to studying the map, and trying to work out just how we might keep pushing ahead towards Qalat Sikar.

It was Jason who finally broke the silence: 'Dave, there's no way through.'

All eyes turned to me now, apart from Steve who was out on sentry. Everyone was waiting for my response. Between the six of us, we had more than sixty-five years of military experience. On exercises we'd covered every possible eventuality, *or at least we thought we had*. Likewise, we reckoned we'd done so on operations in Sierra Leone, Afghanistan and elsewhere. But in truth, none of us had ever been in this kind of situation before – with no route through on all sides, and surrounded by a massively superior enemy force.

We prided ourselves on being cunning and audacious, and on thinking the unthinkable. Yet I was racking my brains and I couldn't seem to see any way through.

The distance between the eight of us on the vehicles was a few metres at most. In the pitch darkness I could hear the lads' quiet breathing, interspersed with the rhythmic *'breep-breep-breep'* of the insect life all around us. Otherwise it was deathly quiet. This silence, coupled with the crushing indecision, was fucking horrible. I hated being trapped like this.

For an instant my mind flashed back to the last time I'd been hemmed in like this, with the enemy on all sides. It was Afghanistan and my very first mission with the PF. I was a captain back then, but I'd been allocated a place as the top gunner on the rear of one of the wagons commanded by one of the old and the bold. He was mentoring me through my first PF combat mission, to ease me into becoming the Pathfinders' 2IC.

It was late 2001 and we'd flown into Bagram air base, tasked with being first into a Kabul freshly liberated from the Taliban. After the decades of fighting, Afghanistan's capital city was shot to fuck. I'd never seen anything remotely like it. It was a ghostly wasteland. Our mission was to establish some ground truth, because no one had a clue what was going on there – which clans controlled which areas, who the key warlords were and what were the chief threats.

It didn't take us long to realise that Kabul presented a very fast-moving, fluid situation, one replete with shifting allegiances and treachery. We drove out to meet a warlord at his base on the city limits. The closer we got to the rendezvous, the more nervous and frightened our Afghan interpreter became. It was a sure sign that the guy we were about to meet was seriously badass.

We pitched up at his base, which turned out to be a mini-fortress with watchtowers, gun emplacements and walkways around the walls. Upon arrival we suddenly found our two wagons surrounded by skinny Afghans sporting Pakuls – their traditional rolled woollen caps – and toting guns. A group of around twelve surged around us. At each corner of the fortress there were guys on the watchtowers smoking these massive hash joints, and the air was thick with the sickly-sweet, heady smell of burning grass.

A guy stepped up to me and offered me his RPG. It was a bizarre kind of a gesture. I feigned interest and accepted it. As soon as I did so he reached inside the wagon and grabbed my SA80, from where it was strapped to the vehicle's side. A second later the guy had it pointed at my head. We'd come in here in 'non-threatening' mode. That meant we hadn't dismounted with our longs – our assault rifles. Now I had a wild, stoned-looking Afghan with my own weapon levelled at me, and his finger white with tension on the trigger.

One glance around the place had been enough to show how totally outnumbered we were. We were surrounded, trapped and outgunned. It had taken some kind of epic standoff to get us out of that warlord's domain alive and unharmed. The memories of that Afghan stand-off triggered a sudden flash of inspiration. It was true that on the face of it we were trapped here in Iraq. We couldn't go north, south, east or west with the vehicles without hitting insurmountable obstacles, or a vastly superior enemy force. *But what about if we did so on foot?*

I checked the faint fluorescent dial of my watch. It was 1900 hours, and the airfield was less than 45 kilometres away. We'd got eight hours until 0300, H-Hour for 1 PARA's insertion. I reckoned it was just about doable. I thought back over the final, endurance stage of PF selection, which involves a 64-kilometre night march over mountains. You had to do it carrying 80 pounds in your bergen, plus your weapon, and you had to achieve an average speed of 6 kilometres an hour.

It was 45 kilometres to the airfield, it was flat terrain, and we'd be carrying far less weight than we do on endurance. I calculated that 45 divided by 6 made it an eight-hour march. *We could make it.* In fact, we might well make Qalat Sikar in under eight hours, maybe even as little as six, if the terrain held good. We might not have time to do a full 360-degree recce of the airfield, but we could secure a HLS, mark it and green light 1 PARA in.

It'd be a beast of a march through the unknown, but moving forwards on foot was the one way that I could see us getting out of here. If we stuck with the vehicles, we were boxed in on all sides by impassable terrain and the enemy. We had to presume that the Fedayeen hunter force had radioed through that they'd lost us. They would know that we'd gone cross-country, which in turn meant that they'd be alert for any vehicles moving off-road. Dumping the wagons and proceeding on foot was the last thing the enemy would be expecting.

It was time to voice what I'd been thinking. I glanced up and my eyes met Jason's. I could tell that he was looking to me for some kind of leadership here and a sense of what we could do. In a hurried whisper I outlined my idea to the guys.

'You're right, Jase, there's no way through *by vehicle*. The only way left for us to achieve the mission is to blow the vehicles, and go forwards *on foot*. That's the last thing they'll be expecting, and it's our only way out of here without heading into a massive contact. If we leave everything but our weapons and grab bags, we'll be travelling fast and light. We'll leave one-hour fuses on the charges, so we're long gone by the time the wagons blow.'

We'd have to blow the vehicles, so as to deny them to the enemy. But we'd leave hour-long fuses, to give us the time to get well away from where they were by the time they exploded. Otherwise, we'd bring the enemy down on top of us. We'd rip out any top secret kit, wreck it, then chuck it into the canal.

For a couple of seconds no one responded to my suggestion.

It was Jason who broke the silence. 'We could try and make it through on foot. Trouble is, we don't know what the fuck lies between here and Qalat Sikar. So far, there's been Iraqis all over the place. We've seen a 200-strong hunter force, plus they've got positions all along the road, and they've been taking a good pop at us. There's no way of knowing what we might be walking into if we push ahead on foot, and we'd be doing so without our heavy firepower.'

'Tricky?' I prompted.

Tricky shook his head. 'I just don't think we'll make it on foot for H-Hour. We could make the distance, but not in time to get the PARAs into a cleared and marked HLS. We'll need to avoid local habitation, dogs, canals, marshes, main roads. Plus we'll have to box around Iraqi army positions and maybe Fedayeen. And all of that will slow us down.'

Tricky was one of the most experienced and positive operators in the Pathfinders, but he was also a realist. Along with Jason, he was the most battle-tested operator that we'd got. If the two of them were against what I was suggesting, maybe going ahead on foot wasn't an option. But still I wasn't ready to let it go.

'Maybe you're right,' I conceded, 'but we've come this far, and we're 80 per cent of the way there. I reckon we can press ahead on foot, and if necessary we can get 1 PARA to delay their H-Hour. If it takes longer on foot to reach, recce and secure the airfield, we can get them to come in later, and we can still make the mission happen.'

'What do we do if we're on foot and we get pinned down by Iraqis?' Jason asked. 'We'll be lacking the heavy firepower provided by the wagons.'

'We do what we always do: we put down fire and try to withdraw from the contact and escape and evade.'

'But what happens if there's no way out?' Jason persisted. 'If we're pinned down and trapped?'

'If that happens we go into a hide, and we call in a CSAR team to pull us out. We call up the Army Air Corps, and if that fails the RAF with a Chinook, or if that fails the Yanks with an MH-53 Pave Low. Either way we get a machine in with some serious firepower, and we get ourselves pulled out.'

There was silence again. I could almost hear people's brains racing. No one else was voicing an opinion now, or even making any suggestions. It was like we were frozen: *was going forwards on foot really an option, or was it a bridge too far?*

Eventually, Jason said: 'Tricky, what d'you reckon?'

Tricky was a combat-hardened soldier and very battle-space aware. That was why Jason sought his opinion.

Tricky said: 'I think we've got to keep the vehicles for as long as we can. We can always end up on foot, but they are our firepower, our speed and our mobility.'

There was one glaring problem with keeping the vehicles: we couldn't drive west, because the terrain was impassable; we couldn't go north due to the Fedayeen ambush, and east we'd hit the canals. The only route open to us was south, and that meant abandoning the mission and heading back through the Iraqi forces that we'd just avoided.

For several reasons we figured there were at least two battalions – so anything up to 2000 Iraqi troops – to the south of us. The Fedayeen force had numbered 200, minimum. We figured there were 1000-odd troops in the last settlement that we'd driven through. South of that, we figured the Iraqis had to have another battalion at the very least, to stand against the US Marine Corps.

Those troops would be stood-to and alert to our presence. They would be more than ready to hit us if for some bizarre reason we came driving back through their positions. Driving south we'd have zero element of surprise, and we'd be heading into a series of ambushes. And we might well have the Fedayeen hunter force bearing down fast on our tail.

Going south was asking for a world of trouble. We'd be facing thousands of Iraqi troops, and most likely we'd get slaughtered. But so too was any other bloody direction. It was crunch time, but it was clear that no one had a fucking clue what to do.

Tricky broke the quiet: 'The constant is the vehicles. Remember Bravo Two Zero? They were fucked 'cause they didn't go in with vehicles.'

'Dez, what d'you think?' asked Jason.

'Same as Tricky and you, mate: we keep the vehicles.'

I asked the Royal Engineer sergeant, Ian, for his take on it.

'Keep the vehicles,' he said. 'Remember what happened to those SBS lads up north: they lost their vehicles and they were fucked.'

'Joe?' said Jason.

'Keep the vehicles,' said Joe.

I called Steve over from sentry. This was everyone's decision. Had to be.

I outlined our predicament to him. 'Steve, we can't go east, north or west with the vehicles. We either blow them and go forwards on foot to the airfield, or we keep the vehicles. Everyone else so far wants to keep the vehicles. We'll have speed, fire and mobility, but we're likely to get malleted big time.'

'I still think we can go forwards on foot,' I continued, 'and that way we can achieve the mission. But there's obviously a high chance of being captured or killed. So, it's like I'm offering you a fucking great boot in the bollocks, or a massive punch on the nose? Which is it to be, mate?'

Steve grinned. Shrugged. 'On balance, I want to keep my bollocks. So I guess we keep the vehicles.'

In life I've always believed that acceptance is a virtue. Sometimes, you just have to accept the shit you're in, and try to see the opportunity that can come out of it. Otherwise, it was your own head and your own fear that would mess you up. But this was still the hardest decision that I'd ever made in my life. What determined it for me was that I would never go against the blokes, especially not when it was a life-or-death choice like this one.

I took a long in-breath and exhaled. 'Okay, so we keep the vehicles. But that has to mean heading south and fighting out way through to the American front line.'

Jason nodded. 'We use the wagons to get as far as we can towards the Americans. When we can't get any further with the wagons we fight on foot, back-to-back if it comes to it.'

I glanced around the rest of the faces. There was a series of grim nods from all. The decision was made, but I didn't kid myself that somehow we were okay now that we'd made it. The reality was that we had *nowhere* to go. North, east, west, or south, we were all but certain to get smashed.

At best some of us might get wounded, captured and tortured by the Iraqis, and I reckoned I'd prefer a bullet rather than that.

CHAPTER TWENTY

There was no time to linger on any of this. We couldn't afford the time to think, or to freeze. We only had one option now and that was to fight. And if we were to do so to the maximum of our ferocity, we had to get up and at 'em pronto and get scrapping.

'Dave, if we're making the run south we could do with some fucking air,' Tricky suggested. 'If we can get some air above us I can call in air strikes on both sides of the road as we drive down it. It'll open up a tunnel of escape and smash the enemy positions as we go.'

It was hardly a subtle or a covert plan, but Tricky's suggestion was a mark of pure genius. It was classic PF. We could turn our presence here to everyone's advantage by calling in air strikes to mallet those enemy positions that no one but us knew were here. In doing so we might not have achieved our mission, but we sure as hell could annihilate a whole lot of hidden enemy units – ones that had just given the US Marine Corps a seriously bloody nose.

Take a totally shit and murderous situation and turn it into a battle-winning opportunity: it was the kind of maverick, lunatic thinking that defined the men of Pathfinder Platoon. As a PF JTAC, Tricky was one of the most experienced air war operators in the British Army. If we could get some serious firepower orbiting above us, I had no doubt that he could pull it off.

I raised a smile. 'Cracking idea, mate. Let's get some fucking air.'

Tricky set up the comms, so we could put the call in to PF HQ.

'*Mayhem Three One*, this is *Mayhem Three Zero*,' Tricky intoned. 'Fetch *Sunray*, over.'

Amazingly, there was an instant response. Within seconds we had John – call sign *Sunray* – on the radio. Tricky passed me the handset.

'*Sunray*, this is *Maverick One*,' I told him, using my personal call sign. 'We're 80 kilometres north of Nasiriyah and we're trapped behind enemy lines. Our exact location is grid 937485. There are enemy forces to all four points surrounding us. We cannot proceed with the mission.'

There was a moment's silence on the net, then John's response: 'Roger. What's your intention?' From his voice it sounded to me like he was tired and shocked.

'We intend to move south on Route 7,' I told him. 'We'll engage enemy forces as we go, and link up with the Americans. Enemy are positioned in significant numbers all along Route 7. The area is not, I repeat not, relatively benign.'

John's voice came back to me echoing over the static: 'Roger.' Pause. 'You need to get back to the American positions.'

I thought: *No shit, Sherlock. What's the point in repeating what I've just said?*

'Tell him about the air plan,' Tricky interjected.

'Request air cover,' I told him. '*Sunray*, we can call in air strikes on heavy enemy positions all along Route 7. The area is not relatively benign. It's crawling with enemy. With air cover we can smash 'em. Requesting air to do so.'

John's voice came back to me instantly, flat and mechanical: 'There's nothing available.'

It was my turn to pause now. *How could there be no air?* We were on a battle-critical mission deep behind enemy lines, and we'd got the might of the British and American militaries depending on us. We'd just discovered scores of enemy in hidden defensive positions, and we were ideally placed to whack them. In those circumstances there had to be a way to find us some air.

I glanced at Tricky. He had this look of total disgust on his features.

How could there possibly be zero air available, especially when we had a golden opportunity to strike such a killer blow? It made no sense at all.

'Ask again,' Tricky mouthed at me.

I tried explaining to John that we'd uncovered the hidden positions of thousands of Iraqi soldiers, and that with air on hand Tricky could direct it in to hit them. I tried explaining that those troops were waiting to ambush the US Marines, as they advanced out of Nasiriyah. I argued that this needed to be made an air mission priority. There was a momentary delay in the comms, and I guessed John was checking with higher command.

'There's no air available,' was his response again.

Of course, we'd been told in the patrol briefings that it was highly unlikely air would be available to us. Air cover is never in limitless supply. But we weren't asking for air to somehow come in and rescue us. We were simply saying that if they gave us air assets we'd smack it into the enemy in all their hidden positions that we'd discovered, and rout them.

'If there's no air, is there a CR capability available to us?' I queried. I was going to push it as far as I could go now. 'Is there a team on standby, in case we need one?'

I wasn't asking if there was CSAR available. You only get Combat Search and Rescue when you're on the run, have zero comms and HQ doesn't know where you are. CSAR gets called in to find you and get you out. I was asking if there was a CR capability that we could call on, if we reached a suitable area where we could clear it in. You call for Combat Recovery when you're at a known location, one where you're able to remain static for long enough to get a rescue force in.

A Combat Rescue force would likely consist of two Chinooks, packed full of infantry, with helicopter gunships in support. I figured that right now 1 PARA must be stood-to for the Qalat Sikar airfield insertion, with Chinooks available and ready to get airborne. So presumably John could get a bunch of those lads re-tasked to fly a Combat Rescue mission for us lot, if needed.

The lads on my patrol knew what CR was, and we'd trained for it relentlessly. I figured the Engineer Recce blokes probably hadn't, but we could nurse them through it anyway. They'd all heard me ask John if CR could be made available. Without any air cover, it was almost inevitable that we were going to need it, because in truth we had *nowhere* to go. North, east, west, or south, we were all but certain to get smashed, and especially without any supporting air strikes.

John came back on the air: 'There's no air cover available. There's no rescue team.'

He told us we would need to extract ourselves. To my mind that meant that we were in effect on our own. For a moment I was totally lost for words. We all knew that forces such as ours could get left to find their own way out of the shit. But we were in a position where we could rain down fire on to a series of enemy positions, ones that no one knew were here until we'd stumbled into them. We'd flushed the enemy out of hiding, and they were clearly here to fuck up the US Marine Corps when they moved north out of Nasiriyah. But there was no sense me arguing this any further over the radio. We didn't have the time for this shit.

I told John: 'Roger. Out.'

I turned to the blokes: 'There's no air. We're on our own. We need to get moving.'

On the few occasions in my life when I've felt I have been really left in the shit, I have prayed. All I had time for now was a quick: 'God, if you get me out of this one, I *promise* I will screw the nut.' We were so deep in the shit that it was only a fleeting thought. We had no time to linger on anything now that was not directly related to getting us the hell out of there, and preferably alive.

We'd just had this massive shit sandwich rammed down our throats. In spite of this, we started sparking. Sometimes in life when you were dealt a shit sandwich you just had to squirt a load of ketchup on it, and get it down you.

Jason started to reel off the actions-on. 'I'll lead us off. Keep the space between the vehicles. Only engage the enemy when we're taking accurate fire. Keep covert and hold fire at all times otherwise ...'

Over the past forty-eight hours I'd totally changed my opinion of Jason. He was fearless, and nothing seemed to knock him back. Like now – when he volunteered to take the lead position on the coming suicide run south towards Nasiriyah. For none of us were kidding ourselves any more: it was a death run that we were facing here.

Jason was right: fire discipline would be everything. We could be fighting for days here, especially if we were forced at some stage to go on the run on foot. We needed to conserve our ammo, and use it only when we were forced to fight and could be sure of making kills.

'I'll lead, throwing smoke,' Jase continued. 'That'll give the two rear vehicles cover from view. If there's a roadblock, I will lead us off the road to try to box around it. If a vehicle gets taken out, everyone else gets the fire down and extracts the blokes from the fucked wagon into the two that remain.

'If all vehicles are taken out or blocked and we're pinned down, then we get the rounds down with the vehicle weapons, break contact and move off on foot. At all times our aim remains to head south, whether by vehicle or on foot, and to make the US front line.'

'What about when we get to the American positions?' Tricky asked.

It was a fair question. If we did make it through against all odds, crossing back over friendly lines was likely to be our most dangerous moment. The Marines were tired; we didn't have comms with them; they'd lost dozens of men; they'd been fighting brutally hard for the last twenty-four hours; and we would have to approach and cross their front line positions from the direction of the enemy. The chances of getting torn to pieces by our own side were all too real.

'When you see me put on my hazard warning lights you put yours on too,' said Jason. 'Lower your weapons. Put your IR Fireflies on. If the Yanks engage us do not return fire: get away from the vehicles and into cover.'

Tricky turned to me. He had this hard, determined look in his eyes, like he was steeling himself for what he was about to do.

'Dave, I'm going to flush the Crypto,' he announced.

I paused. This was horribly fucking ominous. Tricky knew how deeply we were in the shit, and that it was only going to get a lot worse from here on in. The Crypto was the encoded messaging software that enabled us to speak with PF HQ and air cover. If the enemy got hold of the Crypto, they could hack into the comms net of the entire British war effort. By flushing the Crypto Tricky would wipe it off all of our radios, and that would be it – comms gone.

Flushing the Crypto was a pretty terminal move. You only ever did it if you thought you were about to get captured or killed. But I figured Tricky was right on this one. We'd just been told by our OC what our situation was. We were pretty much facing certain capture or death here.

'Yeah, mate, fair enough,' I told him. 'There's no one fucking listening anyway, so flush the Crypto.' I turned to the rest of the lads. 'And whilst Tricky's at it, better ruin any other top secret kit that's in the wagons. You know the form. Tear it out, rip it to shreds and dump it in the fucking canal.'

'How about we drive lights-on?' Steve suggested. 'They'll expect us to be dark. Three vehicles, lights off – they'll know it's us lot right away. All their wagons were lights on, even the Fedayeen hunter force.'

'Let's see what ground we can cover first on black light,' said Jason. 'But if I flick my headlights on you lot follow suit, okay?'

There were murmurs of agreement all around.

I mounted up our Pinkie. I saw Steve laying out a neat line of grenades on the Land Rover's front dash, within easy reach, and then I glanced around at the lads. At that moment I realised how close I was to each and every one of these blokes. If I was going to go down fighting, I couldn't choose to die in better company.

In spite of my gut-churning fear, I forced a smile. For an instant, I found the Pathfinders' collect running through my mind.

Happiness shall always be found by those who dare and persevere; wanderer – do not turn around, march on and have no fear.

In the bars we frequented, on exercises and on ops, it had been short-ened over the years to one word that we all understood: *happiness*. The lads had their eyes on me now: steady, firm, unwavering. They were men of courage. They were showing no visible signs of fear. They were waiting for me to give them the go.

I gave it with that one word: 'Happiness.'

There was a moment's silence, then the lads returned the gesture. 'Yeah.'

'Fuck it.'

'Happiness.'

We started the engines. I checked my watch, cupping it in my palm to shield the faint glow of the hands. We'd been here for twenty minutes – that was all the time it had taken to make the decision of a lifetime.

After the quiet and stillness of the night, the purr of the diesel motors sounded deafeningly loud. The rhythmic beat of the cicadas – '*breeeep-breeeep-breeeep-breeeep-breeeep*' – seemed to falter for a moment, as the engines fired. It had been the constant companion to the silence here, the beat of a million tiny insects marking time as first we considered the impossible, and then accepted it as being the only option left open to us.

Jason led off, the other wagons following. We bumped and kan-garooed over the rough terrain back towards the road. We checked right – north – where we knew the Fedayeen hunter force was lying in wait. It was dark and silent up there, and there wasn't a thing to be seen. Then we turned left and hit the tarmac heading south. I still couldn't quite believe that we were doing this, but we were.

It is what it is.

We picked up speed with the wind in our faces, and I felt strangely, oddly calm. I held on to this moment – a few seconds of peace and stillness before the storm of all storms – for myself. I was sure the lads were feeling the same fear that I felt. We all felt fear – it was how we controlled it that mattered. We kept it real, controlled the adrenaline as it burst and burned through our system, and used it as fuel for the coming battle.

Our speed increased to 70 kph. *Soon now.*

We were on the road speeding through the night, when a line from Monty Python's classic comedy *The Holy Grail* came unbidden into my head. When facing the Killer Bunny the knights of King Arthur's Round Table had opted to 'Run away! Run away!' I told myself there was nothing wrong, or cowardly, about the decision that we'd just made. We weren't bulletproof. We didn't stand and fight Rambo-like when to do so was sheer suicidal stupidity.

Instead, we'd opted to make a tactical retreat, and we'd be fighting all the way through the heart of enemy territory. It was either a moment of complete and utter madness or a mark of sheer genius: *maybe they won't be expecting us.* Either way, I wished we had that air power on hand to really smash them.

But there was no point dwelling on that now.

We'd been on the road for 5 kilometres when I felt a tap on my shoulder. It was Tricky. He leaned forward from his position atop the 50-cal turret.

'Car headlamps,' he yelled above the wind noise. 'About a klick ahead of us, flashing on and off.'

He pointed in the direction of what he had seen. I raised myself up in my seat, and scanned the dark horizon. And then I saw it, just to one side of the road up ahead: a pair of lights like two devil's eyes, going flash-dark-flash-dark-flash-dark.

'You see it, yeah?' Tricky yelled. 'That's it: enemy ambush set.'

Shit: so they knew we were coming.

CHAPTER TWENTY-ONE

I f you want to know where the enemy are and what they're planning, you have to try to think like them. You have to take on their
mindset, and second-guess what they're up to. You've got to figure
out where you would choose to attack a three-vehicle convoy moving
south down the main highway. In any other context, a car flashing
its headlights wouldn't be so unusual. But Tricky had seen it and read
it for what it was: a signal to the Iraqi forces lying in wait that we
were coming.

As if to confirm what he'd just been saying, there was a burst of
sporadic shots from out of the southeast. It was some 500 metres
forwards of Jason's vehicle, and the tracer rounds went arcing high
into the night sky. This wasn't aimed at us. It was signal fire to back
up the message of the flashing headlights.

They're coming.

We were approaching the large settlement where a short while
earlier we'd got mortared, and where the RPG round had skipped
across our bonnet. For a moment I wondered whether we shouldn't
try going off-road, to box around the enemy. But just as soon as I'd
entertained the thought, I'd dismissed it. Now they knew we were
on our way they were sure to have radioed through an alert to the
Fedayeen hunter force.

Any delay, and that hunter force would be on our tail. The Fedayeen wagons were swifter than us, and more manoeuvrable, and we

had to presume they knew the ground here intimately. Our only chance was to keep heading south at full whack, and try to outrun them on the main highway.

Seconds dragged by in a tense silence. The only noise was the rush of the wind. For any soldier there is nothing worse than speeding into a known ambush when you're outnumbered and outgunned by the enemy. But right now any fear that I might be feeling was buried by the pure animal aggression of the coming fight.

I pulled the hard angular steel of the GPMG closer into my shoulder. It felt comforting. *Bring it on.*

We sped past the location from which those warning shots had been fired. Suddenly, the night ahead of us erupted into a volcano of tracer fire. The enemy had opened up from positions 600 metres to the east, high on the ridgeline. From there the fire rippled downwards towards our convoy, until the entire hillside was awash with flame. From out of the flat, empty blankness of the night it was suddenly as if a laser-gun battle from *Star Wars* was being re-enacted on the eastern side of Route 7.

A few hundred metres ahead of our speeding vehicle I could see tracer rounds sparking and ricocheting off the tarmac. There was a wall of fire right to the front of us. I flipped up my night-vision goggles as I clocked the size of the ambush, and the amount of fire we were facing, which would dazzle us. I saw Steve and Tricky do likewise.

The enemy gunners must have got their weapons zeroed in on the highway, for they were hosing down that stretch of tarmac with a murderous rate of fire. This was a well-co-ordinated, concerted ambush, and we were going to have to run 400 metres of solid fire. It was fucking terrifying.

Silhouetted in the harsh glare of the enemy's muzzle flashes I could see row upon row of buildings up on the hillside. They looked a lot like army barracks, and they were alive with stick figures darting in and out of them. Fuck knows where they'd all appeared from, because this place had been pretty near deserted when we had first driven through it.

After our drive north, the enemy must have been placed in their stand-to positions, ready and waiting. We had one small advantage. They obviously couldn't see us, and so they were firing at static points on the road.

As I studied the approaching enemy positions, I could make out purpose-built sandbagged bunkers set amongst the larger, barrack-like buildings. There were thick walls running up and down the slope, providing rat-runs with ample cover between the various positions. We'd missed all of this on the way through, and it was only the weight of fire and the muzzle flashes that were illuminating it for us now.

First time around this had been a dark hillside running up to a ridge with a cluster of dark buildings. Now we could see that it was the perfect defensive terrain from which to hit us. I pulled the GPMG tighter into my shoulder, and flicked the big clunky safety catch to 'off'. I raised myself up on the balls of my feet, so I was ready to swing the weapon from side to side in smooth, killer movements. But still we held our fire.

The enemy tracer groped its way towards our hidden convoy. The roar of belt-fed machine guns joined the staccato crackle of small-arms fire, as more and more weapons opened up. Then I caught the fearful, rhythmic 'chthunk-chthunk-chthunk' of a Dushka heavy machine gun. The road ahead of us was being hosed down by Iraqi gunmen firing AKs, heavy machine guns, and 12.7 mm armour-piercing rounds.

The roar and thump of the approaching fire punched over us in a pounding, crushing shockwave. It was a shooting gallery out there, and I figured we had half a kilometre or more to run before we would be through to the far side.

A thick cloud of grey smoke billowed up from the road ahead. For a moment I feared that the lead Pinkie had driven into the fire and taken a direct hit. Then I realised that it was Jason throwing a smoke grenade, to give cover to the wagons behind. *Jase: what a fucking hero!*

Just as his vehicle disappeared behind that curtain of smoke, I spotted an enemy bunker position up ahead, close by the roadside. We were in amongst them now, which is why Jason had started to chuck the smoke. Fire erupted from that bunker. It was less than 100 metres from the highway, and rounds went tearing into the Engineer Recce wagon. The Engineer lads opened up at the very same instant, angry tongues of flame spitting from the pair of Gimpys mounted on their vehicle.

We were under direct and accurate fire now, and I didn't waste a millisecond. The enemy bunker was a low dugout with a thick, sand-bagged roof. I could see the silhouettes of gunmen in there, hun-kered over muzzle flashes. I was already in the aim, and as I pulled the trigger with my right hand I'd got my left gripping the top of the weapon, to give extra stability.

I sensed Tricky behind me, spinning the 50-cal around, and then it was thumping away above my head, booming deafeningly in my ears. He was firing right across the top of my scalp, and it felt as if the rounds were about to take my head off. Being 'area weapons', both the 50-cal and the GPMG spray out a cone of rounds to saturate the terrain immediately surrounding a target.

I aimed at the central point of the bunker, knowing the Gimpy would plaster all around it with death. At the distance that I was smashing rounds into the bunker, I'd be hitting at least half of it with fire. I saw bullets from my weapon striking sparks from metal, and ripping into the sandbagged walls, kicking up plumes of dirt as they tore the walls to pieces.

Then the bigger rounds from Tricky's 50-cal were blasting the bun-ker apart. I saw sandbags exploding under the impact, and bodies being thrown backwards into the shadows. Finally, we were smash-ing the enemy back. *And man, was it a fucking wonderful feeling.*

It's standard operating procedure in the PF not to use tracer rounds, especially when on a night mission behind enemy lines. It helps you stay hidden, but still our muzzle flashes would eventually give us away. For several seconds we tore that bunker apart, and then we were in amongst the acrid, choking cloud of smoke from the grenade that Jason had thrown. For a further couple of seconds we were rushing through this dark, eerie tunnel of smoke, lit orange and white by muzzle flashes and explosions from the outside.

We held our fire. There was no point trying to engage and kill the enemy when you couldn't see them. *Conserve your ammo.* But still the noise from all around us was deafening. We thundered out of the cover of the smoke, and there was a wall of tracer before us. The enemy would have packed their mags with one tracer round per four or five bullets. What we could see now was only a fraction of the weight of enemy fire. It was only a matter of time before we started taking hits, and got torn apart.

I was dancing the Gimpy around, engaging target after target after target. Every inch of the hillside was awash with fire. I was hitting muzzle flashes, silhouettes of gunmen, windows spitting bullets at us. Everything was instinctive now. All hopes of stealth and conceal-ment were gone. It was fight or die.

A short burst and I was on to the next target, doing what we'd all learned so well during the months of training and exercises with PF. Tricky and I were on our feet in the vehicle, ramping the guns left and right, fighting for our lives. I was back-to-back with the lads, seeking to kill as many of the enemy as I could. And for sure we'd take a lot of them with us, before we were smashed and bleeding out our last.

Every man in our convoy was doing the same. He was doing it for his life, but more importantly for his mates' lives. If we fought with total ferocity for each other, we had a small chance that some of us might make it through. We didn't have to think about this much. There were few conscious thoughts. That was the beauty of the training.

The barrel of the Gimpy juddered and rocked with each burst of fire, the smooth, gun-metal-blue steel of the weapon reflecting the latticework of tracer rounds tearing past above us. Already, the bar-rel was burning hot to the touch, and I figured I had to be a hundred rounds into that first 200-round belt.

I had to conserve my rate of fire. *One burst, one kill.* If we made it to halfway through this ambush and I pulled the trigger and got an empty click, then we were well and truly fucked. I'd have to change the ammo belt, and this really was not the time to stop getting the rounds down, even for the couple of seconds it'd take me to do so.

A wall of smoke like fog engulfed us for a second time, as we sped into the cover of the second of Jason's grenades. I remained hunched over the Gimpy and in the aim, finger on the trigger, for when we came tearing out the far side. All around the wagon the dull, opaque whiteness was threaded with the fiery trails of tracer rounds. I could sense that the vehicle was getting hit, though the overall noise was too deafening to be able to hear the individual bullets strike. I hoped and prayed that a round didn't take out a tyre, or something equally terminal. If we got a puncture here we were as good as dead.

As we thundered out of the smoke, an RPG round came flaming out of the darkness. It tore towards our convoy from 600 metres up on the ridgeline, and straight towards the Engineer Recce wagon. It hit the road to the left-hand side of their Pinkie, then skipped up and shot beneath it, going between the front and the rear wheels.

I couldn't believe it when the RPG round emerged on the far side and exploded in the bush. The white-hot heat of the detonation lit up a wide stretch of the highway in this eerie, smoke-filled halo of light. It had passed clean beneath the Recce blokes' wagon. *How the hell had it missed?*

RPG teams are often positioned in units of three. You have one shared re-loader between two blokes operating the launcher tubes. It crossed my mind that there was probably a pair of launchers up on the ridge, so I could expect another RPG.

I swung the GPMG around and engaged the location from which the RPG had been fired. As I did so there was the blast of a second RPG launching. It was a violent burst of orange-yellow from within the darkness. It was like a mortar flash, only horizontal and aimed right at us. The flame of that second RPG lit up the billowing cloud of exhaust smoke still hanging there from the first launch.

In that instant I spotted the RPG team crouched behind a sandbagged barrier. I unleashed a burst of rounds from the Gimpy, which went tearing into them. There was this massive flash and the bang of secondary explosions, and shredded sandbags went flying in all directions. I figured my bullets must have touched off their spare RPG rounds. *That was one very dead RPG team.*

The very same instant that I'd smashed them, the RPG round that they'd fired went screaming over our bonnet. It wasn't as if it was in front of us, or near us: it was right over the Pinkie's bonnet, like metal scraping metal, a great big fuck-off rocket before our bloody noses.

Instinctively Steve swerved, and started yelling: 'FUCKING HELL! FUCKING HELL! FUCKING HELL!'

I glanced at him in surprise. I figured he must have been hit. But he was eyes front still and doing the drive of his life, as he fought to control the careering wagon.

I was instantly back to my arcs, picking targets and hammering rounds into them. The ground to the east was 500 metres of solid muzzle flashes sparking right to the ridgeline. There were rakes of buildings up on the high ground, and I could see figures on the rooftops, loosing off whole mags on automatic at us.

Their aim was shit, but a lucky bullet was still a lucky bullet. And nearer to the road there were yet more bunkers and dug-in positions. Those had to be my priority. I picked a target, focused, sighted and fired; picked a target, focused, sighted and fired. On and on and on it went, until I was sure the Gimpy had to be down to its last round. And then the next billowing cloud of smoke engulfed us.

I had no idea how many smoke grenades Jase had brought with him. We went thundering out of the far side of that one, and for a moment I sensed that the fire was mostly behind us now. I swivelled the Gimpy around, to engage the last of the enemy positions, but they were too far to my left and behind us. The bonnet-mounted GPMG could cover to the front and side of the vehicle, but not to the rear.

Behind me Tricky swivelled the 50-cal around until it was pointing rearwards, and for several seconds he kept malleting rounds into the enemy positions. Then he too ceased firing. The enemy guns were still trying to hit us, but there was no point making us an easy target by revealing where we were. Somehow, miraculously, we'd made it through that first ambush alive.

I could sense Tricky searching in the darkness of the road behind us. I knew instinctively what he was looking for. *Vehicles in pursuit*. This had become a crazed dash south before the Fedayeen hunter force could catch us.

Acting on automatic I reached forwards and unhooked the ammo belt from the GPMG. I hefted its weight in my right hand, and I could feel that it was all but empty. I chucked the used belt into the footwell and slotted on another 200 rounds of link.

I'd just finished changing the ammo belt when Steve leaned across to have a word. The tension on his face dissolved into this crazy kind of smile. 'Dave, we fucking made it through! Boat drinks, mate!'

I gave him the nod back. 'Yeah, boat drinks it is. But if you want to make it home to all those lovely Scouse girls, there's more of that to come, mate.'

'Scouse girls? I'm making straight for the bloody Shadow Lounge. You with me, or what?'

I bared my teeth and let out this crazed kind of laugh. We were high on the adrenaline, and the sheer knowledge that we were still alive.

We pressed onwards on a dark and deserted stretch of road. I flipped down my NVG and scanned the terrain ahead. Apart from us, it seemed utterly devoid of life out there. After the insane intensity of that ambush, the silence was deafening. Fearful. I had no idea if anyone had been hit on Jason's or the Recce wagon. I couldn't radio to check, because we'd flushed the Crypto and had no comms between vehicles.

I checked my watch. It was 2100 hours. First light was around 0500. We had eight hours in which to complete this death run. If we were to stand any chance of surviving it, we had to get it done during the hours of darkness. With sunrise we'd lose the cover of the night, and we'd be finished. From the drive up here I reckoned that the settlement we'd just driven through was the largest this side of Nasiriyah. I was hoping that we'd just managed to run the biggest force the Iraqis would be able to throw at us.

Maybe they just presumed that we'd never make it through that first ambush alive. We pushed onwards for 7 kilometres in silence. I was hunched down behind the GPMG, continuously sweeping my arcs, the steel sights seeking targets amongst the night terrain all around us. *Nothing.* Just empty bush, with the skeletal silhouettes of palm trees piercing the darkness. The tension was unbearable.

As my senses tuned into the environment, I realised there was a new scent in the air now: the reek of burned gun oil. The barrel of the Gimpy before me was still hot from the battle. The GMPG is a fantastic weapon. It's been tried and tested over many years, and whilst you do get stoppages they're rare. The barrel does get red hot – by which time you have to change it – but only after unleashing a few thousand rounds. I'd got a good way to go before that happened.

I'd freshly oiled the Gimpy when we'd been waiting to move forwards at the Marine Corps command post, just south of Nasiriyah. Some of that gun oil had cooked off during the firefight. When I'd oiled my weapon I'd done so almost subconsciously. It was one of those automatic drills hammered into us in the PF: *Look after your weapon, your weapon looks after you.* And when I'd done so, I hadn't the slightest idea what shitfight we were driving into. *Relatively benign my arse.*

As I scanned the empty night with my NVG, I couldn't help but wonder what it was that had kept us alive during the frenzy of that firefight. My mind drifted to one of the key lessons learned by our predecessors, the Long Range Desert Group, during their epic feats of soldiering in the North Africa deserts. At first, along with their sister regiment, David Stirling's SAS, they had sneaked on to enemy airfields and planted their Lewis bombs, melting away again quietly into the night.

But on one mission they'd decided to change their means of attack.

The favoured weapons of the LRDG were the Vickers 50-cal heavy machine guns, plus the Vickers .303 inch K machine guns, mounted on pivots and often in pairs. In December 1941, the LRDG and the SAS had carried out two raids on the airfield at Sirte, in northern Libya. But this time they decided to drive their trucks right on to the airfield and between the rows of parked aircraft, using their fire-power to shoot them up. The raid was so successful that this became their standard means of attack, and that December they destroyed 151 aircraft that way.

The LRDG operators were skilled at manoeuvring at high speed and making their vehicles difficult targets, whilst putting down accurate and heavy concentrations of fire. They also relied upon the fact that their enemies – more often than not Italian conscript troops – were taken by surprise, and their fire was wild and inaccurate. I figured it had to be the same kind of mobility skills and fire discipline that was keeping us alive.

But as I scanned the empty Iraqi night, the difference with this mission struck me with the force of a speeding truck: the enemy knew we were coming, so we had zero element of surprise; and we were being forced to speed down a main highway, which left us bugger all room for any manoeuvre.

Our turn-around point had been some 80 kilometres north of Nasiriyah. I figured we were around 15 kilometres south of there by now, so we had some 65 kilometres of enemy territory to run before we reached the American front line. That was more or less the distance of the endurance stage of PF selection, which you had to complete in a twenty-hour night march, or fail. That was how far we had to run the enemy gauntlet, before we reached comparative safety.

I was scanning the darkness, and checking for any sign of head-lights in pursuit. But the road seemed dark and totally deserted behind us. It was from way out in front that I spotted the next threat.

There was a line of vehicles speeding towards us, lights on full beam.

CHAPTER TWENTY-TWO

Headlamps probed the darkness, catching on the dust thrown up by whatever was coming at us, and creating a weird glowing halo of light. As the convoy drew closer, I began to make out the details. There were a couple of minibuses in the lead, the headlamps from the wagons behind glinting off their dirty, white bodywork. From the silhouette of the third vehicle, I figured it had to be a Toyota-type pick-up of the type driven by the Fedayeen. There were further pick-ups behind.

After our experiences with Ron Jeremy – the fat Iraqi cabbie-cum-spy – we'd woken up to the fact that the Iraqi military were using civvie vehicles as their key means of transport. In fact, it made perfect sense for them to move around in non-military vehicles. With the coalition forces having total air superiority, our warplanes would be able to blast their convoys from the air, as long as the aircrew could positively identify them as being Iraqi military. However, our air power was far less likely to hit the Iraqi forces if they were buzzing about in minibuses, pick-ups and taxicabs, and making for all the world like civvies.

We had to figure that this was an enemy hunter force. Jason must have reached the same kind of conclusion as I had. With the gap between the Iraqi convoy and ours closing fast, I saw our lead wagon opening fire. Bullets hammered south across the distance between Jason's vehicle and theirs.

The lead pair of headlights suddenly went dark. The minibus slewed wildly across the road before righting itself. I saw muzzle flashes spark from all along the speeding vehicle's windows. It was packed with Iraqi fighters. From the rear the pick-ups joined in the firefight, and all of the enemy wagons began to engage us as we hammered towards each other at a combined speed of over 100 kph.

It was now that a curve in the road opened up a clear line of fire. The guns on the Engineer Recce wagon started pumping out bullets, and an instant later I unleashed fire from the GPMG. I saw my rounds falling just short, sparking off the tarmac to the front of the lead enemy wagon. I leaned my shoulder harder into the GPMG, raised the muzzle a fraction on its pivot mount, and fired another long burst. Rounds tore along the length of the front vehicle, punching out the windows, and sending fountains of glass into the air. The shattered glass glinted momentarily in the light thrown up by the following vehicles, as if trapped in slow motion.

I could feel every one of those windows getting smashed to pieces. Further bursts of fire tore through the bodywork, chunks of metal spinning off in all directions. Finally, the lead minibus swerved violently to the right, left the road completely and careered into the bush. It rolled over several times, and I followed it with the sights of the Gimpy until it stopped moving. It came to a rest on one side, and then there were no more muzzle flashes coming from the wreckage.

I ramped the hot, smoking barrel of the Gimpy back towards the road, and as I did so the second minibus came juddering to a halt. For some reason it wasn't engaging us any more. It looked as if it may have given up the fight. I decided not to mallet the fuck out of it. But in the third and fourth wagons – the Toyota pick-ups – I could see kneeling figures silhouetted in the glare of their muzzle flashes, as they sprayed off long bursts and tried to smash us.

As one, the six machine guns on our three Pinkies swung on to target and opened up. As we sped towards the enemy convoy we concentrated our combined firepower on those two wagons, and within seconds they were riddled with 50-cal rounds. Bullets shredded the lead pick-up from end to end, punching jagged rents in the white bodywork. There was a lick of red and angry flame from the second wagon, and it looked as if the diesel tank had taken one of the big, armour-piercing rounds.

We roared past the wreckage of the first vehicle. It was lying in the bush with the roof crumpled in, and the window struts buckled outwards. Bodies were hanging out of the shattered windows, with others lying face down in the dirt amidst spreading pools of blood. It was too dark to make out what, if any, uniforms they'd been wearing, but their discarded weapons were everywhere.

We roared past the second minibus. It was parked up on the road-side more or less intact, and it seemed to be totally abandoned. There weren't even any bodies that I could see. Maybe its occupants had done a runner, once they'd seen what our vehicle-mounted machine guns had done to the lead wagon. They must have decided discretion was the better part of valour, and made themselves scarce.

We came level with the pickups. The cab of the first one was a shattered mess. I caught the flash of a red-and-white chequered headscarf tumbling out of a half-open doorway. Sure enough, they were Fedayeen. There were more dead and dying Fedayeen in the rear of the vehicle, but it was half-obscured by a thick blanket of choking smoke. The rear pick-up was a mass of seething flame, oily black fumes from the inferno barrelling into an even blacker sky.

We shot past the wreckage with the hungry roar of the fire in our ears, the pick-up's burning tyres popping and exploding as we went. I glanced at Steve, his face lit up tense and ghostly in the searing heat as he focused on the driving. Behind me the fiery orange light flickered across Tricky's features, as his hands gripped the 50-cal and swung it around to cover the enemy to our rear.

Then we were heading onwards into the cool darkness of the night. Those vehicles had been packed full of Iraqi fighters, mostly Fedayeen. I guessed they were a mobile reception party sent out to hit us, or maybe reinforcements heading north to bolster the enemy positions. Either way we'd managed to smash them first, before they got to ambush us.

We drill and drill and drill for how to fire accurately from fast moving vehicles. It's one of the most difficult skills for a soldier to master, and it's one of the key specialisms of the Pathfinders. And right now, it was those skills that were keeping us alive.

We'd rehearsed those drills repeatedly back in Kuwait, just to make sure we were 100 per cent ready and that our vehicle-mounted weapons were properly zeroed in. During transit, sights tend to get knocked and a weapon's zero can go out of true. It's also the case that rounds deliver to target via a different trajectory depending on atmospheric conditions. The hot and baking desert air was very different from the soggy damp of the UK.

Out on the Camp Tristar ranges we'd got ourselves accustomed to how bullets fly in such burning, bone-dry conditions. Tricky and Joe had had to zero in the Thales Kite sights on their 50-cal machine guns. The Kite sight has times-six magnification, plus low-light image enhancement, which means it doubles as a night sight. Under starlight illumination alone it can detect a standing man at 600 metres. We'd been engaging the enemy vehicles of the hunter force from well within that range.

We'd practised firing the weapons from the Pinkies moving at speed, using human cut-out targets, which are radio-controlled to pop-up and pop-down again. They give you just seconds to spot and kill the target.

We'd started by firing single shots from stationary vehicles, with a buddy spotting our rounds to see if they were falling short or long. That way, we'd got the weapons zeroed in. All three of us – Tricky, Steve, me – had rotated around the 50-cal and the GPMG, to ensure we were up to speed on the weapons, and the sights were true. Anyone could get killed or injured when in combat, so we all needed to know how to use the weapons. If we got the vehicle bogged and Tricky was put out of action, Steve would need to be able to operate the 50-cal.

We'd moved on to firing from single vehicles to firing from pairs of wagons, as a patrol. Targets would pop up randomly on the Camp Tristar range, and we'd yell out warnings so as to co-ordinate our fire. Then we'd graduated to both vehicles being on the move, and engaging the targets across all types of terrain. The targets would fall when hit, so it was possible to see if you were aiming too far in front or behind, in an effort to compensate for your speed.

We'd drilled for firing from the Pinkies when moving at speed by day and by night, and hitting targets that only appeared for a split second. We knew that if we were compromised behind enemy lines, it would be the speed, accuracy and lethality of our fire-and-manoeuvre skills that would keep us alive.

As we pulled away from the shattered wreckage of those pick-ups and the minibus, Tricky leaned forwards. 'Remind me to always take the train.'

It was the perfect comment to break the knife-edged tension of the moment. Steve and I cracked up.

'Well, at least until we're old enough to get us a free bloody bus pass,' Steve quipped. 'Did I ever tell you about that Aussie chick I met once on a train …?'

'Will you ever shut the fuck up about women,' I cut in. Now wasn't really the time for another of his shagged-her-in-the-toilet stories.

By now we'd pushed 25 kilometres south, which meant we had more than twice that distance still to go. I was tensing myself for the next fight. No doubt the enemy commanders were radioing warnings ahead, and all along the road. They had to know that we were coming. The distance to the next settlement – the one that we had driven through under the fierce orange glow of the streetlamps – was 15 klicks away. At the speed we were travelling at, it would take us less than fifteen minutes to reach it. That was when I figured we next had it coming – that's unless they sent out another mobile force to try to hit us.

In the down time and the silence, I swept the night with my weapon. As I did so I reached forward and stroked the barrel momentarily. It was burning to the touch, but not glowing red-hot so that I'd have to consider doing a barrel-change. Reassured, I settled back to sweep my arcs. I couldn't quite believe that the three of us in my wagon were apparently unscathed. I couldn't speak for the other vehicles: maybe they had taken casualties. Maybe they'd lost someone even. There was just no way of knowing unless Jason called a halt.

Jason. How my impression of him had changed. I'd found him difficult, and at times even divisive, when back in Kuwait. A part of me had been dreading having him on my patrol when we went to war. Now, he'd more than made good. He was leading our charge south with lightning-fast reflexes and an instinct that was proving close to infallible. As a soldier in combat, he was pretty much second to none. I had to accept that I'd got it badly wrong about him. When it came to war-fighting, he was an invaluable asset to have on the patrol.

Despite the early challenges with the lads, I knew now that these were the blokes to be fighting back-to-back with. I wouldn't change a single one of them for the world. Class, background, rank, personal rivalries – it had all gone out of the window. Here, in the midst of this death run, we were all on a level, and not a man amongst us had been found wanting.

Driving into almost certain death had got me brimful with fear. I had felt the tension and the terror gnawing at my guts. But the brave man was the man who channelled that fear, and used it for the fight. Knowing that we were all in this together, that we were a brotherhood of equals, had given me something incredibly powerful to help conquer that fear. I presumed it was the same for the others: we all felt the fear, yet it was tempered by the brotherhood.

I was torn out of my thoughts by a jab in the ribs. 'Up ahead,' yelled Steve. 'Roadblock!'

I looked forwards, straining my eyes to spot whatever Steve had seen. In the glow of my NVG I could just make out a pair of hot engine blocks a kilometre or so ahead of us. A couple of vehicles had been parked up sideways on to the highway. They formed a makeshift roadblock. Their motors were still warm, and it was that heat which had been picked up by the NVG.

As we drew nearer I could make out more details. The vehicle on the left looked like an empty Toyota minibus parked arse-end on to the highway. It was similar to the two that we'd just shot to pieces. The vehicle on the right looked like a Datsun-type taxicab of the kind that our old friend, Ron Jeremy, had been driving.

They'd left a gap between the two vehicles that appeared to be just about large enough to squeeze the wagons through. It didn't make a great deal of sense to have thrown up a roadblock with a bloody great gap in the middle of it. Or, thinking like the enemy, *maybe it did*. Maybe they'd got that gap covered by a couple of great big Dushkas, zeroed in and waiting for us to poke our noses through. Maybe if we took the bait and went for the gap, that was going to be a sure kill for those waiting Dushka gunners. A dead cert.

Or maybe they'd got a series of hidden explosive charges rigged to either side of the gap and linked to a detonation wire. As we went to pass they'd trigger the detonators, and blow the lot of us sky high. Or maybe they'd got some strands of razor wire strung across the gap at neck height, in an effort to rip our fucking heads off.

Or maybe they'd thrown some tyre-busters across the tarmac, which at their most basic were planks of wood with nails driven through them and pointing vertically upwards. We wouldn't see them until the last moment, if at all. Without the run-flats that we'd asked for back in Kuwait – and been denied – we'd be finished. We'd go roaring over the tyre-busters and they'd blow out our inner tubes. It'd be a crude but very effective way of stopping us.

If they blew out our tyres they'd fucking have us. Images flashed through my mind of what the Iraqis had done to the Bravo Two Zero boys, once they'd captured them. The B2Z lads had claimed to be from a CSAR team sent in to rescue some downed British pilots. The Iraqis hadn't believed them. They'd locked them isolated and alone in cells plastered with shit, and used beatings, mock executions and worse to try to break them, so they would admit what unit they were from. The torture and abuse had lasted for days on end.

From those images my mind flipped into a powerful memory of being in a torture chamber myself for real. 1 PARA were the first troops into Kosovo during that conflict, and I'd led my company into the war-torn capital, Pristina. We were a couple of days into the city and were out doing a day patrol. We had bergens on our backs, our personal weapons in our hands, and we were moving fast through the streets on foot. We came across this building with a bonfire of burning documents outside. I asked our interpreter what was happening here.

It turned out to be a Serb police station that had just been abandoned. The bonfire was intended to destroy all the evidence of their wrongdoing. But there was no hiding what they'd been up to down in the basement. There was blood spattered all over the place, baseball bats studded with nails, bed frames with straps on them to hold down the victims, and even photos on the walls of those they'd tortured. But most disturbing were the heaps of extremely vile vampire-type pornography lying around the room.

That place had reeked of pain, dark perversions and evil. If the Iraqis captured us alive, I guessed they'd have something similar in store for us. Maybe this roadblock was the ultimate trap, and everything up until now has been just some gentle kind of prelude. *Who fucking knows?*

There was little point me worrying about it, or what we should do about it. Jase was leading the convoy of wagons, and it was his call. In any case, we all knew the actions-on for encountering a roadblock. Pretty soon Jason should pull off the highway, so we could box around the roadblock off-road and rejoin the tarmac further on.

Yet Jason's wagon just kept hammering forwards at full speed ahead. The Engineer Recce vehicle and our own had no option but to follow Jason's lead. The PF golden rule number one is not to break the line of march. Do that, and with no radio contact we'd lose each other pretty damn fast.

The roadblock was growing closer and closer by the second, and I just knew that Jason was going to try to run it or die trying.

Balls of fucking steel, Jase, balls of fucking steel.

CHAPTER TWENTY-THREE

The great thing about the Land Rover is that it sits upon a solid hunk of steel, a ladder frame chassis, the solid, chunky build of which hasn't changed much since it was first put together back in 1947. On top of the Land Rover's natural robustness, our Pinkies were specially strengthened. The chassis had been engineered to massively increase load capacity, with fibre webbing encasing all of the welded joints and stress points. So whilst they might not be able to outrun a Toyota SUV, they'd smash one up in a head-on collision every time.

As we careered onwards, muzzles started sparking amongst the shadows between the Toyota and the Datsun taxicab. As one, our guns opened up and tore into the thin metal skins of those vehicles. We were almost upon them, driving down the enemy's muzzles, when the minibus exploded in a blinding sheet of flame. The fuel tank had gone, the massive blast throwing the vehicle half out of our path.

I saw Jason's Land Rover going for the gap, smashing into what remained of the minibus, punching the wreckage out of the way and careering through the scattered debris. Meanwhile, the Recce wagon and us lot were pumping rounds into what was left of Ron Jeremy's taxicab, at very close range. *I fucking hoped it was his vehicle and all.* It was Ron Jeremy the fat cabbie who'd compromised us in the first place, and brought this world of shit down around our ears. There was nothing better than seeing 'his' sedan getting chewed into small pieces of shattered glass and bullet-punctured steel.

We sped past the remains of that roadblock, leaving the twisted wreck of the burning minibus on one side, and the bullet-torn carcass of the Datsun on the other. I felt this crazy blast of euphoria as we did so. *Fuck 'em!* They'd had us at that roadblock. It was there that they should have stopped us, and killed or captured us all. Instead, Jase had smashed the minibus out of the way, and led us through from a totally unexpected direction. If they did have their guns zeroed in on the gap, we'd neatly side-stepped them.

Still, I couldn't quite believe that we'd made it through. As we emerged from the smoke and the flames I caught sight of two bunkers close by the roadside, up ahead of the lead Pinkie. An instant later they opened up, pouring fire into Jase's wagon. It suddenly struck me that maybe the roadblock had been a ruse, designed to screen us from the real threat – our arrival at the second big settlement that straddled Route 7.

Those two bunkers were the trigger for the full-on ambush. As the gunners there unleashed on Jason's wagon, so the entire hillside behind them erupted into a massive wave of fire. For whatever reason – *they know we're coming; we're nearer the Iraqi front line (though we're approaching from behind it!); they're a better calibre of soldier here* – the gunfire was more accurate than ever, and there was even more of it. It was total fucking murder.

There was no smoke being thrown by Jason any more, so I figured either he was all out of grenades, or he was seriously wounded or dead. As the last vehicle, we had no choice now but to run this ambush, and with zero cover from view. I forced myself to concentrate my fire on the closest positions, because they had to present the greatest threat. I swung the GPMG into the aim, and started to hammer the bunkers that were 100, 200, 300 metres forwards of us, all down the roadside, in one long burst of aimed, accurate fire.

I saw the empty cartridges spewing out of the Gimpy's breech, as I kept my finger on the trigger, churning out the rounds. They went

Above Pushing deeper into Iraq, there was almost zero cover provided by the flat desert terrain. My patrol was tasked to drive some 300 kilometres through such terrain to reach an airfield deep behind enemy lines. As Sod's law would have it, once we set out temperatures plummeted and snow and sleet began to fall.

Below The Euphrates bridge at Nasiriyah, the front-line of American forces in the war. Thick palm groves and rivers meant that this was difficult ground to cross. Nasiriyah became the focal point for the Iraqi resistance, and the battle to take the city became known as the 'battle that America nearly lost'.

was nothing better than seeing 'his' sedan getting chewed into small pieces of shattered glass and bullet-punctured steel.

We sped past the remains of that roadblock, leaving the twisted wreck of the burning minibus on one side, and the bullet-torn carcass of the Datsun on the other. I felt this crazy blast of euphoria as we did so. *Fuck 'em!* They'd had us at that roadblock. It was there that they should have stopped us, and killed or captured us all. Instead, Jase had smashed the minibus out of the way, and led us through from a totally unexpected direction. If they did have their guns zeroed in on the gap, we'd neatly side-stepped them.

Still, I couldn't quite believe that we'd made it through. As we emerged from the smoke and the flames I caught sight of two bunkers close by the roadside, up ahead of the lead Pinkie. An instant later they opened up, pouring fire into Jase's wagon. It suddenly struck me that maybe the roadblock had been a ruse, designed to screen us from the real threat – our arrival at the second big settlement that straddled Route 7.

Those two bunkers were the trigger for the full-on ambush. As the gunners there unleashed on Jason's wagon, so the entire hillside behind them erupted into a massive wave of fire. For whatever reason – *they know we're coming; we're nearer the Iraqi front line (though we're approaching from behind it!); they're a better calibre of soldier here* – the gunfire was more accurate than ever, and there was even more of it. It was total fucking murder.

There was no smoke being thrown by Jason any more, so I figured either he was all out of grenades, or he was seriously wounded or dead. As the last vehicle, we had no choice now but to run this ambush, and with zero cover from view. I forced myself to concentrate my fire on the closest positions, because they had to present the greatest threat. I swung the GPMG into the aim, and started to hammer the bunkers that were 100, 200, 300 metres forwards of us, all down the roadside, in one long burst of aimed, accurate fire.

I saw the empty cartridges spewing out of the Gimpy's breech, as I kept my finger on the trigger, churning out the rounds. They went tumbling into the Pinkie's footwell in one long cascade of hot, smoking brass. It was a sea of spent bullet cases down there, and I had to keep kicking them out of the way so as to maintain a good foothold. I could only imagine that our wagon was getting riddled with enemy fire, but the noise from the Gimpy, plus that of the 50-cal thumping above my head, was so deafening that I couldn't tell where we were getting smashed.

I was on my feet ramping the GPMG from side to side, those spent cartridges scrunching underfoot. Time had wound down to a slow, dragging, agonising loop, in which I figured I could all but see the bullets rocketing out of the barrel of my weapon. I was locked into the slowmo, adrenaline-fuelled, tunnel-vision of full-on combat, where a second seemed to last for a whole hour.

My mind felt crystal clear, as it processed sight, sound and smell at the speed of light, and with seemingly all the time in the world to do so. My brain pumped out a million thoughts a second, my body responding instantly to each one: *threat; target; fire; threat; target; fire; threat; target; fire; threat; target; threat; target – FIRE!*

My shoulder muscles were burning from the pain and tension of swinging the weapon from side to side, as I poured rounds into those targets. But as much as I might be smashing those enemy fighters, the fire against us just kept coming. I saw this wave of bullets slamming into the road right in the path of our vehicle, and ricocheting high into the air. I could feel the harsh jab of the shockwave punching over us. I was half-blinded by the tracer flaring like an angry bonfire right before our wheels.

I was used to seeing and hearing tracer on exercises, but I'd never known anything like this. It was like we were driving into the heart of a volcano of solid fire. I sensed the bullets tearing metal all around me, and punching into steel. I figured they were making mincemeat out of the Pinkie, and I just prayed that she fucking kept moving. *We stop here, we're instantly dead.*

And then it just got worse.

High on the ridge, a good 800 metres away, was the silhouette

Above Our arrival in Kuwait by C130, several weeks prior to the war in Iraq starting, as the advance British contingent. I'm standing second from right. Small teams of Pathfinders like us were kept well away from the prying lenses of the media, who were soon to descend on Kuwait in droves.

Below Kuwait, March 2003, making preparations for our move into Iraq. Note all vehicle-mounted machine guns are in dust covers, to protect them from sandstorms. I'm to the right of the photo, along with the five fellow members of my patrol, call-sign *Mayhem Three Zero*: Steve, Tricky, Dez, Jase and Joe.

Right Just prior to crossing into Iraq, March 2003. All weapons uncovered and ready to rumble.

Above Pushing deeper into Iraq, there was almost zero cover provided by the flat desert terrain. My patrol was tasked to drive some 300 kilometres through such terrain to reach an airfield deep behind enemy lines. As Sod's law would have it, once we set out temperatures plummeted and snow and sleet began to fall.

Below The Euphrates bridge at Nasiriyah, the front-line of American forces in the war. Thick palm groves and rivers meant that this was difficult ground to cross. Nasiriyah became the focal point for the Iraqi resistance, and the battle to take the city became known as the 'battle that America nearly lost'.

Top We sported *shemaghs* (Arab headscarves) to help disguise us as locals and wore a personal choice of uniform and kit culled from half of the militaries around the world. Driving at night with Night Vision Goggles, our aim was to slip by Iraqi positions unnoticed.

Centre The cut-down Land Rovers we used on the Iraq mission were nicknamed 'Pinkies'. Ever since David Stirling's SAS ran riot amongst German commander Erwin Rommel's forces in the North Africa desert, pink has been the colour of choice for British Special Forces desert vehicles.

Below Two Pathfinder Pinkies using a wadi – a dry, seasonal riverbed – as a Lie-up Point (LUP) in which to hide from the enemy. Two vehicles, each carrying three men – a driver and two gunners – is the basic Pathfinder patrol unit.

The Iraqi Fedayeen – a militia fiercely loyal to Saddam Hussein – were a mobile, irregular, and very well-armed hunter force.

The intelligence we were given prior to our mission proved hopelessly wrong: whilst we were told the area we had to penetrate was relatively benign – devoid of enemy – it was actually teeming with hundreds of Fedayeen and thousands of other hostile forces including Iraqi Republican Guard, the Iraqi SSO (the feared Secret Police), and regular troops. Many of these units were preparing to fight their last stand in Iraq, for if Saddam's regime fell these people would lose their stranglehold on power.

Above My patrol, *Mayhem Three Zero*, passed through scores of Iraqi positions undetected before the enemy finally had us surrounded. As ferocious battle was joined, Tricky, the rear gunner on my vehicle, used the heavy .50-calibre machine gun to smash through the walls of enemy bunkers and to tear apart their vehicles.

Centre We were outnumbered several hundred to one, but at least we had a serious amount of firepower. On the three Pinkies we had a .50-calibre heavy machine gun (like the one pictured here), five trusted General Purpose Machine Guns (GPMGs), rocket-launchers, personal assault rifles, pistols, and a whole stack of grenades.

Right We train relentlessly for mobile operations and firing accurately from fast-moving vehicles – one of the hardest of combat skills to master – and it was that expertise that kept us alive during hours and hours of full-on combat.

Left Yours truly, in the 'local' gear that we wore in Iraq.

Below Having a much-needed scoff and a brew back at the American front line the morning after our patrol finally fought its way through a series of massive Iraqi ambushes. Steve was the Pathfinder's armourer, and he managed to lob a grenade one-handed into an enemy bunker whilst he was driving through a murderous ambush. Tricky is setting up comms in the background. He was the .50-calibre gunner on my wagon, and more than once on this mission saved my life.

Right Myself, on stretcher and oxygen, having been Casevaced from Iraq into a field hospital in Kuwait. My patrol had been on our second night mission when our Pinkie rolled down a ravine. It was a miracle that I had been pulled out of it alive.

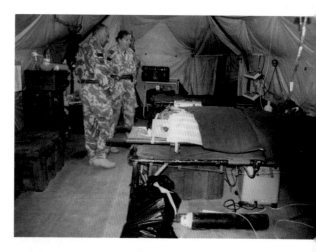

Above My military medals. From left to right; Kosovo, Northern Ireland, Sierra Leone, Afghanistan, Iraq, Queens Jubilee.

Right Myself, with HRH Prince Charles, the Colonel-in-Chief of the Parachute regiment, at Copehill Down Urban Warfare Training Centre, on Salisbury Plain. I'm briefing him on an 'urban warfare' demonstration – fighting through built-up areas.

BIRKHALL

6th April, 2003

dear Jane

I heard of the terrible accident that befell you in Iraq and just wanted to write and send you my very best wishes for a speedy recovery. I am relieved to hear that you should be able to leave hospital soon.

My spies also tell me you had a narrow escape from a carefully aimed Iraqi bullet, just the other day before your crash and that you were saved only by a lucky pair of trousers! The good Lord is obviously still smiling on you...! I hope that, despite your setbacks, you remain in good spirits and that the enclosed "medicine" might help to raise them a bit...

I know you will be desperate to rejoin your comrades in the Pathfinder Platoon as soon as you can but, in the meantime, I hope you are able to enjoy some time for recuperation with your family.

Yours most sincerely

Charles

The letter HRH Prince Charles wrote to me after I was injured. He refers to me being shot through my trousers by a 'carefully aimed Iraqi bullet', which happened during our mission to seize Qalat Sikar airfield. The 'medicine' he mentions sending me is a bottle of whisky from his personal cellars.

of something truly terrifying. There was this big, multi-barrelled weapon swinging towards us – the kind of thing that should be pointed at the sky, to bring down allied warplanes. Instead, it was being depressed to its lowest trajectory so its four gaping barrels could point right at our vehicles.

The muzzles reached horizontal, and then they started to throw out long gouts of flame, one after the other after the other. Rhythmically: 'Kaboom! Kaboom! Kaboom! Kaboom! Kaboom!' Big, long dirty spurts of smoke accompanied each burst, as if the squat, ugly weapon was some kind of primeval monster that ate and vomited smoke and fire.

It had to be a ZPU-4 or something similar. The ZPU-4 is a towed, quadruple-barrelled anti-aircraft weapon, which throws out a devastating barrage of 14.5 mm armour-piercing shells. It is accurate up to 2000 metres when used against ground targets. We were well within its range. If it hit us, it'd shred us.

I aimed in on the ridgeline where those four muzzles were spouting smoke and fire, and I sprayed and prayed. Rounds from the GPMG groped towards the target, but 800 metres is approaching the limit of the Gimpy's accurate range, and it was like a duel to the death between me and the ZPU's gun crew.

I saw rounds from the ZPU tearing into a palm grove just ahead of us, ripping trunks in two as if a giant chainsaw was going to work in there. I figured the ZPU gunners were over-compensating for the speed of our wagon, and firing just a fraction too far to the front of us. But they wouldn't keep doing so for very long. Sooner or later they'd adjust the fall of their fire, and nail us.

I held the GPMG steady, readjusted my aim to account for the distance, and saw my first bullets tear into the four-wheeled weapon. Rounds went sparking off the metal armour, ricocheting high into the dark night sky, and I knew that I'd found my target. I kept my finger hard on the trigger and poured in the fire.

Just at that moment I felt something punch into my leg with a frightening power and violence. It was at the level of my left ankle, so on the side of the enemy guns. With all the weight of fire slamming into us, I guessed it was inevitable that someone on my wagon would take a bullet. We'd probably got wounded blokes up and down the vehicles. And now it was me that had taken a hit.

I tried putting all my weight on the left leg, but I had to be so high on adrenaline that I couldn't feel the pain. I just hoped that it wasn't a round from the ZPU, or it'd be my foot and half my leg that was gone. For an instant I wondered if that was it for me: that I'd be hobbling around for the rest of my life on one peg. Would I ever be able to lead my daughter down the aisle? That's if I lived to have kids of my own...

Either way, I forced myself to ignore whatever injury I'd taken, and keep my weapon churning out the rounds. I'd deal with it later, that's if we ever got out of this shitfight. Through the stark metal sights of the Gimpy I saw figures bailing out of the sandbagged gun emplacement to either side of the ZPU. I followed them with the steel 'V' of the weapon, finger hard on the trigger, and I saw them stumbling and going down hard.

The four-barrelled monster had stopped spitting its lethal, 14.5 mm rounds at us. Finally, unbelievably, we shot out of the far side of the ambush. I could barely believe that we were still moving, and that I was still on my feet and alive. I risked a glance away from my weapon, and I could see Tricky hunched over the 50-cal covering the rear, and Steve hard on the steering wheel.

Steve had been 100 per cent focused on the road, and he'd not once been able to return fire. Being the driver meant that you were prevented from being able to use a weapon to defend yourself, which must have been a totally fucking horrific way to go to war. I saw Steve lift his one hand from the steering wheel and punch high into the air.

He let out this crazed yelp. 'YEAAAHHHH! WE MADE IT! YEAAAH-HHH! DAVE! DAVE! THIS IS FUCKIN' MEGA!'

It was wildly inappropriate what he'd just said – *This is fucking mega!* – but somehow it felt just right. Steve was a total pro, and I couldn't imagine how fucked up it was to have his job – to have to drive through that wall of death, and not be able to lift his weapon and fight – so why not enjoy it now and let rip?

As we sped away from the kill zone Steve was grinning and laughing like a lunatic, and he kept punching the steering wheel in sheer exhilaration. I knew exactly how he was feeling. He was on the pure, incomparable adrenaline high of not getting killed. *Not yet, anyway.*

No one was kidding themselves that this was all over. We were 35 kilometres south of our turn-around point: less than halfway back to the American front line. The truth was we'd got the majority of the death run still in front of us.

It was now that I remembered my injured leg. On previous ops in Sierra Leone and the Balkans I'd seen what horrific damage even a small-calibre round can do to the human body. A 7.62 mm short – the standard AK47 round – hits human flesh at a velocity of 715 metres per second. The bullet ricochets off bone, and rips an erratic course through the body, tearing a ragged exit hole as it leaves.

Fearing the worst, I reached down and felt around my ankle gingerly. The first surprise was that the drawstring of my combats seemed to be undone, leaving them hanging loose over my boot. It was an old habit from PARA Regiment days that I never left my combats unfastened.

I fumbled underneath, trying to find where the bullet had hit. I was sure that my fingers would meet blood, pulverised flesh and shattered bone. But I couldn't seem to feel any damage. No slick of blood. Nothing. I lifted my hand to my face to check. There was no sign of any warm sticky liquid, but it was pitch dark so maybe I'd missed it.

I checked the Pinkie's floor for anywhere a pool of blood would have congealed, but it was thick with bullet cases. I touched my hand to my face, and my lips, but all I could taste was the barest hint of blood. There was just the faintest smear of red on one of my fingers. I knew for sure that I'd been shot. I'd felt the fucking impact. I couldn't understand what had happened. *Where was all the damage and the carnage?*

There was bugger all that I could do about it now. We pressed onwards, Steve gunning the heavily-laden Land Rover, and all of us praying that the vehicle's battle damage wasn't terminal.

In the empty, windswept silence of the night I found my mind wandering. The PF exists as a recce force to prove what's on the ground in enemy territory. We'd done that. It was clear now how totally, hopelessly wrong some idiot had got the intel picture here. *Relatively benign it was not.*

A great deal of our intel had come down from the Americans, and we'd already seen the mess they'd made of predicting Nasiriyah. I didn't blame the Yanks though. As far as I was concerned we were all in this together. The US Marine Corps and the nine of us just happened to be at the harsher and brutal end of things.

If it wasn't for the Yanks, we'd probably be left without any sat photos or proper mapping at all. Nevertheless, the intel picture had proven a total fuck-up. The Marine Corps had expected to face minimal resistance in Nasiriyah. In reality, thousands of Iraqi regular forces and Fedayeen had converged upon that city for the mother of all battles.

And tonight, we'd blundered into the heart of them.

We pushed on for a good 10 kilometres on an open, deserted road. With every turn of the wheels I could feel my heart thumping in my chest, as the adrenaline coursed through my veins. There wasn't a sniff of the enemy anywhere, but it was pretty obvious that sooner or later our luck was going to have to run out. It always does for everyone some day.

Yet right now I was feeling pretty indestructible. You could almost say *bulletproof.* Whatever round it was that had punched into my left leg, it seemed to have bounced right off of me. *Incredible.*

As we thundered onwards the first lines of the poem 'Invictus' – Latin for 'undefeated' or 'invincible' – came into my mind. Almost without noticing, I found myself mouthing those words into the dark void of the Iraqi night.

Out of the night that covers me.
Black as the pit from pole to pole.
I thank whatever gods may be,
For my unconquerable soul.

That last line was whipped away by the vehicle's slipstream. But just as I'd uttered it, I'd heard a voice echoing mine, or at least I thought I had. From out of the corner of my eye I fancied that it was Steve, and that he'd started to mouth the immortal lines of the second verse

In the fell clutch of circumstance,
I have not winced nor cried aloud.
Under the bludgeonings of chance,
My head is bloody, but unbowed.

I figured I caught a third voice joining us now – Tricky, from the wagon's rear – as together we hammered out verse three, and moved into the enduring final lines.

It matters not how strait the gate,
How charged with punishments the scroll.
I am the master of my fate:
I am the captain of my soul.

Those final words were torn out of my mouth by the wind, yet still they sent a shiver up my spine. Or maybe in the heightened, trance-like state of combat that I was now in – the red mist of battle all around us – I'd just imagined it all. Who knows?

Either way, reliving those lines had taken me back to the warm familiarity of the PF Interest Room, and my very first day in the Pathfinders. As soon as I'd stepped into the Interest Room, the difference between this and any other unit that I'd served with had hit me in the face. Here, there were men of all ranks sharing a brew and a chat together, as equals.

I guess the closest analogy to the Interest Room would be a common room at school or college. It was in the Interest Room that the men of the unit gathered, to socialise and share the essence of the Pathfinders' unique *esprit de corps*. As I'd glanced around the room I'd spotted the glory wall, which displayed the mug-shots of those who'd died on past PF operations, and the mementoes brought back from the furthest theatres of war. Finally, my eyes had come to rest on a framed poem, one of several hanging on the wall. They were ones that individuals from the PF had gifted to the unit when leaving, often to move on to the SAS.

The poem that drew my eye was by someone that I'd never heard of before, William Ernest Henley, and it was entitled *Invictus*. In between getting introduced to various members of the PF, I'd read and re-read those lines: '*Out of the night that covers me …*' I'd sense in them the defining feature of this unit that I had fought so hard to be a part of. It was a unit defined by an individualistic, maverick bravery and cunning, and a singular determination to win through.

And it was defined by the kind of action we were now involved in, wherein a small group of determined men could face death together, *bloodied but unbowed*.

CHAPTER TWENTY-FOUR

'd glanced around the PF Interest Room, and I'd realised then that I'd never seen a group of soldiers with such a tight-knit sense of purpose, or who were so relaxed in their own skins. These were guys who'd spend nine months of the year away from barracks, on PF training and exercises. And then, during their weekends off, they'd volunteer to go do some extra HAHO or HALO jumping, just to keep it knife-sharp.

But in spite of the confidence that shone out of them, there was real humility too. There was a lack of arrogance and bullshit that was palpable. It was around then that Tricky had asked me the million-dollar question.

'Dave,' he'd said, 'if you cut a Pathfinder's legs off is he still a Path-finder?'

I told Tricky that I reckoned he was.

'You're right,' said Tricky. 'He is. He can't walk at 6 klicks an hour for 60 kilometres, but he's still got the Pathfinder's state of mind.'

It was David Stirling who'd first said of SF selection that most people failed themselves. They failed themselves due to their lack of self-belief: they just didn't believe strongly enough that they were good enough. Yet a good number also failed themselves due to over-confidence bordering upon self-delusion. They'd never had the humility to make it through. For sure, it was a hard balance to get right. I didn't know if I'd always managed to do so, but

I hoped at least on this mission I was getting there.

I understood now what it meant to experience the ultimate thrill of combat, whilst standing shoulder to shoulder with men like these. More than likely, we were all going to die on this mission. In the wagons up front we may already have lost some. I couldn't but think that we had some seriously injured. But I wouldn't want to be anywhere other than in this battle with these blokes, fighting for our lives.

If against all odds we did make it out of this alive, I would try to do better. I'd try never to hassle Steve because of his crappy jokes. I'd try to stop teasing Dez over his bone questions, and Tricky for forgetting his wet weather gear. I'd never think the worse of Joe because of his youth, and I'd forgive the Recce blokes for not knowing how to change a tyre.

But most of all, I'd never again look askance at Jason because of his insecurity, or his dour ways. We were the team. *We were the team that I'd always been searching for.* I was privileged to be amongst them.

As all these thoughts were rushing through my mind, tumbling over each other to be heard, we had pushed a good 10 kilometres past the roadblock-cum-ambush. But I could feel the tension rising again now, like a vice gripping the pit of my guts. I could feel it pressing down upon Steve and Tricky, like something dark and suffocating that I could almost see and touch.

We knew another attack was coming. We could sense it, animal-like, instinctively. In the ferocity of battle, when soldiers face all but certain death, their sixth sense is said to reach a hugely heightened state. I guessed that was what we were experiencing now – the ability to sense the enemy, and to know when the bullets were coming. And it was the wait – the unbearable tension of anticipation – that was killing us.

It was almost as if we were willing the next attack to come. Almost as if it was easier to fight, than to be poised and waiting and dying for the next battle to start.

'Where the fuck are the enemy! Fucking bring it on! Come and hit us!'

I didn't know whether I'd actually yelled those words out loud, or if they were just screaming inside my head. In a sense it didn't matter. I knew the lads had heard them, and that their minds were screaming out exactly the same kind of challenge.

This time, I saw them before they hit us.

I can't explain how, apart from it being the unknowable power of the sixth sense. Something – something beyond human understanding – directed my eyes to exactly where the Iraqis were waiting in hiding to smash our patrol. And in the moment that I saw them I ramped the Gimpy around and opened fire, my screamed words of warning drowned out by the flaming roar of its muzzle.

'AMBUSH 11 O'CLOCK!'

The darkness ahead of us erupted into fire. There were three hidden bunkers right by the roadside. I could see them more clearly now, the enemy faces being illuminated by the harsh yellow-white thrown off by their muzzle flashes. They were hammering rounds into our lead wagon, ripping them across Jason's exposed flank, then back towards the Recce vehicle. As they did so I felt myself burning up with this blinding rage. *They're trying to kill my fucking team!*

I aimed in with the GPMG, pouring fire at silhouettes of heads and shoulders, squirting ten-round bursts into each. I saw figures go down and bodies jerking under direct hits, as bullets tore into them. I swept the Gimpy left and re-aimed, and as I did so I saw this massive figure rear to his feet just to the front-side of our wagon. He'd appeared seemingly from nowhere and he was hefting the unmistakable form of an RPG-7.

The RPG-7 is the old faithful – unmissable, with its unmistakable bulbous warhead and flared exhaust. He'd got it on his shoulder, and he was pretty much on top of us. I swivelled the GPMG around as he levelled the tube, both of us racing to be the first to open fire.

As I did so, the words from a lecture I'd attended at Sandhurst flashed through my head. The speaker was a veteran of numerous battles against irregular forces, and he sure as hell had known his onions.

'Don't be fooled by its brute simplicity,' he'd announced, in this cut glass officer's accent. 'In the hands of a skilled operator the RPG-7 grenade launcher is a formidable weapon. It is rugged, easy to use and packs a lethal punch. It is one of the most common and brutally effective infantry weapons in contemporary conflict. Whether used against a US Black Hawk helicopter in Mogadishu, or a British Land Rover in Oman, it is the weapon of choice for many militia. It is a weapon for all seasons, and it will haunt the battlefields of tomorrow.'

No shit. Or how about the battlefields of today?

This operator wasn't going to need a great deal of skill: he was going to hit us at point blank range if I didn't get him first. I tried to swing the Gimpy's sights on to him, but he was too far to my left and beyond my arc of fire. I was screaming out a warning when the 50-cal from behind me thumped out a deafening burst. The bullets blasted the guy off his feet and hurled him backwards, but not before he'd unleashed the RPG.

There was the blinding yellow flash of the rocket motor firing right beside us. A millisecond later the grenade streaked across the wagon like some giant firework, barely inches from Steve and me. I felt the pressure wave punching into my face as it tore past, leaving a cloud of choking exhaust gases in its wake.

Steve wrenched the steering wheel to one side, the sharp swerve made by the wagon almost throwing me off my feet. I figured the smack of the RPG-7's shock wave must have thrown him. But then he reached forwards with his one free hand, the other still gripping the wheel, and grabbed for a grenade. An instant later he'd torn the pin out with his teeth, and was lobbing the grenade forwards and to the left-hand side of the road.

'FUCKING GRENADE!'

I didn't have a clue what his target was. I followed the trajectory of Steve's throw with my gunsights, and the grenade landed just in front and to the side of us. There was a fourth and final bunker position at the very roadside – more like a small, sandbagged checkpoint

– but I'd been so focused on smashing the RPG gunner that I'd completely missed it. I hadn't even realised it was there.

The grenade curved in gracefully under the sandbagged roof. First there was the blinding flash of the detonation, and then a blast-wave of shrapnel tore through the position. The roof lifted slightly, bodies were thrown into the air, and a thick cloud of choking smoke billowed out of the open sides. An instant later the heavy, sandbagged roof collapsed in on itself, crushing the bunker's occupants.

A few seconds later we were speeding past that last enemy position, and out of the other side. As we powered ahead the surviving enemy fighters fired off wild bursts into the darkness behind us, but we were fleeing invisible into the black embrace of the night. We were through ambush number three. *Fucking unbelievable. How on earth had they failed to nail us?*

In the PF we have an expression: *to use The Force.* Of course, it's a piss-take from the Jedi Warriors in the movie *Star Wars*, but it still encapsulates much of the ethos of the unit. If you opened up your mind to your soldier's sixth sense, it could enable you to win through the seemingly unwinnable. We had sensed the enemy threat, and that had enabled us to get the drop on them. That was using The Force, and maybe it was that which had saved us.

We pressed onwards, but by now Jason was pushing his wagon to the very limits. Steve increased his speed to keep with him, and soon the convoy was careering along at pushing 100 kph. I kept wondering what it was that had made Dez put pedal to the metal. Maybe they had someone badly wounded, and bleeding out. Maybe it had become a race to get to the American front lines to save him. Or maybe it was the Engineer Recce wagon that had taken the casualties. With no comms between vehicles I had no way of knowing. All I did know was that their wagons, like our own, must have taken an unbelievable hammering.

Steve was wrestling with the steering wheel as the heavily-laden rear of the wagon kept trying to overtake the speeding front, and send us into a horrible, careering tailspin. The only way to drive a Pinkie this heavy in any safety was to do so slowly. It didn't matter greatly that you had four-wheel drive. It didn't make it safe. Whether you were on snow or ice or hard, dry tarmac as we were now, if two of your wheels lost traction you might as well be driving a Nissan Micra.

I kept checking for any sign of the Fedayeen hunter force. Maybe they were catching us, and that was what had made Jason go for maximum speed. But there was no sign of any lights anywhere to our rear. Unless the Fedayeen were like us, driving on black light, they'd got to be way behind us still.

I slapped a third 200-round belt of ammo into the breach of the GPMG. Two boxes down, four to go, including the belt now on the weapon. I figured I was doing fine on the ammunition front. The real miracle was how all three of the wagons were still apparently drive-able. *Or maybe I'd spoken too soon.*

Up ahead, Jason's vehicle began to slow noticeably. From career-ing along at 100 kph Dez decelerated the lead Pinkie to little more than a crawl, using the gears to break the wagon's momentum more than he did the brakes. It was the quietest way to bring a wagon from high speed to a dead slow, for the brakes would emit loud piercing squeals and squeaks.

The Recce wagon slowed in turn, and we slowed with it, and all the while I was wondering what the fuck was the problem with the lead wagon. If we lost one vehicle we could cross-deck Joe, Dez and Jase on to the other two. But if we lost two wagons, we either split the patrol so one wagon carried on alone, or we abandoned the vehicles. That would leave the nine of us on foot and depleted of our heavy firepower, and with the enemy knowing pretty much where we were.

I figured we'd got around 25 kilometres to go before we hit the US front line positions, and no way did I want to be losing the wagons at this juncture. We were creeping along at less than 10 kph, and I had no idea what the hold-up might be. I was dying to get us moving again, for I could almost sense the Fedayeen hunter force breathing down our necks.

I kept scanning my arcs to the east and the south. On the horizon I figured I could just make out the warm, domed-orange halo of street lamps – what had to be Nasiriyah city. It was like an impossible promise of hope. I told myself that we weren't there yet. Nasiriyah might as well be a whole world away.

And then I saw it – the reason why Jason had slowed to a dead crawl. Outlined against the faint orange glow of the city there was what had to be yet another Iraqi army base. I could see vehicles parked up in formation, plus here and there a figure standing sentry and silhouetted against the night sky. Jason must have sensed the enemy position first – *he was using The Force* – hence slowing the convoy.

No one had opened fire yet, or called out a challenge, and Jason had to be trying to sneak past undetected. We crept forwards at 5 kph, tyres humming gently on the road, engines purring softly. I saw a momentary flare in the darkness, but it was only the spark of a match. It was followed by a faint, glowing pinprick of light, as an Iraqi soldier drew in a deep lung-full of smoke and nicotine.

I was dying for a cigarette myself. The Iraqi soldier was almost close enough for me to reach out and grab one. At that moment our wagon hit an unseen bump in the road, and one of the sand ladders banged against the wagon's metal side. The body panels of the Land Rover being aluminium, as opposed to steel, the ladder made a soft, dull, muffled thud, as opposed to a clang. Still, in the harsh stillness of the night it felt to us like a powerful drumbeat. *Booooom!*

I had my gunsights glued to that smoking soldier. I held my breath, as if merely by breathing I could alert him to our presence here on the road. I was praying that none of the Iraqi sentries had heard the thump of that sand ladder, or if they had that they wouldn't recognise it as the noise of a passing vehicle.

We crept past that enemy position without a shot being fired, and with no challenge in Arabic ringing out in the darkness. It was a fucking miracle that we'd done so. We hit open, empty terrain and gradually we picked up speed again. We thundered south, desperate to eat up the miles.

Up ahead, for whatever reason, Jason suddenly flicked on his vehicle's headlights. I saw the driver of the Recce wagon follow suit. After operating for so long on black light it seemed weird and wrong – shocking almost – to be able to see the leading Pinkies. I turned to Steve, and raised a questioning eyebrow.

'Are we nearly there yet?' he quipped, reaching forwards to flick on our own headlights. 'I guess we are … And that's why Jase's putting the fucking lights on, to warn the Yanks we're coming in.'

I felt this rush of excitement. 'What else can it be, mate?'

Steve grinned. 'Dave, I have never loved the US Marine Corps as much as I do right now!'

I grinned back at him. 'First shaven-headed grunt I see I'm going to hug and fucking kiss him!'

Jason's vehicle slowed. I saw it start to make a sharp turn east. I took it he was going off-road, in which case I guessed we had to be facing a major roadblock. Maybe the Americans had moved forward during the hours of darkness, and set up a new front line position here on the road. Maybe Jase was trying to get past their most-forward – and potentially trigger-happy – troops so we could come in to some more relaxed, and hopefully less lethal, Yank positions.

But it was nothing of the sort. As Jason's wagon turned I spotted two bunkers to the right-hand side of the road, and a dark, sinister-looking building behind them. All of a sudden I knew exactly where we were. This was the first compound that we had driven past after we had left the US front line, in which we had seen our first Iraqi soldiers.

We were at the T-junction on the northern edge of Nasiriyah itself. *I couldn't believe that we were this close.* But in the wash of Jason's headlights I could see now that this was no ordinary compound. It was like a bloody great big fortress, with watchtowers and bunkers and sangars (temporary fortifications) all over the place.

Groups of Iraqi soldiers were positioned within each of them, and Jase had to be trying to bluff his way past, headlights-on.

CHAPTER TWENTY-FIVE

The lead Pinkie was side-on to the bunkers, and Jason couldn't use his GPMG, because Dez was directly in his line of fire. They'd almost made it past when one of the figures in the nearest bunker yelled out a warning in Arabic. He must have realised who it was that was trying to sneak past. An instant later the first AK47 opened up on Jason's wagon, with a dozen more following suit.

Joe sparked up his machine gun and began thumping rounds into the bunkers to the side of them. I saw Jase swing the Gimpy around but he couldn't bring it to bear. We couldn't provide covering fire, for fear of hitting Jase's vehicle by mistake. For a moment I was convinced that they were going to get hammered, and then I saw Dez lift his pistol from the dash. The next moment he was firing it one-handed into the bunker, whilst ramping the wagon around with the other.

It was like a scene from some Wild West movie. I couldn't believe it was for real. Dez emptied what looked like a whole 13-round Browning mag into the enemy bunker, and then they were through. Normally, you'd use your pistol for close-quarter combat on foot. One thing we'd never ever drilled for was firing a 13-round Browning handheld from a speeding vehicle! The Pinkies were bristling with machine guns on state-of-the-art pivots, so in theory you'd never need to use a pistol.

An instant after Dez had unloaded with the Browning the Engineer

Recce guys started malleting the bunkers, and both wagons were speeding past. It didn't matter any more how many showers Dez might have had during his time in PF, he was the fucking boy now. In spite of being the driver, he'd got his moment of glory, and what a Hollywood moment it was.

We were last in line, and as we headed towards the enemy positions I opened up with the trusted Gimpy. I saw bodies blasted backwards, as a whirlwind of lead pounded into the enemy position. When we went to make the turn, I couldn't use the GPMG any more, because Steve was in my line of fire. I gazed into the last bunker half expecting to get smashed by Iraqi fire, but all I saw was a heap of bloodied bodies. The occupants of that position had been torn to pieces, and they weren't about to do us any damage any time soon.

Muzzles sparked from windows set back in the darkened building, but they were a good distance away. In no time Steve had made the turn, and we were speeding away from them. Steve leaned forwards, clicked off the headlamps, and put pedal to the metal, the night-dark terrain swallowing us. Just another few kilometres and we'd be there, at the American front line.

Some instinct made me glance behind. Suddenly, I realised there was no Tricky. The 50-cal was swinging around in its turret completely unmanned. *Fucking Tricky's gone!* For an instant my heart stopped beating. I was gripped by this all-consuming panic. We were a man down and we didn't know where we'd fucking lost him!

I started yelling, my voice cracking with panic: 'TRICKY! TRICKY! WHERE THE FUCK'S TRICKY?'

I had visions of us having to turn the wagon around and go back the way we'd come. Either Tricky had been hit at that last enemy position, or he'd somehow tumbled out of the wagon as Steve had made the turn at the T-junction. Whichever, there was no way in a million years that we were ever leaving Tricky.

Steve clocked where I was looking, and then he started yelling too. 'Tricky! Tricky! WHERE'S HE FUCKING GONE?'

All of a sudden a head popped up from behind the big machine gun. Tricky kind of rolled his eyes at us. Grinned this dead cool smile.

'What's all the flap, lads? I was just changing the ammo box on the 50-cal.'

Steve and I cracked up laughing, but it was mostly with relief. He and I exchanged a sheepish glance. For a moment there we'd both been close to losing it. Tricky was the picture of unruffled calm. It was like the last few hours of full-on combat were no big deal, like he'd done it all a thousand times before.

The moment of lightness passed, for now we were approaching the Marine Corps' front line positions. We knew well the state of the Marines stationed here: they were pretty much exhausted; they'd lost a lot of their guys; they were thirsting for revenge. And worst of all, as far as we were concerned, they were maxed up to the eyeballs with some serious firepower.

I looked front and saw Jason's wagon pulling over into the darkness by the roadside. I saw his hazard lights blink on, off, on, off. A couple of American Bradley Infantry Fighting Vehicles loomed out of the distant gloom. As we pulled over behind the Recce wagon, I couldn't help but remember the friendly fire incident that had torn apart the marines of Charlie Company, during the previous day's fighting.

The A10 tankbuster ground-attack aircraft had pounded Charlie Company's armour with their fearsome, seven-barrelled 30 mm GAU Avenger Gatling-type guns. One of the most powerful cannons ever flown, the GAU Avenger fires depleted uranium armour-piercing shells, and Charlie Company's AAVs had barely stood a chance.

The Bradleys up ahead of us were packing a cannon of only a slightly smaller calibre – an M242 25 mm chain gun – one capable of taking out Iraqi T55 main battle tanks. Crossing back across our own front line could well prove the most dangerous moment of the death run so far. If we got opened up on by those Bradleys, we were toast.

We stripped off our shemaghs, and buttoned up and smartened ourselves as best we could. We were dropping the Iraqi disguise, and trying to make like 'proper' soldiers. I grabbed an IR Firefly from out of my webbing, switched it on and placed it in front of me on the bonnet. Anyone using NVG would now be able to see it flashing away, and should recognise that as a signal that we were friendly forces.

We closed up the space between the vehicles, lowered all the weapons, and Jason moved off. With our hazard lights flashing we crawled towards the US front line position, marked by the Bradleys forming a block across the road. As we drew ever closer my heart was beating like it was going to burst. We'd fought our way through some 200 kilometres of enemy terrain. How ironic would it be to have run a series of massive ambushes, evaded hunter convoys, and smashed the enemy's roadblocks, only to be blown away by our own side?

As we crawled closer to the Bradleys, Dez started honking the horn – Peep! Peep! Peep-peep! Peep! Peeeeep! Peeeeep! *The Brits are coming through.* The Recce wagon's driver and Steve started doing likewise. It struck me as being vaguely ridiculous, the six of us doing this whilst sandwiched between two armies that had been tearing each other's throats out. But what other option did we have?

There wasn't the slightest response from the Bradleys. We presumed they had to be occupied, but not a soldier there seemed to see us or hear us, or acknowledge our approach. We reached the two hulking great armoured vehicles, and drove through apparently unseen. On the US front line, in the aftermath of the battle for Nasiriyah, we'd managed to slip through whatever Marine Corps sentries had been posted here, without being challenged.

We pressed on at a crawl until we reached the area where I figured the US command post was situated – the last Americans that we had spoken to before commencing the mission of a lifetime. Then we cut the engines.

We bailed out of the wagons. For a moment we were standing there in stunned silence, staring at each other in complete disbelief. And then I grabbed Steve and I was hugging him, and Tricky was bear-hugging both of us, and we were practically dancing with joy. We simply couldn't believe it. *Fucking hell! We'd made it out of there alive!*

There were serious man-hugs going on all around, and this really wasn't us. Pathfinders, PARAs, whatever unit we hailed from – we didn't generally go in for man-hugs. But today, after the death run south from Qalat Sikar, all that had changed. All our macho attitude and bravado had gone out of the window.

Because, fucking hell, we were alive!

I pulled out our Thuraya satphone, part of our lost comms kit. It's an open, insecure means, and so we'd only ever use it as a last resort, if all other comms were gone. It was the kind of thing that we'd use to call in a CSAR helo, if we were about to get captured or killed. The satphone was about as easy to intercept as your average mobile phone signal. But that didn't particularly matter now that we were in amongst the American lines. My first responsibility had to be to report in to PF HQ.

As I was waiting for the call to go through, I spotted a couple of US marines wandering over to stare at us. It was like they couldn't get their heads around where the nine of us had just appeared from. I guess it was fair enough really. It was pushing 0300 hours, and we'd just emerged from the darkness of the night with our vehicles half torn to pieces by enemy gunfire. And there we were hugging each other like a bunch of schoolgirls.

I spoke to the Pathfinders' signaller and gave him the good news: 'This is *Mayhem Three Zero:* urgent sitrep for *Sunray.* Patrol is back in friendly lines and with no serious casualties. Will send locstat and further details once we have comms on secure means.'

I was speaking on insecure comms, so I couldn't afford to say any more than that short message. I'd yet to check what injuries the blokes might have, but I could see from the way the nine of us were celebrating that no one had lost any limbs, or was about to die out here.

I came off the line, and went to ask the nearest marine for a smoke. I felt ready to hoover up a whole packet of twenty in one long inhalation of sweet, calming *nicotine.* The marine passed me a ciggie, and cupped a lighted match in the palm of his hand. I took the light, and as I did so I realised that my hands were shaking. I inhaled, sucking in a first, deep, greedy drag. *Fucking paradise.*

The marine gave me this look. 'Uh, say buddy, where did you guys just come from?'

I pointed north. *Out there.*

He stared at me, like it didn't compute.

I was past caring.

The lads gathered as we shared around the smokes. Tricky, Steve, Joe, plus Ian, Simon and Stephen from the Recce wagon, sparked up. Jason was down on his knees by his Pinkie and rummaging in his grab bag. I knew instantly what he was after. He was searching for some scoff. I knew from experience that he didn't like to be disturbed when he was eating. God knows he'd earned the space to stuff his face fuller than a fat girl's shoes, if that was what he fancied doing right now.

Dez wandered over to join the smoking party. For an instant he looked a bit uncomfortable, kind of shifting from one foot to the other nervously, and then he said it.

'Tricky, mate, any chance of a drag?'

No one could quite believe it. We were speechless. We watched him take a couple of awkward puffs, then he was honking and coughing his guts up. He was jerking about like a guy riding one of those electric rodeo horses in an amusement arcade.

Tricky was crying with laughter. 'Yee-hah!' he gasped. 'Ride 'em, cowboy!'

'Yeah, we all saw your Hollywood moment on the Browning, mate,' Steve added, 'but you'll never make a proper cowboy if you can't handle a Marlboro!'

We'd all been in contacts before. All of us, even Joe. But none of us had ever known anything remotely like what we'd just been through. We'd been repeatedly ambushed far behind enemy lines, with thousands of hardcore Iraqi soldiers and Fedayeen trying to rip our heads off. We'd never expected to get back alive. And now here we were pissing ourselves laughing as Dez choked his lungs up over a Marlboro.

Jason chucked some food down his neck, and got a hexy stove

going for a brew. Whilst he was waiting for the water to boil, he pulled out his map. We spread it on the bonnet of his Land Rover. There was a sense of urgency about the two of us now, for there was work to be done. We started comparing notes, working out exactly where the main Iraqi positions were. We configured a series of six-figure grids. The biggest surprise was how close the last ambush point had been to the US front line. As the crow flies, it had to be less than a kilometre away.

I asked one of the marines for direction to his CP (Command Post). He pointed out a group of vehicles 300 metres to the east of us. As I started walking, I realised how totally and utterly exhausted I was. The adrenaline was pissing out of my veins now, to be replaced by a crushing, leaden fatigue. I made my way silently through the sleeping positions, and stepped inside the US command post. It was little more than some canvas sheeting strung between two Bradleys, but even at this hour the place was buzzing.

There was one figure that I recognised instantly. It was the Charlie Company CO. He stared at me like I was some kind of apparition. He'd got a couple of blokes on his shoulder, and they looked equally mystified.

'David, the British Pathfinder patrol,' I announced. 'Remember? We've been having a bit of fun north of here ...'

'Yeah, got ya.' He cracked a smile. 'Good to see it's not just us Americans gettin' down and dirty out there. So what's cookin?'

'Well, we've just been on a long drive north on Route 7, pretty much all the way to Qalat Sikar airfield. We hit a bit of trouble, and fought our way back again. I thought I should report to you what we found.'

The entire place had fallen silent. You could hear a pin drop. These guys made up the US Marine Corps' most forward positions in Iraq. They'd spent the day fighting for their lives in Nasiriyah and pretty much getting hammered. Then night had fallen and it all had gone quiet. But a little over an hour ago they'd have seen this massive shitfight erupt on the night-dark horizon to the north of them. Now

I'd walked in and told them that it had been the nine of us, fighting through the Iraqi lines in three open-topped Land Rovers.

'We got to within 40 clicks of the airfield,' I continue in a tired, but matter-of-fact way. 'We ended up being surrounded by the enemy, Iraqi regulars plus Fedayeen. There was no way of pushing further north, so we decided to head back the way we came. En route we were hit by a series of ambushes, each of which corresponds to a major Iraqi position.'

The marines had eyes like saucers. They clearly thought we were some kind of Mad Max bulletproof James Bond lunatics. Either that, or we were on some serious drugs. They couldn't seem to get their heads around the fact that we got that far north and back again, without getting annihilated. One of the guys passed me a brew, another some Hershey's chocolate. But mostly, they were staring at me in stunned silence.

'You advance any further from here, that's the force you're going to run into,' I told them. 'They're in good, dug-in and sandbagged defensive positions. They've got bunkers, trenches, rat-runs, the works. They're got light arms, HMGs, RPGs, some big four-barrelled anti-aircraft cannon and God only knows what else we didn't see. We figure that each of those positions corresponds to a company strength force, maybe more.'

I glanced at the major and his men, and I could read the thoughts in their eyes. This was some kind of nightmare. The battle for Nasiriyah was far from over: just ahead of them lay thousands more fighters, in well-camouflaged, well-constructed defensive positions, and they were clearly ready to rumble. In terms of numbers that Iraqi force – regular soldiers plus Fedayeen – was far larger than the force that had halted the Marine Corps in Nasiriyah, and had cost them so dear.

I figured it was time to give the major the good news. 'Whilst we failed to reach our mission objective, we did identify a shed load of Iraqi positions en route. We can provide you with a series of six-figure grids for each of those.'

I saw the major's face light up. We went into a huddle over the maps. I talked him through each ambush point, and gave him my best guess as to what the enemy strengths were in each. At ambush point one – the most northerly attack point – Jase and I had figured there was a battalion of Iraqi troops, plus the 200 men of the Fedayeen hunter force.

At the second ambush point we figured there had to be a further battalion. At ambush point three we reckoned there was a company. Then there was the company that never saw us, plus the ambush point at the T-junction, just north of Nasiriyah. All told, we figured that made some 2000 Iraqi infantry plus militia at a minimum, and probably a whole lot more.

Our estimates were based upon the volume of fire that rained down upon us from those positions, plus what we'd seen of the hardware. I told the Marine Corps major that those numbers were conservative. Those 2000 fighting men would have an equal number of logistics, signallers, and reserve troops in support.

'My take on this is that you've got to get air strikes on to those positions fast,' I told him. 'Hit them hard before you move forwards, and that'll clear the way for you guys.'

The major looked at me. Nodded. I saw this glow of excitement lighting up his tired eyes.

'You betcha, soldier,' he growled. 'You're damn right we will.'

With that he started barking orders. I sat there savouring my coffee – a fine cup of Starbucks homebrew – as his men went scurrying about, getting those co-ordinates reported up the chain via their radio net. It was one of the best brews I'd ever had in my life, and I drained it to the last. Then I headed back to the wagons, where I found the blokes getting ready to crash out on the deck, next to the trusted Pinkies.

To a man we were all totally done in. But before getting comatose, there was one more thing that had to be done. We needed to organise sentries, for if we could drive through the US front line completely undetected, so we figured could the enemy.

I was too wired to sleep, so I took the first stag along with Dez. As I stared out from the island of light that was Nasiriyah and into the darkness to the north of us, I said a short prayer. I was born and raised a Catholic, although I guessed I was pretty lapsed these days. Still, I took a quiet moment to thank my God that both I and all the blokes in my patrol were alive.

And I offered up an apology for only ever praying when I was in the shit, and in desperate need of help.

CHAPTER TWENTY-SIX

Apart from my stint on stag, I slept the sleep of total exhaustion. At first light we were all nine of us up, and locked and loaded for stand-to. No one was going back to sleep, so Tricky and Joe set up our 319 HF radio. Although Tricky had flushed the Crypto on the TACSAT and the VHF radio, we still had the HF system via which we could in theory send secure, text-type messages, but only when it chose to work.

Long-range HF comms are a nightmare to establish, and it was a shit piece of kit anyway. We managed to get a short text message back to PF HQ, or at least we hoped that it had gone through: 'Sitrep: enemy grids at 937584 ... Our grid with US forces at 738295. No casualties.'

We got a brew and a scoff on, and the sun rose fine and bright. In the clear desert light we started to notice stuff. I realised that the pull string on my left bottom trouser leg hadn't come undone: it was missing completely. I took a closer look, and noticed that there was a hole punched through the material. I checked the leg, and there was barely a graze.

I inspected the puncture marks more closely. They consisted of a circular entry and exit hole of the type a 7.62 mm round would make. Somehow, I'd been shot through my trousers but the bullet had missed my leg. As my hands felt around those bullet holes, I noticed how swollen they were. I had fingers like sausages. It must have been from the hours spent gripping a juddering GPMG, as I ramped it back and forth across the targets.

Fingers like sausages. I kind of smiled to myself: that phrase took me way back. I'd always associated it with Prince Charles, the colonel-in-chief of our Regiment. On the day that I was due to be commissioned into the Army Prince Charles was scheduled to have lunch with us on our Regimental table – the PARA Reg table. My mum, my dad and my sisters had come down for the ceremony, plus my nan and grandpa from Liverpool.

Grandpa had told me that he'd got to meet Prince Charles once, and if I ever got to shake his hand I was to get a good look at his fingers. They were like little sausages. I didn't get the chance just then, but I'd always remembered what Grandpa had said. A while later the Parachute Regiment was scheduled to receive new regimental colours, for after twenty-five years in service our flags were well battle-worn. As one of the youngest officers in the regiment, I was picked to receive the colours from Prince Charles. Afterwards, there was a dinner in the marquee, and I shook his hand and made conversation with him.

Prince Charles didn't do meaningless 'small talk'. He was focused and involved, and I admired him greatly. He struck me as being genuinely interested in who I was and what I had to say. We met once more when I was on operations in Kosovo, and the PARAs were first on to the ground in that war-torn country. He flew out to meet and greet us personally, and to lend his moral support to the campaign. I did get to have a good look at his fingers, and Grandpa was right. Prince Charles did have fingers a bit like sausages.

Grinning stupidly to myself at the memory, I did a quick check of my Bvlgari watch. There wasn't a scratch on it. The thing was fucking bulletproof. I went to fetch my grab bag from where it was hanging on the door of our battered Land Rover. I unhooked it, and took a good long look. The grab bag resembled a bloody sieve with all the bullet holes torn in it. Inside, even my brew kit was shot to pieces, which pissed me off no end because I couldn't make a brew any more.

There was one upside to all the battle damage. My sexy French girlfriend Isabelle's crappy future-world alien novel had taken a round clean through it. I figured I'd lucked out here. I'd take it to her when I got home, and it had to be worth the greatest shag of my life. *What better reason not to have got myself killed?*

I pulled out my Persol sunglasses from my smock pocket. They were smashed to pieces. It was hardly surprising, and my fault entirely. I'd not bothered to collapse them, or put them away in their hard, protective case. Hand-made they might be, but even they couldn't survive the kind of punishment I'd put them through, when ramping the GPMG back and forth. It was 200 quid down the drain, but a small cost to still be alive.

I retrieved the medical kit from my grab bag. There was a neat hole punched through the middle of my can of Savlon antiseptic spray. It was a perfect round hole blown clean through it. I held it up for Steve and Tricky to admire, shaking my head in amazement.

In response, Steve pointed out the fuse box in the Land Rover. It was a black plastic rectangle the size of a shoebox and it sat in the centre of the dash, between the driver and the passenger's knees. Right now it looked like a bloody great Swiss cheese. But it wasn't nice neat bullet holes that it was riddled with: it had great rents torn in it by what looked like chunks of shrapnel.

I turned to the other blokes: 'Fuck me, have you seen our vehicle?'

No one seemed particularly interested. They were all staring at their own wagons, and checking out their own kit, which was likewise shot to buggery. I heard Ian, the Engineer Recce sergeant, let out this low whistle of amazement. He held something up for all to see.

'Fucking check this out.'

Unlike us, Ian had carried his Browning 9 mm pistol strapped to his body in a chest holster. We PF blokes had ours strapped to our thighs. Ian's positioning of his pistol had been unbelievably fortunate, for it had quite simply saved his life. There was a big, fat ugly bullet embedded in the steel of the weapon. He rolled up his shirt, and there was a bloody great angry red and purple bruise spreading across his torso, where the pistol had taken the force of the round.

It was a sobering reminder of how we weren't bulletproof. We'd just been incredibly, insanely lucky.

Joe pointed to the 50-cal on the rear of Jason's wagon. 'Fuckin' take a look at that,' he muttered.

The circular, ring-like mount of the heavy machine gun was horribly bent and twisted, where it had been hammered by fire. When Joe had been pumping rounds into the enemy positions, they had been aiming in on the muzzle flash of his weapon. It was impossible to comprehend how the young lad could still be alive.

We were counting the numbers of bullet holes in the Pinkies, and taking bets on who had the most, when the distinctive form of a US Cobra attack helicopter came barrelling over the horizon. It circled once over the enemy position at the T-junction, just to the north of us, then gave it the good news. The Cobra plastered the target below with 30 mm cannon fire, flying strafe after strafe after strafe.

It was great to see the airpower coming in so quickly, to act on the intel that we'd provided. The Americans were bringing up the big guns. *Result.* We may have been prevented from JTACing in the warplanes, but this was the next best thing. It was our intel that had got this air strike in and bang on target.

A runner appeared from the Marine Corps Command Post. Charlie Company's OC wanted a quick word, if I was free. I wondered what was up. I strolled across to the CP. When I got there I was treated to this long, piercing look from him, one of awe mixed with disbelief. He offered me a brew – coffee again, being as he was an American – before getting down to business.

'We just got a recce flight over those co-ordinates you gave us north along Route 7,' he began. 'You guys are dead right: there are shit loads of Iraqi positions up there. But the aircrew says a lot of those Iraqi units have been smashed to fuck.' He paused. 'Just what the hell were you guys *doing* out there?'

I eyed him for a moment. I was unsure what to say. The truth would sound so totally absurd, so utterly far-fetched. *We were fighting for our lives. We thought we were all dead. Somehow, against all odds we made it through.* The truth just didn't add up, so I said nothing.

'I got it. Yeah.' He gave me a nod and a wink. *'Need-to-know, right?* No worries.'

I saw his eyes searching my combats for some indication of rank, or even the unit we hailed from. Of course, there was none.

'Captain,' I offered, as helpfully as I could. 'David. Pathfinder Captain.'

'Captain, Dave, Pathfinders, I want you to know this,' he announced, somewhat formally. 'Thanks to your intel we got air strikes racked up to go in all along the grids that you gave us. All along Route 7 there'll be US F15 fast jets, Cobra gunships, A10 ground attack aircraft and other warplanes giving those positions a seriously good hosin'. And Captain, we got you guys to thank for that. Hoooo-ahhh!'

I'd spent a deal of time with US Marine Corps types before, and I was used to their 'hooo-aahhhing'. It might sound strange to us, but it was their equivalent of 'Yes, sir!' We chatted away for a while longer, and the major kept stressing what an intel bonanza we'd delivered to them. If not for us, he figured his forces would have advanced right into those hidden Iraqi positions and on to their guns.

Then he had this for me: 'You know, Captain, I got dead bodies from Charlie Company that we've yet to recover. We're heading back down Ambush Alley this morning, and then east into the marsh area to recover the vehicles, and search for our dead. 'Cause we leave no man behind, you know'

'Yeah, that's important. Same with us.'

'Now, I got a favour to ask you Pathfinder guys.' He paused. 'Captain, you figure you guys could provide an armed escort as we do that recovery mission, and maybe give my boys some top cover?'

It struck me that this was a somewhat insane request. We'd got three open-topped, soft-skinned Land Rovers that were shot to fuck. His men were operating in heavily-armoured Bradley fighting vehicles, each packing an M242 25 mm chain gun. It'd be a little challenging for us to provide some top cover for them. But I told him that we'd do what we could, although we'd likely get re-tasked on to another mission any time now.

We said our farewells, and for a couple of hours me and the lads busied ourselves doing damage assessments and checking the vehicles, in preparation for departure. Our position kept coming under sporadic but inaccurate fire, but we didn't take much notice. We left it to the Marines to deal with.

At one stage a yellow garbage truck came thundering down the road towards us. It stopped a good distance away, and a couple of guys with long greasy hair leaned out of the window and unloaded AK47s in our general direction. It was all a bit laughable compared to the death run from Qalat Sikar, and we didn't pay it too great a mind.

The truck started moving again, and it built up speed until it was careering towards the US front line positions. One of the Bradleys sparked up and tore the truck to pieces with its M242 chain gun. It was only right that they'd malleted it. It could well have been packed full of explosives, those Iraqi gunmen being on a suicide mission.

At 0100 we received a response from PF HQ to our text message. We were ordered back to the FOB. Dez had spent the entire morning tweaking, talking to and patching the Pinkies, with the other lads helping wherever they could. As long as we took it slow, he reckoned they'd make it back to base okay.

At 0130 we departed, heading back into Nasiriyah and along Ambush Alley. As we did so, there was a long stream of US Marine Corps vehicles coming in the opposite direction. I guessed they were preparing for the big push north. We saw the Regimental Combat Team 2 (RCT-2) headquarters unit coming forwards – the same guys we had spoken to before first moving into Nasiriyah. We stopped to speak to their Ops Officer.

He gave us a flashing smile and a heartfelt thank you. The intel that we'd provided was dynamite, he told us. It was being used to find, fix and smash the Iraqi positions all along Route 7 to the north of their front line.

By the time we were through to the southern outskirts of Nasiriyah, we'd started to relax a little and enjoy the drive. This territory was owned by the US Marine Corps, and there was unlikely to be enemy for many kilometres in any direction.

Steve turned to me, and yelled a comment in this hammed-up American accent: 'Ya know what, buddy, a few weeks from now and we'll be in Li-ces-ter Square, meeting the loves of our lives in The Shadow Lounge.'

'Mate, I've never needed Smudge in his Elvis rig more than I do now!' I yelled back at him. 'Fuck it: I'm even going to fucking sing …'

We were all three of us laughing.

As we headed south on Route 8 I found I'd got the lyrics from the song 'Hands of Time', by Groove Armada, running through my mind. It's a cool, mellow track, which kind of embodied my emotions right now. I was feeling the pure, total joy of being alive, and of having survived the unsurvivable.

Plus there was something else. We may not have reached the mission objective, Qalat Sikar airfield, but we'd been sent into a tsunami of enemy fire with no warning, and we'd ended up conducting a recce-by-fire through some 200 kilometres of enemy terrain. In doing so, we'd uncovered what amounted to two Iraqi divisions hidden in the desert north of Nasiriyah. We'd done our bit to mallet them, and now the American air power was going in to smash them big time.

The US Marines now knew what lay ahead of them, and they were forewarned with six-figure grids of each position. So whilst we might have failed in our mission, I reckoned we'd done something pretty extraordinary out there. I liked the American people and their military. I'd trained alongside them and served alongside them, and warmed to their generous, open-hearted spirit. I was thankful that we'd helped prevent some of those young US marines from getting the shit kicked out of them as they pushed north of Nasiriyah.

We'd been able to add something of incalculable value to their war effort – pinpoint-accurate intel. Plus I'd seen how much we'd boosted their morale by just being there. They'd taken the mother of all beatings in Nasiriyah. They'd had their arses kicked and their heads were down. They were licking their wounds, when suddenly us lot of lunatics appeared from out of the night. We'd been out there, way out front, taking the fight to the enemy.

Hoooh-ahh! as they say in the Corps.

As we sped south the chorus of that Groove Armada song, 'Hands of Time', kept running through my brain. The lyrics speak of the impossibility of turning back the hands of time. Well, I had no regrets. It had been a good mission. Not the one that we set out to achieve, maybe, but still the mission of a lifetime. As 2IC Pathfinders I was proud of what we'd achieved. And I was lit up that every man on my patrol was coming home alive. I wouldn't want to turn back the hands of time, even if I had the power to.

It was 2200 and pitch dark by the time we made it back to PF HQ. We hadn't slept much for several nights, and we'd been on the go for hours on end in the fight of our lives. We were totally and utterly chinstrapped. We said a quick, yet heartfelt goodbye to the three Engineer Recce lads, then bedded down wherever we could on the hard sand.

As I drifted off to sleep, I thought about those Engineer Recce blokes who'd been with us. They had come up trumps on this mission. There was the tyre-changing incident, which had set a bad tone at the start, but they'd more than made up for it in the heat and the fire of battle. Their wagon looked as smashed about as ours, and when the rounds went down they gave as good as they got. I was absolutely certain that the weight of fire they put down from their GPMGs was a battle-winner, and one that helped us break through in the death run from Qalat Sikar. It was good to have had them with us.

I slept the sleep of the dead. After stand-to and a brew the following morning, the lads from the other patrols gathered around. By now, word had got out about our murder run south from Qalat Sikar. Everyone seemed curious to know more, but that didn't stop the messing. Bryan Budd, Steve's best mate, was there, and as always he was playing the fool. He strutted around doing his best impression of a typical nose-in-the-air officer type.

'Hello, corporal, is everything all right?' he announced, to Steve. 'Mail getting through?'

Steve was trying not to laugh. 'No, it fucking isn't, and no, it's fucking not. I haven't seen a woman in days. I might as well be in the Shadow Lounge. Oh, yeah, and there's been a load of fucking blokes I've never met trying to kill me.'

After the Qalat Sikar mission, it was good to see the blokes having a laugh again, because by anyone's reckoning they'd earned it.

I felt an ominous rumbling in my guts. I headed over to the thunder boxes. I was sat there having the biggest dump ever, and really savouring the moment, when a familiar figure plonked down next to me. It was Brigadier Jacko Page, the CO of 16 Air Assault Brigade, and seemingly he needed a shit too.

I was tortured with embarrassment, because my enormous crap was polluting the atmosphere big time. Plus I was dehydrated and seriously constipated, so it was all taking one hell of a long time, but by all appearances Jacko didn't seem to mind.

He turned to me and gave me this half smile. 'Well, that all sounded rather interesting. Qalat Sikar: quite a mission. Bloody well done for getting everyone out of there safely.'

Jacko was a man of few words, and he was known for not giving praise lightly. He must have commanded countless covert operations whilst serving with elite units. I'd just had a well done on the quiet from the brigade commander, whilst we were sat together on the bogs. It didn't get much better than that.

But it seemed as if not everyone felt the same way as Jacko.

CHAPTER TWENTY-SEVEN

I returned to the vehicles feeling on a real high. It was then that I got called to have a one-on-one with one of the more senior officers in the Brigade. In theory there were eight or more ranks above me who might have a direct interest in the Qalat Sikar mission and in debriefing me, so I wasn't particularly worried.

I made my way over to his tent. He was sat at a makeshift wooden desk, and as I entered he didn't look up, which struck me as being somewhat odd.

He gestured to a chair: 'David, take a seat.' I could sense immediately that something wasn't quite right. 'So tell me, David, how did you end up being so far north pinned down by loads of contacts?'

I was immediately thinking: *What the hell is this*? Where was the small talk, the chat, maybe the offer of a brew? I tried to keep my cool. In fairness, it was important for high command to get as full a debriefing as they could and as soon after the mission as possible. That way, lessons could be learned which could be passed on to other PF patrols, not to mention the wider British military.

'There was only the one route in towards the mission objective,' I replied, 'one that we'd been ordered to make overland by vehicle.'

He scribbled a note on a pad on his desk. I realised then that he was effectively giving me a formal interview, what we in the military call 'an interview without coffee'. This was priceless. When missions went well and everyone on a patrol was bathed in glory, all wanted to claim they were involved. But when you were asked to achieve the impossible and the shit hit the fan, everyone began searching for a scapegoat.

He stayed silent for a moment. Then: 'I understand you missed your 1600 Sched?'

Up until that moment I hadn't realised that we had missed it, and neither had Tricky. I thought back to the first bridge crossing in Nasiriyah, where we'd tried and failed to raise PF HQ on the TACSAT. I guessed it was shortly after that we must have missed the Sched. But we were mobile and crossing enemy lines at the time, which must have been why we had forgotten to send it.

I could imagine what a nightmare that would have been. For several hours after we'd missed our Sched headquarters might well have feared that we were compromised and on the run. Having to list our patrol as 'missing in action' would have been one of the worst of all possible outcomes for the Brigade.

'We tried once, just before 1600, but couldn't raise PF HQ,' I told him. 'We must have forgotten about it in the heat of the mission. But we'd maintained constant comms throughout the day, and headquarters was well aware of our intent. In any case, we were mobile and moving through enemy lines. You can't send Scheds when you're mobile, because you've got to stop to set up the radio antenna.'

Again, he noted down my answer. Then he asked: 'Why did you move ahead of the Marine Corps' front line positions?'

'We did so because that was our mission – to move ahead and recce and mark a HLS at Qalat Sikar.'

'At Nasiriyah the US Marines were getting pinned down. Why did you think it was safe to move forwards?'

'I didn't think it was safe. We are at war. We work behind enemy lines. It's never safe. But the intel we were given said the area north of there as far as the airfield was "relatively benign". We checked with the most forward units of the Marine Corps. They'd seen nothing in terms of the enemy in front of them. We went forwards on the best available intel. It happened to be entirely wrong.'

It was only with great difficulty that I was holding myself in check. The point about us missing the Sched was a fair one, but this was feeling more and more like a Spanish Inquisition. My fists were starting to ball with pent-up fury.

'Why did you keep going north after the first compromise?' he demanded.

'It's standard operating procedure for Pathfinders to drive through ambush points, plus it was the only way to achieve our mission.'

'Why did you only send one basic text sitrep when you got back to the US frontline? Don't you think headquarters could have used more info?'

'That's because the comms guy on my wagon, Tricky, had flushed the Crypto, because we were surrounded by the enemy and thought we were all about to die.'

'Even so, why didn't you send a proper combat rep with ammo states?'

I couldn't believe this. It was akin to asking why I'd broken health-and-safety procedures, when I was convinced that we were about to get slotted. He was giving me shit because we didn't file a report telling him how much ammo we had left, when we'd just escaped from the fight of our lives.

'Funnily enough, we were more concerned about getting accurate intel to the Americans, so they could smash two divisions' worth of enemy with air strikes, intel for which the US Marine Corps were very, very grateful. Funnily enough, ammo stats just didn't seem that important at the time.'

I had nothing more to say. I got to my feet, dismissed myself and left the tent.

I went for a good long walk around the FOB in an effort to calm myself down. Why had I just had this crap dumped on me? An interview without coffee after all that we'd been through, and us saddled with a crock of shit as the intel. *What was his fucking problem?*

I reckoned headquarters must have got a massive flap on when the mission went tits up and they thought they might lose an entire patrol. Had we got up there unscathed and recced the airfield, and 1 PARA had gone in and secured it, then we'd all have been in clover. As it was headquarters must have presumed they'd lost us, and hence they were somehow trying to disown the patrol.

Instead, we'd come out of the death run from Qalat Sikar alive and with crucial intel, which had the potential to turn the tide of the war. As far as I was concerned we'd pulled off a crucial mission, one that we should all be proud of. I'd just had a quiet 'well done' from the brigade commander whilst sat on the shitters, so he clearly felt the same. I'd had similar and better from the US Marine Corps commanders. More the pity, then, that someone at headquarters couldn't share that sense of satisfaction in the mission.

As I stomped around the base there was one thought at the forefront of my mind. We'd gone forwards to carry out the orders that we had been given, but had we all been killed or captured out there, I wondered if there were those in headquarters who would have tried to distance themselves from the patrol?

I knew that as 2IC Pathfinders the final burden of leadership for field operations lay with me. If we fucked up, rightfully I'd be held responsible by Brigade Command, and that was probably what lay behind the interview without coffee that I'd just had. I'd been using the blokes by breaking down mission planning, and giving each a specific area of responsibility, but it was still my gig. It was me in command of my patrol. When the shit hit the fan, the buck stopped with me. But I felt we'd done good out there and I was proud of my team and of our mission.

When I tired of stalking the base perimeter I returned to the lads. I found Tricky resting by the side of our wagon, enjoying a cuppa.

'Just made a jack brew, have you, mate?' I quipped. Making a 'jack brew' was PF speak for brewing a cuppa for yourself only.

'Fuck off, you were in seeing the slipper city gang.' Tricky eyed me for a second. 'How did it go? You look like shit.'

'I was told to take a seat and given an interview without coffee.'

'What the f – !' Tricky spluttered, half spilling his tea. 'After a mission like Qalat Sikar, you get given that kind of crap?'

I did my best to shrug it off. 'Don't worry about it. They were just doing their job.'

I didn't want to make a big deal out of this, and for resentment to fester amongst the lads and for problems to escalate.

We spent most of that morning dozing in the shade by the vehicles. I felt demotivated and bitter, but my anger was tempered by what the brigade commander had said to me on the bogs. I knew that he had got it, even if there were others who hadn't.

As the day wore on my mood cooled. I figured this was what must have happened: at this stage of the war there had been few, if any, British combat casualties. There'd likely been a major flap on by senior officers and politicians, when it became clear that an entire Pathfinder patrol was missing in action behind enemy lines.

Very likely there were people higher up the chain than Brigade banging on about 'Britain's Black Hawk Down' – the infamous 1993 incident in which scores of elite US soldiers were trapped, shot up, captured and tortured by Somali gunmen, in Mogadishu. I ran that scenario through my mind a good few times, and I started to feel a little better about that interview without coffee. I was sure they had their reasons.

In the Pathfinders operations are fast-moving, and we'd shortly be onto our next mission, of that I had no doubt. If that interview led to lessons being learned that would improve future ops and save blokes lives, then maybe it was fair enough. But still, it had left me with a bad feeling.

All that day the lads from the other PF patrols kept wandering over for a natter. They'd heard about our mission, and were unable to comprehend how we had got out of there alive. They were welcome to join the party: I had no idea how we'd done so, either.

If there was one positive thing that came out of all this, it was the collective realisation of how unusable the intel was that we'd been given. Areas slated as unoccupied or benign were far from it, and the Iraqis were more than ready to put up a fight. An order came down from the brigade commander: all Pathfinder patrols would now deploy four-up in terms of wagons. That way, we'd double our firepower.

The following morning we did a Brigade move northeast towards Basra. We thundered through the open desert to link up with the Royal Marines, who'd air-assaulted into southern Iraq during the opening hours of the war and seized the Al Faw peninsula. Once there, we made for an abandoned Iraqi army camp, which would be our base for some weeks now. We found an old hangar where we could set up camp together with our beloved vehicles. We'd been kipping in the open up until this moment, so this was sheer luxury.

The camp was a big old compound, consisting of a cluster of stark concrete structures that looked to have been abandoned for some time. But the key thing was that it had a big solid building within which Brigade HQ could establish their ops room and planning cells. They had complex and sensitive computer and communications kit, and they were busy as fuck with a million and one moving parts relating to the war effort, including the air missions that were being flown. There was only so long they could operate in tents in the desert.

The Brigade engineers strung some razor wire around the compound's perimeter, and constructed sandbagged sangars at the entry and exit points. We soon had teams of blokes buzzing in and out for orders groups, including a group of lads from the SAS. They pitched up to brief the brigade commander on what they were up to in the area, and for an information exchange. A couple of the SAS lads were ex-Pathfinders, and they wandered over to our hangar for a natter.

The SAS blokes were dressed in civvies, and they were driving four-by-four Toyota-type jeeps. They were running operations in and around Basra, and although they loved what they were doing you could see just a hint of envy in their eyes when they heard about the Qalat Sikar op. They knew there was little chance of them getting HALO'd deep into Iraq, or of being sent on a mission to drive hundreds of kilometres behind enemy lines.

Hereford is a much bigger unit than the PF. It's less personal, and you could go for years without seeing the others in your squadron. Inevitably, you'd lose some of the feeling of togetherness we had in the PF, and the closeness and brotherhood. There was a phrase we used a lot in the PF: *Grip change by the hand, before it grips you by the throat.* For a lot of the blokes who moved on from the PF, only when they left did they realise what they'd lost.

When you leave the PF, you get given a statue of an operator doing a HALO jump. In return, one of the blokes had given the PF something for the Interest Room. It was a statue of an SAS bloke tabbing through foul weather across Pen-Y-Fann. Across the bottom was the inscription: 'To the PF: enjoy it while it lasts.'

But in truth, as we swapped war stories there was a bit of envy both ways. The SAS lads were at the top of their game, and they were doing their edgy, sneaky-beaky work relentlessly. The last time we'd seen them was at Hereford for a piss-up after a funeral, when another ex-PF operator had been killed on ops. There was a high mortality rate in the kind of work that we did, and none of us ever knew whose funeral it might be next.

Our hangar was actually an old agricultural kind of barn, with brick walls and a corrugated iron roof. It was fine for our purposes, and similar in size to our hangars back in the UK. All six of the wagons had been brought inside for much-needed maintenance and repairs. We knew for sure now that the Iraqis were going to fight – as opposed to surrendering in their droves – and we needed the Pinkies in tiptop condition.

We ignored the scores of bullet holes torn in the alloy bodywork. They posed no threat to ongoing operations. We taped the worst over with khaki gaffer tape, and they were good to go. A couple of fuel pipes had been damaged and needed replacing, and luckily we had the spares on hand to do so. Amazingly, the fuse box in our wagon was still just about working. We replaced the broken fuses and gaffer-taped it up, after which we figured it might well last out our war in Iraq.

As we worked on the wagons, we learned about what the other PF patrols had been up to, whilst we'd been busy on the Qalat Sikar mission. They'd been out observing road junctions and other NAIs, and some had cued up air strikes on enemy positions.

But the banter that flew was mostly about our own op, Qalat Sikar. It was in a whole different league entirely, and the other patrols were itching to get their teeth into something equally meaty. We were barely a week into the conflict, so there was every chance of them doing so, and we were excited to see how the next few days and weeks might unfold.

Qalat Sikar had changed things for me personally. It was the most outrageous operation that anyone here had ever heard of, including the old and the bold. As a result, the grumpy officer-hater types seemed much warmer now. I hadn't done any single-handed bayonet charges to save my men, but I had commanded a patrol that against all odds had come out more or less unscathed. I'd not been found wanting, and that hadn't gone unnoticed.

There was another factor at play too. Word had got around about my altercation with the senior officer. I'd not said anything other than the few words to Tricky, but everyone seemed to know. I hadn't tried to bring anyone else into the line of fire, or blame any of the others. I alone had carried the can, and in a way they respected me for it.

A day or two after our arrival at our new base I went to pay a visit to the Brigade HQ building, situated about 100 metres from our hangar. I was used to the hustle and bustle of the place. People were working feverishly hard, but still there was always some banter. This time I walked in and the atmosphere was like death. There was this horrible edge to the air, and people everywhere were flapping.

I spotted Josh, one of my longstanding mates from my Sandhurst days. I grabbed him by the arm. 'Mate, what's happened?'

'An American plane has just done a drop on one of the Household Cavalry vehicles,' he told me. 'We think they're all dead.'

He hurried onwards to the bank of radios. I glanced over at the air cell, where a handful of RAF blokes were tasked with co-ordinating ground and air missions. There was a horrible air hanging over those guys, and one in particular looked ashen-faced and in shock. If the air cell had failed to pass the right warnings to the US warplanes, that might have accounted for this blue-on-blue, but it was more than likely simply the fog of war.

There was nothing more that I could do, so I returned to the hangar. I'd been sat having a ciggie with the Household Cavalry lads just a couple of weeks back, in Kuwait. We'd been on a shake-out exercise together, in which we were practising moving in tandem with their Scimitar light tanks. They, like us, had the Blue Force Tracker gear, plus the friendly forces recognition panels, so what on earth could have gone wrong this time?

Over the next few hours further details started to emerge. A squadron of Scimitar light tanks had been moving north of Basra, at the vanguard of the British advance. They were trying to recce the road northwest of the Iraqi town of Ad Dawr. Once again, intel had suggested that they'd face little resistance. Instead, the lads of the Household Cavalry had advanced into a barrage of enemy fire.

During fierce gun battles with Iraqi armour, they'd discovered there were hundreds of Iraqi T55 main battle tanks dug in and hull-down in the desert sands. As with the Qalat Sikar mission, the Iraqi positions had been skilfully camouflaged and hidden from aerial view, and no one had had the slightest idea they were there until the Household Cavalry had stumbled into them.

The British Scimitars were heavily outnumbered and outgunned. They'd ended up playing a deadly game of cat and mouse with the Iraqi armour, as they tried to make a tactical withdrawal. The British forces had proceeded to take a hammering, just as the US Marine Corps had done at Nasiriyah. The Household Cavalry had called in air strikes, as they tried to break out of the trap set by the Iraqi armour. But a US A10 tank-buster warplane had shot up two Scimitars, killing one British soldier and wounding three.

This blue-on-blue had taken place some 40 kilometres north of

Basra. It had happened despite the giant Union Jack painted on the roof of one of the armoured vehicles, and their friendly forces recognition gear. It struck me that this was fast becoming our own Nasiri-yah. Even with multiple intel sources – satellite imagery, human intelligence, Predator UAV overflights – you never knew what was on the ground until you sent men in up close to get eyes-on.

And that, of course, was the *raison d'être* of the Pathfinders.

CHAPTER TWENTY-EIGHT

I t was hardly surprising when we got stood to for a rush mission. Our patrol was tasked to join forces with Geordie's, one of the two patrols originally slated for the Qalat Sikar para-insertion. We were to push ahead of the British front line, to recce and verify the strength of the enemy positions. Our orders were to move out almost immediately, and wherever possible we were to call in air strikes to smash the Iraqi armour, once we'd positively identified their locations.

There were hundreds of Iraqi T55 tanks out there, hull-down and perfectly camouflaged. Each was a 40-tonne beast, with 20-centimetre-thick armour on the turret. Each boasted a 100 mm rifled cannon as the main weapon, a direct hit from which would pretty much vaporise a Pinkie. As secondary weapons, they were fitted with either two 7.62 mm machine guns, similar to our trusted GPMGs or our old friend the Dushka.

We were twelve men in four, thin-skinned wagons. Nice one. Yet another peachy mission.

We loaded up the Pinkies with a couple of MILAN anti-tank rockets, newly arrived in theatre, in case we did have a close encounter with one of those armoured beasts. The MILAN Anti-tank Light Infantry Missile is the French equivalent of the American Javelin, and it is equally user-friendly and potent. It employs SACLOS wire guidance to target, being accurate up to 2000 metres. It was an Aston Martin Vantage compared to our LAW-90s, which were Citroen 2CVs. But even so, I'd prefer it if we avoided getting up close and personal with too many Iraqi T55s.

Geordie, a corporal, was small, wiry and hard as nails, and he punched well above his weight. A highly-respected member of the Pathfinders, he was seen as being a very capable patrol commander, and he was placed in overall command of the mission. After Qalat Sikar, everyone in my patrol was feeling pretty much burned out, and we were happy to let Geordie take the lead. Our role was to provide protection and support to his wagons.

The mission plan was for us to move through our own lines and cross into enemy territory, whereupon our patrol would occupy the high ground, so we could give covering fire to Geordie's lot in case they got compromised whilst probing the Iraqi positions. We were doubly aware of the danger of friendly fire now, and it was crucial that we liaised closely with 3 PARA, for it was their forces that were manning our front line in that area. We had to let them know we'd be recceing the terrain to their north, as well as where and when we'd be crossing over their front line positions.

As we weren't leading the mission we weren't involved in the detailed planning, so I spent a lot of time studying the maps and inputting waypoints into my GPS: the location of 3 PARA's front line units went in, plus their forward HQ; and I marked up any potential routes into and out of enemy territory. Late that afternoon Geordie gave his patrol orders. It was a rush mission, and he made it clear we'd follow SOPs if we hit any trouble.

At last light Geordie's patrol led off, our vehicles following. Fairly quickly we moved off the tarmac road and on to a small track, driving northwards on black light and using night vision goggles.

I felt Tricky lean forwards to have a word. 'So it's Operation Death or Glory again?'

'No, mate,' Steve cut in. 'It's Mission Impossible Two, this one.'

I smiled. It was good to see that the lads were still sparking.

It was sod's law that tonight of all nights the cloud base was low and glowering, and the ambient light minimal. I could see bugger all with my NVG, and I figured Steve was struggling to see the way ahead. After a half-hour's drive we passed through the last of 3 PARA's positions, which meant we were moving into enemy terrain.

We reached a small bridge, the far side of which was heavily-vegetated marshland. We knew that there were enemy units positioned in there, hidden amongst the thick swampland and the bush. It was our role to find exactly where they were, and to start smashing them. As we bumped across the rough bridge, the side door on one of the Pinkies popped open. In the rush to leave the base someone had forgotten to check the latches on their vehicle. A load of cooking kit fell out. It was deafeningly loud in the night-dark quiet.

Fuck. Nothing like signalling to the enemy that we were coming.

Not securing your stowage was a rudimentary error of recce patrolling, and it was the kind of mistake that happened when missions got rushed, and operators got tired. Over the past week Geordie's patrol had been bounced from one mission to another more or less without a break, and they'd got little proper sleep. We just had to hope and pray there were no Iraqi positions near enough to have heard anything.

We crept ahead for another 4 kilometres at a dead slow. The only noise was the swish of the thick undergrowth against our wagon's smooth alloy sides, plus the faint purring of the diesel engine. The Pinkies were fitted with a 300Tdi engine, as opposed to the civvie Land Rover, which had a more powerful but complicated Td5. The Td5 unit requires diagnostic computers to repair any faults, and there was no way we were going to have that kind of kit in the field. Plus there was always the danger that the Td5's electronic control systems could be scrambled by electromagnetic interference put out by an enemy.

We had Iraqi units to all sides of us now, and one of the few comforting thoughts was that they wouldn't have the means to mess with our engines. There was little chance of pinpointing exactly where those units were, for the darkness and the bush obscured everything. We were nearing the point where our patrol would head for the high ground, leaving Geordie's lot to probe the enemy terrain.

Geordie pulled over. I presumed this was where he wanted us to split up. We came to a halt in all-around defence, but I could see that Geordie was looking flustered, which was not like him at all.

'Fuck it,' he muttered. 'I've forgotten to warn 3 PARA what we're doing, and to give 'em the mission plan.'

He was angry with himself, and for good reason. Without us having given them a heads-up, 3 PARA wouldn't know that we'd gone past their front line, and more importantly where and when we'd be coming back in again. Geordie was an über-committed PF soldier, and a well-experienced patrol commander. But this was what happened when operations were thrown together hurriedly by men who'd been on the go for days on end.

Geordie knew he'd made a serious fuck-up here, one that could cost men's lives, and he was kicking himself. Geordie and I considered our options. For sure, 3 PARA were going to be hyper-alert and ready for any enemy forces trying to infiltrate their lines. If we tried to cross back blind we'd be asking for trouble. We couldn't radio 3 PARA, for we were not on their net, and even if we tried to patch a call in via PF HQ, using the radio might well compromise us.

We were in the midst of a mass of Iraqi infantry and armoured positions, so we had to presume they had the ability to intercept our comms. Also, we were on strict radio silence for this op, and for good reasons. The Iraqi military were known to have excellent DF (Direction Finding) equipment, from which they could pinpoint the source of any radio signal. To break radio silence might well prove the death of us.

I'd been surrounded and trapped once by the enemy in the past few days: I didn't fancy going through all of that again. Geordie figured he needed to study the maps, so he could work out the best route to get us back to the nearest 3 PARA position, whereupon he could give them a verbal heads-up as to our mission. But even the pinprick of light thrown off by his wagon's map-light might well compromise us.

Geordie and I gathered around the dash of his wagon. He pulled out the mini Maglite he had strung on some paracord around his neck. Light discipline was everything in the PF, especially when surrounded by unknown enemy positions. As with the rest of us, Geordie had wrapped some black gaffer tape over the end of his Maglite. He'd pierced that with a needle-sized hole, which meant that when he twisted it on it let out the barest pinprick of light.

I cupped my hands around the map, as Geordie shone his Maglite on to it, like a tiny laser beam. With my palms shielding even that tiny amount of illumination from any watching eyes, we did a detailed map check without having to worry about getting seen. We located 3 PARA's nearest position, which as a bonus just happened to be their forward headquarters.

I told Geordie that I'd got that location way-pointed into my GPS, along with most of the roads and tracks lying between them and us. I offered to lead the patrol direct to it, which would mean that Geordie wouldn't have to keep illuminating his maps every five minutes, to try to navigate our way there. In the circumstances, Geordie thought this a blinding suggestion.

We readied the patrol, turned the vehicles around, and my wagon led off with the others following. The thick cloud cover meant that neither the stars nor the moon were visible. The lack of ambient light made driving on NVG a total nightmare. I couldn't see more than 5 metres ahead of me, and it had to be the same for Steve. We moved at a painfully slow crawl in the opposite direction to that which we had driven in on, but the terrain was proving horrendous.

I was navigating along this network of narrow tracks, using the GPS as my guide. We pushed back 3 kilometres and were approaching the nearest 3 PARA position, which was the moment of maximum danger. It was black as a witch's tit out here. We hit the junction of two dirt tracks, and I reckoned from my GPS that 300 metres to the right of us we'd find 3 PARA's forward HQ.

As we made the turn right, a challenge rang out in the darkness. 'Halt! Who goes there? Identify yourselves!'

We'd practically driven into a 3 PARA sentry post. Luckily, we were crawling along at 3 kilometres an hour, so Steve managed to stop before we ran the sentry over. He was a young private with his weapon gripped tight in the aim, and he was on the verge of slotting us.

'Pathfinders!' I hissed into the night. 'Pathfinder patrol. We've been on a mission into enemy terrain. We need to liaise with your HQ.'

I saw his shoulders sag as he visibly relaxed. He lowered his weapon. 'Bloody hell, sir, I was just about to open fire.' He jerked a thumb in the direction of the track behind him. '3 PARA HQ is that way'.

With a few words of thanks we pulled away and pressed onwards in the darkness. We'd gone another 15 metres at a dead crawl when I felt this weird sensation. It was like a giant hand was lifting the Land Rover and flipping it over, and suddenly everything was spinning out of control. There was a horrendous falling sensation, then a tremendous, crushing impact.

A moment later my world turned black.

I came to and opened my eyes. There was a crushing weight on my chest. I was trapped in the pitch darkness with something massive lying on top of me. I sensed that I was upside down, but I couldn't seem to right myself. I was trapped. I had this horrible, piercing ringing in the centre of my head, screaming out towards my ears. It felt like the devil himself had been let loose inside my skull, and it was agonising and totally deafening.

I tried to free an arm, so I could press my fingers into my temples, to try to stop the pain. But I didn't seem able to move at all. I heard Tricky's voice from somewhere, echoing and faint, as if it was coming from down the end of a long tunnel.

'DAVE! DAVE! WHERE THE FUCK'S DAVE?'

I could only hear his voice. I couldn't see him. I heard Steve yelling the same.

'DAVE! WHERE THE FUCK'S DAVE?'

Then Jason: 'HE'S UNDER THE FUCKING WAGON! HE'S GOT TO BE!'

I tried to shout a response, to give some form of confirmation. *I'm here! I'm here!* But my mouth was blocked with mud, which was smeared in thick globules all over my face and nose. I couldn't speak and I could barely breathe. I realised that the vehicle must have rolled off the track. It had fallen down a massive drop, and it was upside-down on top of me.

Neither Steve nor I had noticed the precipice in the darkness. Now I was trapped in my seat and pinned under the Pinkie, with my face thrust into some kind of fetid Iraqi swamp. It was standard operating procedure for Pathfinders not to wear seatbelts. It was pretty obvious why. They restrict your arcs when you have to spin the weapons around, and they delay you debussing from your vehicle. Just an instant's hindrance could prove fatal, hence the no seatbelt rule.

Tricky would have been stood behind me in the 50-cal turret as the vehicle rolled, and he must have been thrown clear. Steve was on the driver's side, and I figure it must have rolled over him, leaving him to tumble out unharmed. Which left júst me. I was lying almost vertical beneath the upturned wagon, horribly twisted and unable to move.

I felt utterly helpless and totally alone. Terrified. Almost imperceptibly, I felt the Land Rover start to settle, compressing my chest and my legs a fraction more. It was a horrifying feeling, like being sucked into the dark heart of hell.

Suddenly I heard Jason yelling orders. He was trying to work out how the fuck to get me out from under the wagon, or to get it off of me. I heard Dez and Joe arrive beside the upturned vehicle. I heard Steve's hurried explanation – *the Pinkie's rolled and Dave's trapped beneath.*

The pressure on my neck and back kept growing. I was short of breath. I heard blokes scrabbling to my left and my right, but I couldn't see anyone. I counted the minutes. Ten went by. It seemed like an eternity.

Another ten. With each minute the vehicle settled a little further into the quagmire, forcing my head deeper into the gunk, and twisting and crushing my neck and spine. I could smell the rotting leaf matter, plus whatever animal or human shit had been draining into the swamp. The stench was thick in my nostrils.

We were right on 3 PARA's front line. The enemy would be positioned in the darkened terrain to the north of us, and within visual range. The NVG were barely working in the pitch darkness, but no one could risk showing any lights. To do so would draw a whirlwind of enemy fire.

The Pinkie was full of all the usual heavy ammo, supplies and weaponry, and the weight was forcing it deeper into the mud. I'm a tall bloke at 6 foot 4. When sitting in the front seat my head would be up against the rollbar. That was all but submerged now, rammed into the swamp by the mass of the vehicle above it. Gradually, my head was going the same way.

I felt this nauseating tide of panic rising up inside me. *I'm going to fucking drown in this mud and shit down here!* And then I heard the guys start digging for me. Jason was at the front urging them on. But I was so far under the vehicle, and already it had sunk so low, that the more they dug with the shovels the more the Pinkie settled. It was a horrible, vicious circle, a zero-sum game.

I felt the muck and gunk seeping into my eye sockets, and then it was over my eyes. I was blinded by it. I could taste the acrid, metallic tang of blood in my mouth. I figured I had to have internal bleeding, as the wagon slowly but surely crushed the life out of me. It was clear that digging me out wasn't working.

I felt so alone. What a way to die.

CHAPTER TWENTY-NINE

I heard a body crawling beneath the vehicle. A hand reached out for me, scrabbling desperately, groping in the thick mud. Fingers touched my fingers; reached to hold my hand. Whoever it was didn't try to pull me out. The hand just held my hand, tightly. He knew there was no moving me.

A face wriggled nearer to mine, ghostly-white in the darkness. It was Tricky. He started talking to me. He wasn't asking stupid shit like – *Dave, are you okay*? All he was doing was chewing the fat, talking about the bars we used to frequent and the lines we used to pull on all the women.

'I never told you, mate, but when you met Isabelle, that gorgeous French bird, in the Backroom Bar. Remember? Well, you went for a slash and she said:

"Wow. Who's your mate – the tall, dark, silent one?" I told her the only reason you were silent was that you'd send her to sleep if you opened your bloody mouth.'

I was trying not to laugh through a mouthful of mud and blood.

'I told her you'd talk about PF lost comms procedures, or selection, or some such bollocks all night long. I told her I was the man she needed. You only managed to pull her, mate, 'cause she got you on to the dance floor, and she saw what a crap dancer you are. She took pity on you, that's all.'

I tried giving it back to him. I wanted so desperately to talk, to laugh, to share a little human warmth. But I could barely breathe. My words came in hoarse, rasping gasps. I couldn't really hear all that he was saying even, but I was glad that it was Tricky who was with me.

He never said any of the shit that you hear in the movies – *You're gonna be all right. We'll get you out of there.* He figured that was a lie, and how the fuck would he know, anyway. He was just there to be my brother and to show me that I wasn't alone.

The weight of the Pinkie was pressing on me more and more. It was squeezing the life out of me. I felt my lungs start to fill with liquid. I could taste the stagnant water as they flooded with liquid gunk from this rancid Iraqi swamp. I tried talking to Tricky, but the words came out as frothy gargles and spurts. It was terrifying. I could hardly breathe. I stopped talking.

The pressure kept increasing, until finally I started to feel this weird sense of peace and happiness wash over me. I started to have this freaky out of body experience. I was feeling euphoric, like I was stoned out of my brain. I realised this was what it had to feel like to die. I was glad Tricky was with me, and that I wasn't on my own. He was a good guy to be with when it was your time to die.

I started to have flashbacks to my childhood and my family. These weren't slow daydreams, but rapid flashes of all the good stuff and the joy. I could see myself on a summer camping holiday in Wales, with the family. I was around seven years old and my dad was taking me fishing. We hired a little chugging boat and caught eighteen mackerel. There were too many for us to barbecue and eat, so my mum sent me around the campsite giving the spare fish away.

I flashed forwards a year or two to another family holiday. Wales again. This time my dad and I were up at the crack of dawn, and climbing the sheer cliffs around Abersoch. He'd sussed out this great fishing spot, but we had to scale the rocks to get there. I felt a rush of fear – fear of heights and fear of falling – and my father's protective arm around me. We caught some mackerel, and then my dad hooked a dogfish.

A dogfish? What's a dogfish? Half a fish, half a dog?

He reeled it in triumphantly, and there was this mini-version of a shark on the end of the line. We took it back to the campsite, and my father taught me how to prepare it for the pan, by ripping off the tough, sandpaper skin. My dad was so proud of the job we'd done with the dogfish, he put me on his lap and let me drive the car from the campsite across the farm and up to the main road. My little sisters were in the back, giggling their heads off.

I flashed forwards to my mum training me to showjump horses. She'd drive me all around the country so I could compete at the best competitions. She'd worked so hard at her job, and to care for the family, and so she could provide horses for us all.

I jumped forwards again. My sisters were fourteen and eleven years old, which meant they'd been sent to the same secondary school as me. I was constantly looking after them, just as I have done all my life ever since. It struck me as being so sad that now, after this accident, I'd never get to look after them again.

I saw my family gathered around the Christmas dinner table, all laughter and joy and light. Mum had cooked a wonderful meal, for a second night running. My older sister Anna's birthday fell on Christmas Eve, so it was always like having two Christmases in a row. There were double presents. Double the celebrations. And double the cooking for Mum to do.

I saw my Mum and Dad in their beautiful, sunlit rose garden at home, their cottage pretty in pink, and my two sisters playing amongst the flowers. Weirdly, I felt happy as these snatches of memory spooled through my head. I loved my family, and I knew they loved me back. I'd got my patrol out of Qalat Sikar and I had brought every one of them out alive. It had been a good innings. I accepted that it was my time to go.

Then a thought occurred to me. My life was a room in the mess back at our base in the UK. My shit army mattress, a stack of books and DVDs, and a crappy video system. Plus my army gear. There was almost nothing in there that was personal.

When my room was emptied my life would be summarised by that. That was what my parents would get to see. I didn't really have anyone permanent in my life. No wife. No kids. I was going to leave no one behind me, no lasting human legacy.

I remembered then that there was a pile of porn mags in my room. *Shit*. That's what my mum was going to find. She'd be so disappointed in me. It was even worse because some of the other lads had dumped their porn in my room, whilst their girlfriends came to visit one last time before they went to war. All those mags were stacked up high in one corner, like a shrine to the gods of porn.

I tried asking Tricky to sanitise my room, to ditch the porn before my mum could get to it. I was desperate to get him to do so. But I couldn't seem to speak any more.

It was a nice and warm druggie feeling now. I'd got a head full of pink cotton clouds, and the pain started to fade away into rainbow shades of grey. I started drifting in and out of consciousness. I was halfway gone, and I felt pretty happy and complete. I didn't have a regular girlfriend or a wife. There was the lovely Isabelle, of course, but we'd only just started dating. I had no kids. This was my life – *the Pathfinders*.

I managed a whisper to Tricky: 'Mate, I love the Pathfinders.'

'What d'you say, mate?' Tricky asked, trying to wriggle his head even closer to me.

I was kind of annoyed that I had to repeat myself. I was dying here. Why wasn't he listening? I gargled out the same words – *'Mate, I love the PF.'* It struck me that it might be a stupid thing to be saying, but it was exactly how I felt right now. I was fading, floating and flying towards somewhere ethereal and fantastic. I was HALOing into the balmy sunlit heavens, Supertramp's 'Goodbye Stranger' on repeat full blast, as I turned and twisted in the golden slipstream. And all around me echoed sounds of chattering and laughter, as images from my family and childhood zipped past me.

Tricky started going crazy. He was scrabbling frantically at the mud with his bare hands, trying to dig out a scoop large enough for me to breathe. I heard him shout: 'GET ME A FUCKING MUG OR A MESS TIN!'

An arm reached in with a tin mug. Tricky started to shovel out water and mud and shit as fast as he could. I got a tiny bit of relief. I grabbed a breath or two. The euphoria started to recede. As it did, I could feel how crushed and twisted my body was. Every part of me was screaming in total agony.

I was making spluttering noises with each tiny intake of breath. I tried to move my legs, or my arms, or even wiggle my fingers. Nothing. I heard a commotion outside. I heard Jason dragging the high-lift jack out from its stowage place on the vehicle.

I heard his voice: 'Get jacks under it, as many as you fucking can! We got to lift it off of his chest!'

I heard grunting in the darkness. Muffled curses. Then Dez's voice, thick with tears and frustration: 'It's not fucking working!'

I felt Tricky disengaging his fingers from my own. An instant later he was gone. I didn't know why he'd left me. I figured he'd stuck with me until the last possible moment, before his arm got crushed beneath the vehicle and he got trapped with me. I was on my own down here again, and I hated it. I'd been abandoned.

A while later I regained consciousness. I sensed that the downward force of the vehicle had eased slightly. It was barely perceptible, but maybe the wagon had lifted just a fraction. I guess the jacks had to be working. I could hear a new voice now. It was an officer issuing instructions. Then whoever was speaking stopped yelling orders and crawled beneath the vehicle. He took up position where Tricky had left off, and started speaking to me.

'David, it's Andy Jackson, 3 PARA. Are you okay?'

It was a bit of a bone question. Of course I wasn't okay. I wished Tricky was still with me. I guessed he was outside, working on the jacks. I heard scores of voices all around the vehicle. It sounded like a gang-fuck out there. There were people trying to get chains under the Pinkie, and I guessed they had to have a REME recovery truck on the track up above.

There was this debate raging about how they were going to lift the vehicle off me. There were long patches where nothing seemed to be happening, and still I was drifting in and out of consciousness. But at least the Land Rover seemed to have stopped sinking.

The chains were on but the vehicle wasn't moving. I didn't know why. Water kept seeping back into the breathing hole that Tricky had dug for me. I was spluttering in mouthfuls of mud and gunge. I gave up struggling to breathe. I was so fucking tired. I just wanted it over with now.

I hear 3 PARA's RSM start yelling for his men to stand back, as they were going to lift the vehicle.

'Everyone back! Back! We're lifting now and I need everyone back, or you'll get crushed! The vehicle's going to swing left when we lift, and it might crush you lot if you don't bloody move. So everyone back now!'

With all the noise he was making I couldn't believe the enemy hadn't pinged us, and opened fire.

Andy Jackson yelled something at the RSM. 'I'm fucking staying with him!'

I felt him scrabbling with his hands, and then the tin mug, as he tried to bale out my breathing hole. He grabbed my arm and told me he wasn't going anywhere. The bloke was a fucking hero, but I still wished Tricky was there. It was just that I trusted my own blokes so completely.

I heard a winch start to whine, as it took up the strain. Finally, the vehicle jerked up a few inches, creaking and groaning horribly with every lurch. Hands reached in and dug me out and dragged me back, away from the Pinkie's crushing weight.

This bloke was straight on to me. His voice said: 'David, it's going to be all right. I'm a London paramedic out here with the TA, and I've got you …'

I felt somewhat reassured. I'd come across some seriously dodgy Army medics in my time. At least this one was the real deal. I couldn't speak. I couldn't even think any more. I was barely conscious. Just flying. Gone.

I felt myself lifted on to a stretcher. I was carried up the bank and slid into the rear of a field ambulance. A mask went over my face. I felt the sweet release of gas and oxygen. The pain faded, as tubes and needles went into my hands and face. Everywhere.

One of the ambulance doors opened a fraction. I sensed someone leaning in. A hand touched my hand.

'Dave! Dave The Face. Boat drinks, mate.'

It was just a head stuck around the door and a couple of rushed words, but it did the world for my morale. I couldn't move my head to see who it was even. The voice was gone. The door closed and the vehicle moved off.

With those words running through my head – *'Boat drinks, mate'* – I drifted out of consciousness.

CHAPTER THIRTY

I came to in some sort of stretcher bed. I'd got blankets piled over me, but still I was freezing cold. I'd got a tube in my mouth, my neck was in a brace, and I was pinned down in some sort of strait-jacket. I couldn't see properly. My vision was swimming. I was doped up to the eyeballs.

A voice told me that I was still in Iraq, but I was about to be flown out to a field hospital in Kuwait. I heard a helicopter land. It struck me as being ironic that they could manage to get a helo in for one wounded guy, but there was no air available for my patrol when we were trapped behind enemy lines.

Shit happens.

I was loaded beneath a whirling set of helo blades, and I passed out again. I came to in some sort of field hospital. I guessed I was in Kuwait. I looked around me. There were military doctors every-where, in stiff white medical tunics and with clipboards. Plus nurses. It looked like a scene from *M*A*S*H*.

I spotted a figure out of the corner of my eye standing by the bed-side. This one was wearing a horribly mud-stained uniform of sorts, and was sporting a thick growth of stubble. It was Steve. What the fuck was he doing here, I wondered? Why the joker and the slacker? Why not Jason? *Or Tricky?*

A nurse came over. I saw Steve's eyes light up. They followed her every move. *Now I understood.* I knew exactly why it was Steve that was here and not one of the others. *Nurses.*

I saw the nurse start to slice my clothes off me, using a pair of scissors to do so. My combats were ripped and soaked in mud, blood and shit, and she threw what remained of them into a refuse sack by her side. She got to my trousers and I managed to signal that I wanted her to stop.

She lifted the oxygen mask so I could speak. 'I was shot … A few days back … Through the trousers.'

I managed to make her understand that I wanted to keep the trousers. Somehow, in spite of the total mess that I was in, it was important to me. They were the only memento I had of the mission of a lifetime – of the suicide run south from Qalat Sikar – plus I had my silk escape map sewn into the waistband.

I asked her to give them to Steve, for safekeeping. As I did so I could tell that he wasn't listening. He was gazing into her face with his most alluring, trust-me-come-to-bed eyes. *The bastard.*

Somehow, I just knew that I was never going to see those trousers again. If Tricky were here, I'd bet my life he'd bring them home from war for me. But not Steve. He was only there for one thing – the women. I didn't hold it against him. He was what he was.

Once the nurse was gone, Steve decided he could afford me a bit of attention.

He shrugged, uncomfortably. 'Mate, I'm dead sorry that I rolled the vehicle. I didn't see …'

I silenced him with a wave of my hand, and gestured for him to come closer. He brought his face nearer to mine.

'Not your fault, mate,' I murmured. 'We both missed the drop. No one's to blame. So, how's the nurses, you jammy bastard?'

A couple of specialists came to speak to me. They explained they were orthopaedic surgeons, here with the TA. They told me I'd be back in the UK in twelve hours. My lungs were full of blood and water, so I had to remain on the oxygen. They were here to drain the liquid out of my lung cavity. They inserted some big needle device under my right armpit, and explained that the water and blood would drain out over time.

Hours passed. I was put into some sort of cocoon. I couldn't move at all. It was really comfy and warm in there. I guessed I'd got a lot of broken bones, hence all the cushioning. I was carried out to the air-field. We hung around for a while. There was the scream and whine of jets taking off and landing. I killed time by watching Steve charm and schmooze the nurses.

Finally, we started to board a military aircraft with all the seats removed.

I didn't have to move a muscle, which was great because I couldn't. I was placed on a stretcher with tubes, bags and drips attached. There were two nurses with me, and they'd keep an eye on me until we reached the UK.

Steve left with a last joke and a laugh for me, plus a few choice words for the nurses. I figured I saw a scrap of paper change hands. Phone numbers. *Slick.*

We took off and I drifted into the sleep of the dead.

I came to lying on a bed in Taunton Hospital. I was at the back of a ward, and my body was full of tubes and needles. I was feeling a bit of culture shock, to put it mildly. I was classed as VSI (Very Seriously Injured), so they had decided to put me in a ward with the old and the dying. The average age must have been seventy-five plus.

Less than twenty-four hours ago I'd been in Iraq, on my second mission behind enemy lines. I was there with my mates, fighting for my life. I'd now been crushed by our Land Rover, so my war was over, and I'd been placed in a ward with those about to die. I figured they'd put me here because my prognosis was likewise.

A pretty young nurse came over. She perched on my bedside and asked if I needed anything. I started to cry. I didn't know why or what for, but I couldn't stop the tears. She held me and told me it was all going to be all right. She smelled good. Her skin was soft. I passed out in her arms.

When I woke again my mother was there. I felt this massive sense of relief just at the sight of her. I knew she'd get all over this and sort this shit out. Sure enough, she got me moved into a private room where I could be alone with my morphine drip and my addled, woozy brain, plus my dark thoughts.

Over the next few days I had dozens of X-rays. I had eight broken ribs on my right side. I had a badly dislocated shoulder. I had flooded lungs. But the main problem was with the right brachial plexus (a network of nerves). There was severe nerve damage to my right arm. In fact, it was so badly damaged that I might never be able to use it again. My right arm might remain withered and dead for the rest of my life, being left to flop by the side of my body.

It was my right arm. My trigger arm. And without it I had no reason to be a Pathfinder any more.

But at least I was alive.

A week in and I was released into my mother's care. I was wrapped in blankets and I was still on the morphine, but at least I was out of that place where people were sent to die. When I reached my parents' pretty Lincolnshire cottage, my dad helped me into the house and on to the sofa. It was so good to see him again.

There was a brown envelope on the coffee table. It looked official and it was addressed to me. My mum opened it. It was a template letter from the MOD. It stated that following my injuries I was posted away from the Pathfinders to the 'Y-List'. This was the Army's sick and injured list. I didn't have a unit any more. I was out of the PF. It was like a massive kick in the bollocks.

My mum explained how they had got the news that I'd been injured. She'd heard the garden gate go, and leaves scrunching underfoot. She'd glanced through the door to see a grim-faced man in a suit walking up the garden path. She dropped to the floor, screaming: 'No!' My dad fell to the floor and hugged her, crying.

The man in the dark suit had put his mouth to the letterbox, and shouted: 'It's okay! David's not dead! He's just injured.'

I'd only ever seen my dad cry once, and that was after his mother died. This was only the second time that I'd even heard of him being in tears. If I didn't know it before, I knew now how much my parents loved and cared for me. They lay me on a sofa in the lounge with a duvet over me. I found it impossible to sleep, the broken ribs were so painful.

The next day another letter arrived, plus a long, odd-shaped parcel. The envelope looked posh. It was a letter from Prince Charles, personally written on his Birkhall-headed paper. I read it, and it did so much to cheer my soul.

Dear Dave,

I heard of the terrible accident that befell you in Iraq and just wanted to write and send you my very best wishes for a speedy recovery. I am relieved to hear that you should be able to leave hospital soon.

My spies also tell me you had a narrow escape from a carefully aimed Iraqi bullet, just the other day before your crash and that you were only saved by a lucky pair of trousers! The good Lord is obviously still smiling on you …! I hope that despite your setbacks, you remain in good spirits and that the enclosed 'medicine' might help to raise them a bit …

I know you will be desperate to rejoin your comrades in the Pathfinder Platoon as soon as you can but, in the meantime, I hope you are able to enjoy some recuperation time with your family.

Yours most sincerely,

Charles

I opened the parcel. The 'medicine' Prince Charles referred to was a bottle of vintage Laphroaig from his own personal cellars. My dad told me we'd keep that bottle forever. He'd buy me the same Laphroaig vintage, and we'd drink that one together to toast my homecoming.

A few days later there was a bluey in the mail. It was from Tricky. He didn't ask how I was. Instead he chatted away for a while about what the rest of the PF lads had been up to, and then he asked after my two, beautiful sisters. *The cheeky fucker!*

After I'd been casevaced out of theatre, the blokes had been told that I was VSI, but that I would live. At that stage I was ripe for a slagging. That was when they had started the rumour that when I was trapped under the Pinkie, all they could hear me screaming was: 'Not the face! Not the face!'

Oh how I love 'em.

The bastards.

EPILOGUE

I spent many months in recovery in the UK, during which time my parents nursed me back to health. With time, many of my injuries would heal naturally – the broken ribs, the damage to my lungs. The chest drain worked well, and the bag soon filled with this nasty red and yellow fluid as my lungs drained.

During the time I spent in recovery I remembered that whilst lying in the Kuwait hospital I'd been visited by an Army mate. He'd told me that there was a friend of the family in the UK who was a specialist in treating arm and shoulder injuries. Get in touch with his girlfriend, he said, and she'd sort out an introduction between me and that medical specialist.

My mother got on the case and made an appointment. The specialist, Professor Rolf Birch, was a consultant orthopaedic surgeon, and I was taken by my mother to see him, with my right arm in a sling. There was severe nerve damage to my arm, and I'd been warned that it might never fully recover movement or feeling.

Professor Birch turned out to have wild white hair and a long, white walking stick. He really looked the mad professor part. After examining me, he told me that I would come under his personal care for several months, whilst he treated my arm. He told me how he hoped we'd get it working again, but with nerve damage there were never any guarantees.

Before leaving I asked him when I could start doing some fitness training again, even if it was simply some sit-ups. He gave me this look as if he thought I was bonkers. I was still on the morphine, and I guess I was quite high, but I was also deadly serious. I was desperate to get back to the Pathfinders, and I wasn't about to let my injured arm get in my way.

The professor told me that it was 'best just to rest for now'. Largely, I ignored his advice. I put in place my own training regime, based in part on the kind of gentle exercises we do in the Pathfinders after completing a proper workout. Over the weeks and months I built up my body strength and fitness again, and I began to sense the return of some feeling in my arm. But after periods where I progressed a little, then regressed, it became clear that I needed some serious shoulder surgery. Due to a mess-up within the NHS I waited eighteen months for the operation, by which time I lost patience.

I sold my car and used the proceeds to pay to have the operation done privately. Some six months later I rejoined the Pathfinders. It had been very much a triumph of mind over matter, but I'd managed to regain the full use of my right arm. I felt physically and mentally fit enough to rejoin the unit as a fully-fledged operator, but I was restricted to doing desk duties until I could be vouchsafed as such by the MOD. Eventually, I would rejoin the PF as a fully-functioning operator, and take up my post again as 2IC.

When I received the letter from the MOD on the day I returned home from hospital, being put on the Army's sick and injured list, the Y-List, was the cruellest blow imaginable. It was a computer-generated automatic mailing. Whilst I can appreciate the logic behind sending it, the MOD showed about as much sensitivity as a charging elephant in doing so.

The letter stated that if I had not fully recovered within eighteen months, the Army reserved the right to kick me out of the armed forces. It didn't even wish me a get well soon. Nice. I was a war-wounded soldier just a day out of hospital. I'd taken a look at the name of the MOD pen-pusher who'd signed it, and I'd memorised it. I resolved to meet up with him in a dark alleyway sometime in the near future, and get even. It's still on my list of things to do.

It was only the letter and the bottle of whisky that I had received from Prince Charles that in part made up for such insensitive and shoddy treatment. That personal, hand-addressed letter from Prince Charles – plus that bottle of single malt whisky – did the world for my morale when I was so badly wounded. It made me think that maybe the Army was a reasonable, humane force to serve with, after all.

One of the biggest mysteries surrounding our mission to Qalat Sikar airfield was why there was no air available for our patrol, when we had called for it *in extremis*. At the moment that we asked for it we had no idea what the rest of the British forces were up to. For all we knew there could have been soldiers fighting for their lives all over southern Iraq, and they could have monopolised the air power.

In reality, that wasn't the case. Apart from our unit of Pathfinders, very few if any British troops were at that time facing serious combat. With the benefit of hindsight, and having spoken to competent people within the UK armed forces, I believe that air could have been found from somewhere – or re-prioritised from a strategic tasking.

It could have been made available, because we had discovered a massive hidden Iraqi force that needed to be taken out, and it might have been the means of saving our lives. It is also a fact that the Americans had masses of air available to cover Nasiriyah, and they proved how swiftly it could be brought to bear once we'd passed over the co-ordinates of the Iraqi positions to them.

However, any rescue force sent in to try to lift out our patrol would almost certainly have flown into a barrage of fire, considering the concentration of Iraqi forces equipped with heavy machine guns all along the route north of Nasiriyah. That force would likely have consisted of two Chinooks carrying PARAs and with helicopter gunships in support, and to send them in may well have risked getting them shot out of the sky.

This may explain why John, the PF OC, felt he was unable to send in any kind of airborne rescue force. It doesn't however explain why no air cover was provided at the time we asked for it to call in air strikes on the enemy positions we had discovered.

The battle for Nasiriyah has been written up in several books, and is the subject of several TV films, including HBO's *Generation Kill*. The best account is perhaps Tim Pritchard's *Ambush Alley: the most extraordinary battle of the Iraq War*, named after the road through Nasiriyah along which the Marine Corps advanced, and along which we subsequently followed.

The book *Ambush Alley* recounts the story of the March 2003 battle for Nasiriyah from the perspective of the three US Marine Corps companies – Alpha, Bravo and Charlie – who fought to take the city and seize the two vital bridges. Those are the same Marine units with whom we liaised, both before crossing over their front lines and once we had made it back again safely.

The following words are quoted from the final page of *Ambush Alley*. They recount the reaction of one Charlie Company marine to seeing our patrol return from the Qalat Sikar mission.

> He couldn't tell if anyone was moving out there or not. *They might still be out there. They can kill us whenever they want.* Out of the darkness a group of figures did appear. They weren't Iraqis. They were British. They came over to Robinson and his buddies and asked for some cigarettes. In their strange accents they started saying that the Marines shouldn't go north, that it was heavy up there.
>
> Robinson was impressed by them. They were older, with beards and moustaches and shit. They were loaded with ammo and their all-terrain vehicle was bristling with rockets and M240s. And then they just disappeared into the desert with no support and no word of where they

were going or what they were up to. Robinson could guess who they were, and in spite of what he'd just been through he yearned for the romance of life in the Special Forces.

Eighteen US marines died in the battle to take the Southern Euphrates Bridge and the Northern Saddam Canal Bridge. Some thirty-five were injured. There were also eleven US Army soldiers killed in Nasariyah that day, bringing total US casualties to twenty-nine. That represents the single greatest loss suffered by the American military during the taking of Iraq, reflecting the bloody intensity of the battle for Nasiriyah.

Notably, every US Marine captured during the week of our mission north of Nasiriyah was executed by the Iraqi enemy. This was very different from the 1991 Gulf War. One American Recon Marine was reportedly crucified in the town centre where he was captured, and left on display. Something similar would no doubt have been our fate, had we been captured.

One of the reasons for the ferocity of the Iraqi resistance experienced at Nasiriyah and north only became clear to us long after the war. Apparently, Saddam had sent his Special Security Organisation (SSO) forces – his 'most feared security forces' according to the CIA – to defend Nasiriyah and routes north of there, along with his Fedayeen.

Both the SSO and the Fedayeen consisted of die-hard Saddam loyalists who understood that they would have no role in the rebuilding of Iraq should Saddam's regime be defeated. Nasariyah was their last-ditch stand, and the SSO and Fedayeen would have believed they were fighting for their very survival. In retrospect, it seems highly likely that 'Ron Jeremy' and others we blundered into on the route north from Nasariyah were SSO operators.

The day after the battle for Nasiriyah, and following the air strikes that went in north of the city, using the intel that we had gathered, the Marine Corps 2nd Light Armoured Reconnaissance Battalion spearheaded the 1st Marine Expeditionary Force's lightning push north of Nasiriyah to seize Baghdad.

It was several days before the last bodies of the US Marines KIA (Killed In Action) in Nasiriyah were found. They had been buried in shallow graves in some of the city's residences. On 1 April 2003 marines from Task Force Tarawa launched a rescue operation to free Private Jessica Lynch, one of the soldiers from the US Army's 507th Maintenance Convoy, whose capture in Nasiriyah had caught the attention of the world's media.

We were nine British soldiers tasked with the Qalat Sikar mission, and as far as I know we were the only British troops present in, and forward of, the battle for Nasiriyah. For the tiny, lightly-armed force that we were, I like to think that we played a vital role in enabling the Marine Corps to advance out of that city and take Baghdad.

Qalat Sikar airfield was never seized by an elite force along the lines planned in our original mission, and that of the PARAs who were to follow us. As events transpired, the lightning advance of the Marine Expeditionary Force north out of Nasiriyah pushed far into Iraq, and the airfield fell into coalition hands anyway.

John, the OC of the Pathfinders, submitted recommendations for honour and awards after our Iraq tour. Jason received the Military Cross for his actions during the Qalat Sikar mission. Deservedly so. He was a flawless, superlative operator, and in spite of the ups and downs in our relationship before the war he was solid in his support of me, and his bravery was second to none when leading the patrol out of almost certain death.

His clarity of mind while riding in the front vehicle and leading the convoy down Route 7 was incredible, and he was a fine example for us all to follow. He showed calmness and consideration for those behind him by throwing smoke grenades, which helped save the lives of all in the two wagons following, the Engineer Recce lads included. I have immense admiration for Jason as a soldier and an elite operator.

Though he was put forward for a medal, Tricky received no

decoration for his soldiering in Iraq, and despite the fact that the plan to move back south down Route 7 and link up with the US Marines at Nasiriyah arose from his insistence that we keep the vehicles. Tricky was a fearless, professional and cool operator, and the safety of the patrol was heavily dependent on his experience, not to mention his use of the 50-cal.

He was unflappable when handling that heavy weapon, despite the fact that he was the most vulnerable person on our wagon, for the 50-cal operator sits higher and is more exposed than the rest of the team in the Pinkies. At the end of the day I've no doubt that Tricky didn't particularly give a damn about the lack of medals he received from Iraq: he wasn't in the Pathfinders for the glory.

I will feel indebted to him for the rest of my life, for it was Tricky who was under the upturned wagon holding my hand, and trying to pull me out of there.

Sergeant Ian Andrews – the Engineer Recce sergeant – was also awarded the Military Cross. That was fair enough and well-deserved. When the shit went down the Engineer Recce lads delivered on that mission, and were not found wanting in the heat of combat. He was also allowed to keep the pistol that saved him from the Iraqi bullet that struck him on the side, as a souvenir. I hope he has it framed, and displayed in a prime position on his glory wall.

None of the other patrol members received an honour, including Steve, Joe, Dez and the other Engineer Recce lads, although a number of us were put forward for medals of one sort or another. Although I understand that honours given out are limited in the British Army, I firmly believe that every bloke on the Qalat Sikar mission deserved a Military Cross, or something similar.

After I was medevaced out of theatre John went on to command the Pathfinders exceptionally well for a further five months of operations deep in Iraq.

Each of us on the Qalat Sikar mission went through a baptism of fire, and came through a changed man. Consider Dez. Whilst he didn't get a medal, his modern-day Wild West gunslinger moment with the pistol has gone down in Pathfinder legend. He wiped John Wayne off the map, and in the secretive world of elite forces operations people will be talking about Dez's stunt for years to come. Half in jest, Pathfinders refer to battle-hardened blokes as having had 'more action than Chuck Norris'. I can't recall any Chuck Norris film in which he's trapped behind enemy lines, facing thousands of enemy forces as we were, and does a Dez and fights them off with a pistol.

Some senior officers have argued that as the patrol commander tasked with the Qalat Sikar mission, my decision to push forward beyond the US front line in an effort to complete the mission was the wrong one. I hope from the telling of the mission in this book it is clear why that decision was made – a decision which crucially was shared by every man of my patrol. As the patrol commander I know the buck stops with me: but I believed then and still firmly believe that we made absolutely the right decision to proceed with the mission, in light of the intelligence that was available to us, and the outcome of the mission in itself proves our decision the right one. I am sure the men of my patrol feel likewise.

In the final analysis, the immense sense of satisfaction that we got from being able to pass those enemy co-ordinates to the Americans meant a huge amount to every man on the Qalat Sikar mission. Apart from the blindingly obvious fact that it was vital intel – especially when satellite, aerial and human intel had already proven so disastrously out of kilter – it was fantastic to be able to contribute to the American war effort in such a crucial way.

Throughout my Army career I've been on joint operations and training with the Americans many times. I've been used to being their poor brother, and borrowing from them whatever we might need: airframes first and foremost, but other kit as well. More often than not we're the paupers, and it has been embarrassing at times. Our blokes have as much skill and can-do attitude, but never the right kit, or enough of it.

In Iraq, 16 Air Assault Brigade had initially sat in the rear with little or no air assault capability, and yet we'd seen thousands of Marine

Expeditionary Force troops advancing into combat, with massive air support. In Iraq two different wars were being fought by two very different militaries, and we were there to support the Americans with our hands tied behind our backs a great deal of the time.

We were doubly hamstrung by the lack of will, which made a para-insertion into Qalat Sikar somehow militarily and politically unacceptable. Had we been allowed to HALO into Qalat Sikar, I have no doubt that we would have achieved the mission we had been given, which might have shortened the length and lethality of the war. As it was, the ability of our patrol to pass vital intel to the Americans meant that the British forces added something of enormous value, and of almost equal import, in my view, to seizing Qalat Sikar airfield.

Nasiriyah held the key to the jewel in the crown of Iraq, which was Baghdad. The fight to seize Nasiriyah has become known as 'the mother of all battles'. The US Marine Corps had been fought to a standstill, and the losses on the American side speak for themselves. I believe we truly helped change the course of that battle, and that in turn was a decisive moment in the war.

The Americans have always been so respectful and supportive of us as British soldiers and Pathfinders, so to be able to deliver something back was returning a favour to them – a favour that was well due. Our patrol's achievements in gaining that intel, *and coming back alive to deliver it*, should have been something HM Forces trumpeted from the rooftops. Hopefully, this book will go some of the way to making known what was achieved by a small body of British soldiers in the opening days of the war in Iraq.

Pathfinders regularly train with American elite forces, and our relations with our American fellow warriors remain strong. I hope the Qalat Sikar mission – and its telling in this book – helps strengthen that relationship. In recent years we have started doing more HALO and HAHO training in South Africa, and the operation written about at the start of this book concerns a training mission undertaken by myself and other Pathfinders in South Africa.

The Pathfinders remain the most decorated platoon in the British Army. Pathfinder sergeant Stan Harris was awarded a Military Cross when fighting the West Side Boys, a rebel group in Sierra Leone. Bryan Budd was awarded the VC in Helmand province – sadly post-humously – and he'd just come out of the Pathfinders to join a regular unit. In his heart he was and remains a PF. Plus there are scores of MIDs (Mentioned in Despatches), and the 2 MCs awarded for the Qalat Sikar mission.

This tiny unit of men can justifiably stand proud. Rest assured that on the ground right now, in remote and hostile parts of the world, there are small groups of very determined men spreading chaos amongst the enemy.

If you ask them, you probably won't get any answers, but they're very likely Pathfinders.

GLOSSARY

Belt kit   *pouches a soldier wears on a belt to carry his ammunition, survival equipment etc.*

Blue Force Tracker   *military term for a GPS-enabled system that provides military commanders and forces with location information about friendly (and, despite its name, also about hostile) military forces*

Browning   *Browning 9 mm pistol*

C130   *Hercules aircraft used by many armies for troop, vehicle and logistic transportation. Also used to transport and dispatch parachutists*

CR   *Combat Recovery*

CSAR   *Combat Search and Rescue*

CTR   *Lose Target Recce*

DPM   *Disrupt Pattern Material – commonly used name for camouflage pattern*

EPs   *Emergency Procedures*

ERV   *Emergency Rendezvous*

HAHO   *High Altitude High Opening*

HALO   *High Altitude Low Opening*

HAPLSS   *High Altitude Parachut Life Support System*

HLS   *Helicopter Landing Site*

IA   *Immediate Action*

intel   *intelligence*

IP   *Impact Point (at which a parachutist lands)*

LONG   *slang for long-barelled weapon, i.e. rifle*

LUP   *Lie-Up Point*

M16   *US-made assault rifle once used by the SAS and Pathfinders*

NAI   *Named Area of Interest*

NBC   *Nuclear, Biological, Chemical (warfare)*

NVG   *Night Vision Goggles*

Op Massive   *soldiers' slang for undergoing an intense training regime whereby they bulk up in muscle*

OPSEC   *Operational Security*

PARA   *term for a Parachute Regiment Battalion of about 650 soldiers or an individual Parachute Regiment member*

PJHQ   *Permanent Joint Headquarters – UK headquarters which commands military operations*

Roger   *military speak for 'understood'*

SA80   *standard-issue British Army rifle*

Sched   *scheduled time for a patrol to send a radio update*

SCUD   *tactical ballistic missiles developed by the Soviet Union during the Cold War and exported widely to other countries, including Iraq*

SH   *support helicopters – usually refers to Chinook CH47 but can include Pumas, Wessex, Lynx, etc.*

Sitrep   *situation report*

Snap Ambush   *hastily made ambush to observe any enemy who can then be fired upon*

SOP   *Standard Operating Procedure*

SOPHIE   *thermal imaging system*

Watchkeeper   *an operational appointment in the army in which an experienced officer or non-commissioned officer has limited control over a headquarters or its radio operators while the commanding officer is resting or on other tasks*

PHOTO CREDITS

Early days in the Parachute Regiment (© Chris Page 2002)
HALO training in Nevada (© David Blakeley)
Dressed in full equipment (© Andrew Chittock)
PF jumping out of a C130 Hercules (© Andrew Chittock)
P-Hour plus (© David Blakeley)
Skydiving at sunset (© David Blakeley)
Patrol in freefall (© Andrew Chittock)
Chutes pulled (© Andrew Chittock)
Still images of author performing HALO jumps (© David Blakeley)
PF with M16 rifles (© Peter Russell Photography)
Conduct after capture training (© David Blakeley)

Moving into Iraq (© David Blakeley)
Euphrates Bridge at Nasiriyah (Courtesy Everett Collection/Rex
    Features)
Shemaghs (© Andrew Chittock)
Pinkies (© Andrew Chittock)
Fedayeen soldiers (© Getty Images)
.50 calibre machine gun (© Crown)
Firepower (© Crown)
Firing from fast-moving vehicles (© Crown)
Author in 'local' gear (© David Blakeley)
Brew with Steve at American front line (© David Blakeley)

Author on stretcher (© David Blakeley)
Author's military medals (© David Blakeley)
Author and HRH Prince Charles (© David Blakeley)
Letter from HRH Prince Charles (© David Blakeley)

If you have enjoyed

PATHFINDER

don't miss David Blakeley's thrilling new book

MAVERICK ONE

Available from 23 May 2013
in Orion hardback

ISBN: 978-1-4091-4412-0

CHAPTER ONE

I am one of the first to arrive.

I've heard all the rumours. It's best to get here early and claim a decent billet – ideally one tucked away in a corner, and definitely on a lower bunk. It's only a thin, khaki green sheet of foam that I'm claiming here, but this is where I'll lay my battered and tortured body every night for the weeks to come, wracked with pain and exhaustion and craving sleep.

If you're a late arrival you'll be left with a place by the door, and that could make all the difference between passing or failing whatever hell lies ahead of us. Every time someone opens the door you'll get a blast of bitter, icy, January weather down your neck. And for sure people will be banging in and out for a piss all night long, as we'll need to drink bucket-loads in an effort to rehydrate.

I throw my Bergen onto my chosen billet – the one that's the furthest from the door – and tuck a rough green Army dog blanket into the bottom of the bunk above. That way, the blanket hangs down like a curtain, providing just a touch of privacy and separation from the doss-pits next to mine.

Enshrouded in my dog blanket curtain it'll be total darkness, almost like a makeshift basha in the jungle. After each of the tortuous days that lie ahead I'll need that sanctuary, and some proper sleep, if I'm to stand any chance of making it through.

There's one other crucial advantage to getting a bottom bunk. You avoid the risk of jumping down from one above on sore and battered legs, and the impact further straining or breaking already torn and shredded limbs.

My makeshift dog blanket shelter done, I settle down to wait for the next arrivals.

I'm six foot four, and the steel and corrugated iron bed feels like it's been built for a dwarf. My head's jammed against the wall, and my feet dangle way over the end. I'll have to sleep curled up like a foetus. But at least with a lower bunk, if I do roll out I don't have so far to fall onto the bare concrete below.

I glance around at the inhospitable, spartan billet. It's an old Nissen hut – a thin, corrugated steel construction not a great deal more substantial than a chicken shed. There are ten bunks ranged like skeletal ribs down either side of the room, their paint chipped and fading, the frames sagging in places. It's enough for forty blokes in all, which makes up a full complement for what's coming.

The thin mattress beneath me is encased in a horrible, wipe-clean, sweaty plastic covering – the kind of thing you wouldn't wish on a young kid who pees the bed. It's there so that those who bleed, or puke or piss themselves through exhaustion don't leave a permanent legacy for the next batch who're mad enough to volunteer for this self-inflicted torment.

Welcome to Sennybridge Camp, I tell myself wryly, the base for all British Special Forces selection – including that of the Special Air Service (SAS), the Special Boat Service (SBS) and the tiny, elite unit that I burn to be a part of: the Pathfinders.

British Special Forces selection is widely regarded as being the toughest in the world. The American military model their own selection on what we do here, at this run-down, grotty, rain-lashed dump of a place. Those who founded Delta Force came here to attempt UKSF selection so as to ascertain just how hard they could afford to abuse their own soldiers.

In a way I've been lucky in my training, for I've been briefed in detail about what to expect. Jack Quinn, a fellow PARA Regiment bloke, had made it into the SAS but was returned to unit (RTUd) due to a bit of lightweight skulduggery. He'd switched the wheels from a hire car they were using on SAS business onto his own motor.

Unfortunately, he'd been rumbled and RTUd – at which point I offered him a deal. If he helped me train for selection and briefed me on what to look out for, I'd buy him a new set of alloy wheels for his motor. Pathfinder (PF) selection is basically the same as that for the SAS, only it's shorter – being five weeks of initial torture, as opposed to six months. Jack Quinn would make an ideal mentor.

Some claim that PF selection covers the same ground as the SAS in less time, which makes it more intense and challenging. Others argue that it's quicker, which lowers the attrition rate. Jack didn't particularly give a shit either way. As far as he was concerned, I needed to be every bit as physically and mentally prepared for PF selection as he had been for that of the SAS.

And it was Jack who'd given me the nod to arrive early so as to claim the best billet.

The next bloke to pitch up takes the other corner bunk furthest from the door, so the one directly above mine. He's a little, wiry lance corporal from 3 PARA. He tells me he's an ultra-marathon runner, and he shows me the 'NO FEAR' tattoo he's got emblazoned on one shoulder. He's got a broad Welsh accent, and it's no surprise to learn that everyone calls him 'Taff'.

I tell him I'm a captain from 1 PARA and that everyone knows me as 'Dave'. Because this is selection, it's all first-name terms here regardless of rank. It's very likely the first time that Taff has ever addressed an officer by name, as opposed to 'sir'. It's that kind of classless ethos that has drawn me to the elite forces.

As a young captain not many years out of Sandhurst, I'd always believed that those who wish to lead have to earn the respect of those they expect to follow. Merit, regardless of rank – in my book, that's how the best military units should operate. The Pathfinders, I know, live and breathe that egalitarian kind of a spirit.

– 3 –

A second bloke pitches up. He's a massive, hulking Arnie Schwarzenegger lookalike. Typically, he's from the Royal Engineers, who only ever seem to come in the one size – monstrous. The Royal Engineers are well-respected, hard and toughened soldiers, and after the PARAs they make up the second biggest cap badge in the Pathfinders.

There's a good deal of rivalry between the PARAs and the Royal Engineers. The Engineers joke that PARAs are 'mince' – thick in the head – and that Engineers have a higher level of intellect, because they have to build stuff and not just shoot it up. The set PARA retort is: 'Mate, just concentrate on building us some shitters.' I don't think too many of us will be saying that to our Arnie double.

He dwarfs Taff, and I've got no doubt he's going to be the biggest bloke on selection. He looks absolutely fearsome, but that's not my main concern. As one of the next biggest blokes, what I'm really dreading is getting teamed up with Arnie buddy-buddy fashion and having to carry his massive frame across the rain-and-sleet-lashed moors.

Arnie chooses the corner bunk opposite mine and Taff's – so a fine choice, with ours being taken. Next to arrive is another bloke from 3 PARA. He's got a long and morose face. It reminds me of a horse. Taff and the new arrival seem to know each other, for Taff breaks into a wide grin just as soon as he lays eyes on him.

''Ullo, Mark, mate … but why the long face?' he quips.

Often, the old jokes are still the best ones.

The new arrival tells Taff to 'F-off', and the ice is well and truly broken.

He's a private, Mark Kidman, and he hails from New Zealand. That country produces some highly regarded soldiers, and I've no doubt Mark is a class act. More to the point, he tells us he was offered a place as an officer in the regular British Army but refused it. He did so simply because he wanted to try for selection into the Pathfinders – and that deserves a great deal of respect.

Two blokes arrive together, and they're more 3 PARA lads. Al

I know of old. He's tall, lean, scruffy and wolfish looking, and he doesn't give a toss about his appearance. The only time he looks in the mirror is to shave. If anyone comments on his looks, he gives a set response in a thick Leeds accent: 'Not fucking arsed, fucking am I?'

Al doesn't talk much, and he's not the sharpest tool in the box, but he's known as being a superlative operator. He greets me with his typical dour humour.

'Fucking all right then, Dave. We're gonna be fucking going on a fucking tab, then, eh?'

Jez is the other 3 PARA lad, and he's the real enigma. He's a private, but he's balding and well spoken and he sounds distinctly educated. He looks as if he's in completely the wrong kind of place right now. He'd be well at home in a tweed jacket and tie in the Officer's Mess, being addressed as 'the Colonel'.

One of the last to arrive is Pete, who hails from the Grenadier Guards. He has no option but to take a bunk right next to the door. He is a chain-smoker and a ranker, and he's been in the Guards for a very long time. He wears nothing but Army-issue kit, and he seems to pride himself on being able to take any shit the Army can throw at him – including getting the bunk from hell.

Pete has got zero civvie mountaineering kit, and even his boots are standard Army issue. They've got cheap, flimsy soles, and they look like they've been designed for a stint as a petrol-pump attendant. As far as I can see he's the only one in the entire hut wearing Army-issue boots. The rest of us all have civvie footwear – either Altbergs or Scarpas, or in my case Lowes.

My Lowes are made of a tough leather upper with a Vibram sole to soak up the pounding impact of the forced marches. They're not Gore-tex lined, because that would make the feet sweat too much, plus the Gore-tex keeps the water in when wading through bogs, and there'll be plenty of that to come. It's the last thing you need on selection.

The Grenadier Guards are famed for their smartness, plus their drill. Sure enough, all of Pete's standard-issue kit is polished and pressed to perfection. The lads can't help ripping the piss.

'Hey, Pete! They've got a trouser press in the wash-house, mate.'

'Hurry – soon be time to get on parade.'

'You boys need some fucking drill,' Pete retorts. 'Bloody ill-disciplined PARAs.'

Oddly, one of the last pieces of kit that Pete pulls out of his Bergen is a book – some battered sci-fi thriller.

Al stares at it for a long second. 'What – the – fuck – is – that?' he asks, each word punctuated by a disgusted silence.

'It's a book,' says Pete. 'Sorry. Forgot. You PARAs can't read, can you?'

There's something hard and unshakeable in Pete's look, and he doesn't seem the least bit fazed by the slagging. He and I get talking, and it turns out that he's a 'pad'. He lives on the pad – in Army accommodation and in the married quarters. It's another thing that marks him out as being a misfit, for the rest of us are very much not attached.

'So, erm, Dave, you were in SL with 1 PARA, weren't you?' Pete asks.

'Yeah, I was.'

'It was a NEO, wasn't it?'

'Yeah.'

SL is short for Sierra Leone, a nation in West Africa that had been torn apart by civil war. My battalion, 1 PARA, was sent there a few months back to carry out a Non-combatant Evacuation Operation (NEO) – in layman's terms, pulling out all British and allied civilians. The rebel forces were poised to take the nation's capital, which would have caused a horrific bloodbath. We were flown into the teeth of that conflict to get our people out and to stop the carnage.

'You'd have to be a fire-pisser to be on that one,' Pete remarks.

'A what?'

Pete mimes as if he's holding his cock. 'Someone who pisses fire.'

'Fair enough.' I raise the obvious question. 'So, mate, why're you doing selection?'

Pete knows why I'm asking. He's an older, married family man, and he's clearly a well-established, regular Army kind of a bloke.

He shrugs. 'Last shot to do something exciting … I love the Guards. I'll always be true to my roots. But I don't exactly think they'll make me RSM, 'cause I've had more than a few run-ins. Pathfinder selection – it's my last chance at being a fire-pisser.'

The crack with the guys is good and morale is high, but none of the agony has started yet. Plus there's something else that I'm painfully aware of. I'm not just here to undertake PF selection. I'm here to see if I can make it through as second-in-command (2IC) of the unit, and that's the added pressure that I'm under.

By midday we're all forty of us present and correct. We head for the cookhouse, each of us carrying our own plate, mug, knife and fork. Sennybridge Camp is a temporary kind of a set-up, and too much of the Army-issue cutlery has been nicked by those who went before us. These days, if you want to eat you have to bring your own tools.

We queue for food. It's hot dog and chips, and we pile it high. There are a couple of urns, one serving coffee and the other tea. It's the cheapest, shittiest brew the Army can find, and whichever you choose it all tastes pretty much the same.

As we move off with our brews I spot a row of familiar figures, but there's not a flash of recognition amongst them. They're stony-faced and pretending they don't know me.

One is Lenny, the present 2IC of Pathfinders. He and I were on the piss together directly after Sierra Leone, and we got so hammered we woke up in bed together. I actually thought he was a bird at first, that's until my hand felt the stubble on his jaw. But right now he's acting as if he's never set eyes on me before.

Then there's Gavin and Tricky, two more PF stalwarts that I know well. But right at the moment they're the Directing Staff (DS) on selection, and they're here for one reason only – to beast us through the weeks of hell to come. In fact, the entire PF unit has pitched up so as to better handle the murderously intense pace of what's coming.

The PF lads have got their own, separate accommodation block and their own, separate showers. To a man they're pretending they don't know me. I don't try to greet them, either. I understand there can't be even a hint of any matey-matey shit between us. No special allowances. Zero favouritism. No exceptions made for any man who doesn't of his own accord make it through.

We get the food down us, and there's a lot less piss-taking and high spirits now. A massive bloke rises from the Pathfinders' end of the cookhouse. Stan Harris is the PF Platoon Sergeant. He's a giant of a Yorkshireman with a face as hard and chiselled as a rock face.

He's also a living legend in such circles. Among the many feats of soldiering he's renowned for, he won the Military Cross when the Pathfinders took on the rebels in a pitched battle in the Sierra Leone jungle.

'Right, all youse want to join the Pathfinders, the first event is the eight-miler,' he announces with zero ceremony. 'You must be with the DS at the end of the tab. If you're not, it's a fail.'

'This is not like any other course in the Army.' He eyeballs the lot of us. 'If you're sick, lame or lazy, at any point you can voluntarily withdraw – VW. None of us is here to motivate you. If you want to go back to Battalion and do guards and duties with your mates for the rest of your life, then you're more than welcome to go.

'This isn't a face-fits unit,' he continues. 'There are some right criminal-looking bastards in the PF. We're looking for a few good men – those who can survive and deliver against all odds. All of us here in the PF – you call us "Staff". No one wears rank in our unit, so you don't need to worry about that. PF selection is fast and intense. It's not like the SAS, where all you've got to worry about for the first five weeks is tabbing. We've only got youse for six weeks, so after your tabs you've got lessons and more tests, and then if you're lucky you might get your head down.

'I'm sure you know the basics, so I won't waste any more of my precious breath, 'cause by the end of today some of youse won't be here.' He pauses for a second, just to let the words sink in. 'If you do pass selection, you'll go on to continuation training, including combat survival and resistance to interrogation. You're on probation for the first year, in which time you must pass your HALO and HAHO courses, plus your comms and mobility cadres.'

He glances at the watch strapped to his massive, hairy wrist. 'It's 13.45. The armoury is two blocks down from your accom block. Go draw your weapons. Be on the parade square at 1400 hours with Bergens in front of youse, ready for weigh-in. If you're not at minimum weight, we'll add it to your Bergen, plus a big rock so you'll be over weight for the tab. And remember, everything in your Bergen must be useful kit for winter in the mountains.'

For a moment, his laser-eyed stare sweeps the room. It comes to rest on Pete. 'Well done, Sergeant Terry. You've just volunteered yourself to be in charge of the tea-urn roster. Perfect work for a Guards sergeant. Make sure everyone takes a turn, and make fucking sure every time we go out there's two on the back of each of the four-tonners – that's one for you lot and one for the DS. If anyone forgets the tea urns, I will be extremely pissed off, and you'll be going up and down an additional mountain. Now, get away.'

We split.

The atmosphere has utterly changed. It's silent and tense, and there's real urgency in the air. I've got serious butterflies in my stomach, and I'm worried about whether I should have eaten as much as I have. I know I'll need the energy, but doing a forced march like what's coming on a full stomach can easily make you puke.

We head for the Nissen hut, grab our Bergens, then there's an argy-bargy at the armoury to be first to draw weapons. We're each issued with a dummy SLR – an ancient, self-loading rifle. It's the kind of weapon the British Army soldiered with a few decades ago, and we've only got it for the weight and the discipline, plus the added realism. But woe betide anyone who disrespects their weapon …

Until recently, those doing selection used to be issued with real assault rifles. But too many were lost during the more extreme stages

– 9 –

of selection, high on the hills and in atrocious weather conditions. Search parties had to be mounted to bring in the lost kit, and it all got a bit too much – hence the introduction of the dummy rifles.

We form up on the parade ground in three ranks with our Bergens propped in front of us. Some of the blokes have laid their dummy SLRs on the ground beside their packs. It's another thing that Jack Quinn had warned me about: unless you're sleeping, you never, ever let your weapon leave your hand, and even then it's got to be just a quick grab away.

Stan Harris stops dead in front of the first bloke who's committed this heinous crime. 'First fucking thing is this,' he yells into the offender's face. 'In the PF you NEVER, EVER put your weapon on the fucking ground! If you EVER need to put your weapon down, rest it on your feet or your pack!'

'Staff,' the offender confirms, grabbing his dummy rifle.

'Your weapon must at all times be within arm's reach,' he continues. 'If you fuck up, we run a fine system. You'll be fined every time, and you'll soon fucking learn. Money goes into a fund, and we drink it in a piss-up at the end – that's for those who pass. Anyone got a problem with that?'

Silence.

'If I catch anyone using their weapon as a walking stick when you're out on the hills tabbing, you're fucked. You'll be RTUd, no messing.' He turns to a lean and hard-looking bloke beside him. It's Tricky, his fellow DS. 'Time to weigh in their kit.' He turns back to us. 'You lot – remove your water and food.'

We're each supposed to start with a Bergen laden with 35 pounds of kit, not counting water and food. As the days progress, we'll keep upping the weight in increments until we're tabbing under a crushing load. The DS will keep checking us at the start and end of each stage to make sure no one's shirking.

As we pull out all the scoff and the bottles from our Bergens, most blokes are carrying high-energy drinks and protein bars. But I always have at least one Ginsters Cornish pasty in my Bergen. It's real, hearty food, and I've got it as a special treat. Just the knowledge that it's in there can prove a real boost to morale.

Tricky sees the pasty and shakes his head in disgust. 'What – the fuck – is that?'

'Ginsters pasty, Staff.'

Tricky lets out a snort of disbelief. 'What, a Ginsters Cornish pasty as recommended by the British Olympic Committee?'

'Staff.'

No one so much as sniggers. We all of us know that if you laugh at the DS's jokes, they're just as likely to turn on you.

Tricky and I know each other from the Sierra Leone op, plus we've been out on the beers together. But right now I realise that the DS are very likely to give me a doubly hard time. First, so as to be absolutely certain they are not showing any favouritism, and second because I am trying for the 2IC's slot in their closely guarded unit.

I decide I'm going to have to try to be the 'grey man' here – the bloke who does nothing to get himself noticed or singled out still further. In that way, I might just escape from the worst of the DS's ire.

We weigh in fine with our Bergens, all apart from the one bloke who's a kilo under. Tricky glances at Stan Harris, who indicates a sizeable boulder lying at the edge of the parade ground.

'Right, go fetch that fucking rock,' Tricky tells the offender.

I can see the sheer panic written on the bloke's face as he realises what's coming. He scuttles off, lifts the rock, brings it back and Tricky piles it into the top of his Bergen. He gets the scales and weighs it for a second time.

He smiles. 'You're two kilos over. Tough shit. I'll be weighing your Bergen at the end of the eight-miler, and it'd better be the same fucking weight.'

'Right, enough fucking around!' Stan Harris yells. 'On the back of the four-tonners!'

We double-time it over to the battered khaki-green Army trucks. Two are needed to carry the forty-odd blokes starting selection. The tailgate on a four-tonner is heavy, and it takes two blokes to unlatch the first one and lift it down. We're about to start mounting up the truck when Stan Harris stops us with a look that could kill.

He's staring into the nearest truck with eyes like murder. 'Fucking Guards sergeants … So, tell me: who's forgotten the fucking tea urns?'

The PF Platoon Sergeant has got lock-on with Pete already. On the one hand, I feel sorry for him. But on the other, I know I'm going to have to give Pete a wide berth from now on. If you're mates with the guy who's got lock-on from the head DS, you'll likely get hit in the back blast.

'Staff!' Pete yells, acknowledging his failure to sort out the tea roster. He turns to Jez and Al. 'Lads, let's get the fucking urns sorted.'

Jez – 'the Colonel' – has already got his Bergen and dummy rifle loaded onto the four-tonner. He turns and makes a run for the cookhouse, but he's left his weapon lying where it is.

Stan Harris practically explodes. 'WHERE THE FUCK IS YOUR FUCKING WEAPON?'

Eyes bulging, Jez stops in his tracks. 'Staff!' He runs back, grabs his dummy SLR, and turns to go and fetch the tea urns.

'What's your fucking name?' Stan Harris barks after him.

'Rowlands, Staff.'

'Fucking *Rowlands*? Sounds like a poofy bloody officer's name!'

'Staff.'

No one is laughing. No fucking way. And no one answers back. All it takes is for one of the DS to decide he doesn't like you, and you'll get beasted half to death by the lot of them.

Jez returns with a tea urn under one arm and his rifle under the other. We mount up the four-tonners. As Jez climbs aboard, he's got a box of sugar and a carton of milk balanced on top of the tea urn. Predictably, the whole lot goes over.

Luckily, the milk's unopened, but the sugar ends up scattered all over the bed of the truck. Before the DS can notice, Pete scoops it up as best he can and throws it into the tea urn, presumably working on the assumption that the mud and grit will sink to the bottom, whereas the sugar will dissolve.

'Fucking hell, lads,' he hisses, 'use your fucking heads. Don't bring the fucking sugar and the urn separate. Dump it into the urn back in the cookhouse, and bring it like that. Otherwise, it'll keep getting knocked over, and we'll keep having shit in our tea.'

I take my place on the hard wooden bench by the rear of the truck so I can keep a check on where we're going. I quickly realise my mistake. As soon as we're under way, the wind starts whistling in through the open canvas back, and it's freezing.

There's a heavy, oppressive silence as the four-tonner trundles along this narrow country lane. No one's chatting now, and there's zero crack.

It's day one of PF selection, and we know we're going to get thrashed.